Spirituality
for All Times

Spirituality for All Times

READINGS FROM THE CATHOLIC CLASSICS

Ronda Chervin, Ph.D.
and Kathleen Brouillette

En Route Books & Media

Contact us at contactus@enroutebooksandmedia.com

© 2014, Dr. Ronda Chervin, Ph.D
All rights reserved. This book, or parts thereof, may not be reproduced in any form without permission.

Cover design done by TJ Burdick

Book Design & Production
Columbus Publishing Lab
www.ColumbusPublishingLab.com

Print ISBN 978-1-950108-32-9
E-book ISBN 978-1-63337-052-4

Printed in the United States of America
1 3 5 7 9 10 8 6 4 2

CONTENTS

Introduction   1

EXCERPTS FROM SPIRITUAL CLASSICS THROUGH THE 18TH CENTURY FROM:
St. Augustine: The Confessions of St. Augustine   5
St. Benedict: The Rule of St. Benedict   27
St. Bernard of Clairvaux: Sermons on the Song of Songs   51
St. Hildegard of Bingen: Selections   73
St. Francis: The Little Flowers   87
St. Gertrude the Great: The Revelations of St. Gertrude   117
Bl. Julian(a) of Norwich: Revelations of Divine Love   139
St. Catherine of Siena: The Dialogue   155
Thomas a Kempis: The Imitation of Christ   173
St. Thomas More: Selections   191
St. Ignatius Loyola: The Spiritual Exercises   209
St. Teresa of Avila: The Interior Castle   231
St. John of the Cross, The Ascent of Mt. Carmel   253
St. Francis de Sales: Introduction to the Devout Life   281
Brother Lawrence: The Practice of the Presence of God   297

SHORTER EXCERPTS FROM 19TH CENTURY SPIRITUAL WRITERS:
St. Louis Marie de Montfort: True Devotion to Mary   315
Blessed John Henry Newman: Selections   323
St. Thérèse of Lisieux: The Story of a Soul   339

Conclusion   349

INTRODUCTION

When I, Ronda Chervin, began teaching a course on the great writings of spirituality in the Catholic tradition, I asked for feedback from my students. Kathleen Brouillette, a Coordinator of Religious Education in a parish in Connecticut, and also a student in that course, thought how wonderful it would be to have a version of the excerpts we studied in a format for parish adult education. Since I have written numerous books on spirituality for the laity, the idea of an anthology of writings from the classics designed for student use but also for parish use was a natural.

Spirituality for All Times is offered in the hope that it will inspire those who seek a deeper union with God. We have chosen to offer short selections to enable the readers to wade in from the shallow end of the pool, so to speak, until they are comfortable enough to take their feet off the bottom and swim toward the deeper end - someday reading whole books by the same writers.

Once the beautiful images in these writings speak to your heart and make sense to you, you can surely find more to read on a deeper level. We suggest that you read these excerpts when you have time for quiet reflection, so that you are not rushed and can absorb and digest what God may be speaking to your heart.

We ask God to bless this work, and each one who will pick it up and read it. May each of the faithful ones whose work we have included pray for us that we may, through their writing and inspiration, come closer to the good God who so loves us.

A bit about Ronda Chervin: I am a professor of philosophy and of spirituality. I have taught in many universities and seminaries. As well I have written numerous books and appeared as a presenter on EWTN, mostly in the area of lay spirituality. A widow, mother, and grandmother, I try always to relate ideas from saints who were often priests, monks, nuns, sisters or brothers to the daily life of people in the world.

Kathleen Brouillette: I met Dr. Chervin as a student in her classes at Holy Apostles College and Seminary in Cromwell, CT. A convert to the faith, I was introduced to the lives of the saints by a very faith-filled woman who was significantly instrumental in my coming to the Church. As a wife, mother, and grandmother, I can't think of anything more important than living this faith of ours, and taking advantage of all the guidance and assistance on our spiritual journey offered by these wonderful examples of holiness. It is our hope that you will find inspiration in these writings to spark your interest and help you get closer to God.

Spirituality for All Times, is formatted for use in small parish groups as well as for individual reading. Each chapter has: a little bi-

Introduction

ography, an excerpt from the classic, contemporary applications and personal reflections by us, and questions for the reader's personal reflection and group sharing.

Before you read more of *Spirituality for All Times*, I, Dr. Ronda, want to convey to you a specific concept underlying Catholic spirituality: one size doesn't fit all! In the year 2006, I wrote an introduction to spirituality entitled: *Called by Name: Following Your Own Personal Spirituality*. What follows is a brief account of this challenge.

"You've got to read this spiritual book, it will change your life." "You've got to join this lay movement, it will make you holy." "You've got to say these exact prayers, the graces that follow will convert everyone you know." Sometimes those enthusiasts are absolutely right. What they love is just what you will love and it will transform you. But often what is good for them just doesn't feel good for you.

It is important to distinguish between God's way for everyone, proclaimed in Scripture and taught by His Church such as going to Holy Mass and receiving the sacraments, and venerating Mary, Mother of our Savior; and other spiritual practices that are optional. Discovering your own personal spirituality involves openness to the Holy Spirit to bring you out of what I call in my book "No Way" times when we feel stuck because of our sins or our problems. It means realizing how God brings you closer to Him, for instance, more by the beauty of nature than by being alone with Him in your bedroom. It means learning also from the ways of others since sometimes, indeed, what they have found, will be a new step for you with unexpected joys.

Now, as you read the excerpts from the writings of famous saints and mystics throughout the centuries, we hope you see their stories and thoughts as invitations. Some concepts will just seem so different from anything you've experienced that you need to read swiftly or move on. Others may seem hard at first, but then unexpectedly come back to you later to explain an experience or inspire a conversion.

For more from *Called by Name* go to www.rondachervin.com and click on books; then free e-books.

Spirituality for All Times can be used for any group of Catholic adults. A leader would simply add his or her own opening introductions, lecture on highlights, have the group ponder the readings between sessions and have group sharing on the themes at the end of each chapter. I, Dr. Ronda, would be happy to help in any way by e-mail at chervinronda@gmail.com

Our prayer:

Holy Spirit, we ask that you bring the truths in *Spirituality for All Times* into the minds, hearts and souls of our readers. May they catch the fire that led each of our writers to intimate union with the Trinity and to overflowing love for all those they encountered.

SAINT AUGUSTINE (354-430)
THEME: THE RESTLESS HEART

Augustine lived a very dissolute life, taking a mistress at age seventeen with whom he had a son. At nineteen he fell under Manichaeism, believing there were two forces in the world: good and evil. Evil was associated with matter and so an ascetic life was necessary. Manes, the founder of Manichaeism, claimed authority from Jesus and held that sin comes not from man but from the force of evil alone, thus making Manichaeism a heresy.

In 383, Augustine left Manichaeism, finding it to be more a cult than a religion. He studied Neo-Platonic thought, closer in philosophy to Christianity, accepting an immaterial world higher than the material world. He heard of St. Ambrose and attended his talks, meeting with Simplicianus, a mentor of Ambrose. St. Monica cried copious tears for Augustine's waywardness and was assured by St. Ambrose that the child of so many of his mother's tears would not be lost.

Augustine was attracted to the truth and mercy found in Christianity. He saw that there was an immaterial realm, and found a way to become part of that realm in the Christian Church. Christ offered a way to know truth, but also a way to live it.

One day Augustine heard a voice in the garden say, "Take up and read." Believing it to be an instruction to him, he opened to Romans 13:13-14 regarding sexual excess, lust, and drunkenness, putting on the Lord Jesus Christ, and giving up desires of the flesh. Certain that this was an admonishment to change his life; he did so and was baptized.

In 391 Augustine went to Hippo, where he became a priest. In 395 he was made a bishop. In 406 he wrote his *Confessions*, and in 426 his *City of God*. He saw history as a struggle between the earthly city and the heavenly city, and wrote to instruct the people of his time in truth. Correcting the perception that the fall of Rome was due to weakness and humility in Christianity, Augustine asserted it was due rather to a loss of virtue among the decadent Roman society.

After living much of his life in contradiction to Christian principles, Augustine became one of the greatest saints and doctors of the Church, influencing Christian thought and teaching even today.

St. Augustine

Excerpts from the *Confessions* of St. Augustine[1]

Book I

Great are You, O Lord, and greatly to be praised; great is Your power, and Your wisdom infinite...yet would man praise You; he, but a particle of Your creation. You awaken us to delight in Your praise; for You made us for Yourself, and our heart is restless, until it reposes in You...I will seek You, Lord, by calling on You; and will call on You, believing in You...My faith, Lord, shall call on You, which You have given me, wherewith You have inspired me, through the Incarnation of Your Son, through the ministry of the Preacher.

...Oh! that I might repose on You! Oh! that You would enter into my heart, and inebriate it, that I may forget my ills, and embrace You, my sole good! What are You to me? In Your pity, teach me to utter it. Or what am I to You that You demand my love, and, if I give it not, are angry with me, and threaten me with grievous woes? Is it then a slight woe to love You not? Oh! for Your mercies' sake, tell me, O Lord my God, what You are to me. Say to my soul, I am Your salvation. So speak, that I may hear. Behold, Lord, I am listening to You… say to my soul, I am Your salvation. After this voice let me hurry, and take hold on You. Hide not Your face from me. Let me die—lest I die—only let me see Your face.

---

[1] Augustine, *Confessions,* Translated by Edward Bouverie Pusey (Chatto and Windus, 1921), Book I, Book VIII, at About, ancienthistory.about.com/od/staugustinetexts. In common domain but changed in parts to modernized English.

Narrow is the mansion of my soul; enlarge…it, that You may enter in. It is ruinous; repair…it. It has that within which must offend Your eyes; I confess and know it. But who shall cleanse it? or to whom should I cry, save You? Lord, cleanse me from my secret faults, and spare Your servant from the power of the enemy. I believe, and therefore do I speak…Have I not confessed against myself my transgressions to You, and You, my God, have forgiven the iniquity of my heart?

…Is there, Lord, any of soul so great, and cleaving to You with so intense affection…who, from cleaving devoutly to You, is endued with so great a spirit, that he can think as lightly of the racks and hooks and other torments…as our parents mocked the torments which we suffered in boyhood from our masters? …And yet we sinned, in writing or reading or studying less than was exacted of us. For we wanted not, O Lord, memory or capacity, whereof Your will gave enough for our age; but our sole delight was play; and for this we were punished by those who yet themselves were doing the like. But elder folks' idleness is called "business"; that of boys, being really the same, is punished by those elders; and none commiserates either boys or men. For will any of sound discretion approve of my being beaten as a boy, because, by playing at ball, I made less progress in studies which I was to learn, only that, as a man, I might play more unsuitably? And what else did he who beat me, who, if worsted in some trifling discussion with his fellow-tutor, was more embittered and jealous than I when beaten at ball by a play-fellow?

And yet, I sinned herein, O Lord God, …I sinned in transgressing the commands of my parents and those of my masters…For I disobeyed, not from a better choice, but from love of play, loving the pride of victory in my contests, and to have my ears tickled with lying fables, that they might itch the more; the same curiosity flashing from my eyes more and more, for the shows and games of my elders. Yet those who give these shows are in such esteem, that almost all wish the same for their children, and yet are very willing that they should be beaten, if those very games detain them from the studies, whereby they would have them attain to be the givers of them. Look with pity, Lord, on these things, and deliver us who call upon You now; deliver those too who call not on You yet, that they may call on You, and You may deliver them.

As a boy, then, I had already heard of an eternal life, promised us through the humility of the Lord our God stooping to our pride; and even from the womb of my mother, who greatly hoped in You, I was scaled with the mark of His cross and salted with His salt. You saw, Lord…with what eagerness and what faith I sought…the baptism of Your Christ, my God and Lord…I then already believed: and my mother, and the whole household, except my father: yet did not he prevail over the power of my mother's piety in me…For it was her earnest care that You my God, rather than he, should be my father; and in this You did aid her to prevail over her husband, whom she obeyed, therein also obeying You, who have so commanded.

I beseech You, my God, for what purpose my baptism was then deferred? …How many and great waves of temptation seemed to hang over me after my boyhood!

In boyhood itself, however…I loved not study, and hated to be forced to it. Yet I was forced; … for, unless forced, I would not have learned. But no one does well against his will... Yet neither did they do good who forced me, but what was good came to me from You, my God. For they didn't care how ere regardless how I should employ what they forced me to learn... But You…did use for my good the error of all who urged me to learn; and my own…

This was the world at whose gate unhappy I lay in my boyhood…with innumerable lies deceiving my tutor, my masters, my parents, from love of play, eagerness to see vain shows and restlessness to imitate them! Thefts also I committed, from my parents' cellar and table, enslaved by greediness, or that I might have to give to boys, who sold me their play, which all the while they liked no less than I. In this play, too, I often sought unfair conquests, conquered myself meanwhile by vain desire of preeminence…And is this the innocence of boyhood?...For these very sins…are transferred from tutors and masters…to magistrates and kings, to gold and manors and slaves, just as severer punishments displace the cane. It was the low stature then of childhood which You our King did commend as an emblem of lowliness, when You said, Of such is the kingdom of heaven.

…I learnt to delight in truth, I hated to be deceived, had a vigorous memory, was gifted with speech, was soothed by friendship, avoided pain, baseness, ignorance. In so small a creature, what was not wonderful, not admirable? But all are gifts of my God: it was not I who gave them me; and good these are... Good, then, is He that made me, and He is my good; and before Him will I exult for every good which of a boy I had. For it was my sin, that not in Him, but in His creatures—myself and others—I sought for pleasures, ecstasies, truths, and so fell headlong into sorrows, confusions, errors. Thanks be to You, my joy and my glory and my confidence, my God, thanks be to You for Your gifts... For so will You preserve me, and those things shall be enlarged and perfected which You have given me, and I myself shall be with You...

(Note from editor, Ronda Chervin: There follows a long account of how Augustine fell into sins of theft and then of sex outside of marriage and then gives birth to a son out of a long term relationship to a woman he didn't marry. Then he writes of how he became entangled with the Gnostic section of Manichaeism. He goes to Milan to teach and there meets St. Ambrose and becomes interested in the Church but is torn between his sins and his desire to become a Catholic. Book VIII narrates the graces that led to his final conversion.)

Book VIII

...I was displeased that I led a secular life; now that my desires no longer inflamed me, as of old, with hopes of honor and profit, a very grievous burden it was to undergo so heavy a bondage. For, in comparison of Your sweetness, and the beauty of Your house which I loved, those things delighted me no longer. But still I was enthralled with the love of woman; nor did the Apostle forbid me to marry... But I being weak, chose the more indulgent place; and because of this alone, was tossed up and down in all beside, faint and wasted with withering cares, because in other matters I was constrained against my will to conform myself to a married life, to which I was given up and enthralled. I had heard from the mouth of the Truth, that there were some eunuchs which had made themselves eunuchs for the kingdom of heaven's sake... Surely vain are all men who are ignorant of God, and could not...find...Him who is good. But I was no longer in that vanity; I had surmounted it; and by the common witness of all Your creatures had found You our Creator, and Your Word...For You have said to man, Behold, the fear of the Lord is wisdom, and, Desire not to seem wise; because they who affirmed themselves to be wise, became fools. But I had now found the goodly pearl, which...I ought to have bought, and I hesitated.

...But I still under service to the earth, refused to fight under Your banner, and feared as much to be freed of all encumbrances... Thus with the baggage of this present world was I held down pleasantly, as in sleep...And as no one would sleep for ever, and in all men's sober judgment waking is better, yet a man for the most part, feeling a heavy lethargy in all his limbs, defers to shake off sleep, and though half displeased, yet, even after it is time to rise, with pleasure yields to it, so was I assured that much better were it for me to give myself up to Your charity, than to give myself over to my own desires; but though the former course satisfied me and gained the mastery, the latter pleased me and held me mastered.

...Who then should deliver me thus wretched from the body of this death, but Your grace only, through Jesus Christ our Lord?

And how You did deliver me out of the bonds of desire, wherewith I was bound most strictly to carnal concupiscence, and out of the drudgery of worldly things, I will now declare, and confess to Your name, O Lord, my helper and my redeemer. Amid increasing anxiety, I was doing my wonted business, and daily sighing to You. I attended Your Church, whenever free from the business under the burden of which I groaned…

…But I wretched, most wretched, in the very commencement of my early youth, had begged chastity of You, and said, "Give me chastity and abstinence, only not yet." For I feared lest You should hear me… and…cure me of the disease of concupiscence, which I wished to have satisfied, rather than extinguished.

…But now it spoke very faintly. For on that side where I had set my face, and where I trembled to go, there appeared to me the chaste dignity of abstinence, serene…honestly alluring me to come and doubt not; and stretching forth to receive and embrace me, her holy hands full of multitudes of good examples: there were so many young men and maidens here, a multitude of youth and every age, grave widows and aged virgins; and Abstinence herself in all, not barren, but a fruitful mother of children of joys, by You her Husband, O Lord. And she smiled on me with a persuasive mockery, as would she say, "Cannot you [do] what these youths, what these maidens can? The Lord their God gave me to them…Cast yourself upon Him, fear not He will not withdraw Himself that you should fall; cast yourself fearlessly upon Him, He will receive, and will heal you." And I blushed exceedingly, for that I yet heard the muttering of those toys, and hung in suspense. And she again seemed to say, "Stop your ears against those your unclean members on the earth, that they may be mortified. They tell you of delights, but not as does the law of the Lord your God." This controversy in my heart was self against self only...

(Note to reader from Kathleen: Part of Augustine's lengthy description has been omitted here. Please know that his friend, Alypius, a faithful Christian convert, was present with Augustine during this emotional conversion as you read the part below.)

But when a deep consideration had from the secret bottom of my soul drawn together and heaped up all my misery in the sight of my heart; there arose a mighty storm, bringing a mighty shower of tears. Which that I might pour forth wholly, in its natural expressions, I rose from Alypius: solitude was suggested to me as fitter for the business of weeping; so I retired so far that even his presence could not be a burden to me. Thus was it then with me, and he perceived something of it; for something I suppose I had spoken, wherein the tones of my voice appeared choked with weeping, and so had risen up. He then remained where we were sitting, most extremely astonished. I cast myself down I know not how, under a certain fig tree, giving full vent to my tears; and the floods of my eyes gushed out an acceptable sacrifice to You. And, not indeed in these words, yet to this purpose, spoke I much to You: and You, O Lord, how long? how long, Lord, will You be angry forever? Remember not our former iniquities, for I felt that I was held by them. I sent up these sorrowful words: How long, how long, "tomorrow, and tomorrow?" Why not now? Why not is there this hour an end to my uncleanness?"

St. Augustine

So was I speaking and weeping in the most bitter contrition of my heart, when, lo! I heard from a neighboring house a voice, as of boy or girl, I know not, chanting, and oft repeating, "Take up and read; Take up and read." Instantly, my demeanor altered, I began to think most intently whether children were wont in any kind of play to sing such words: nor could I remember ever to have heard the like. So checking the torrent of my tears, I arose; interpreting it to be no other than a command from God to open the book, and read the first chapter I should find. For I had heard of Antony, that coming in during the reading of the Gospel, he received the admonition, as if what was being read was spoken to him: Go, sell all that you have, and give to the poor, and you shall have treasure in heaven, and come and follow me: and by such oracle he was forthwith converted to You. Eagerly then I returned to the place where Alypius was sitting; for there had I laid the volume...I seized, opened, and in silence read that section on which my eyes first fell: Not in rioting and drunkenness, not in sexual sin and wantonness, not in strife and envying; but put ye on the Lord Jesus Christ, and make not provision for the flesh, in concupiscence. No further would I read; nor needed I: for instantly at the end of this sentence, by a light as it were of serenity infused into my heart, all the darkness of doubt vanished away.

Then putting my finger between, or some other mark, I shut the volume... He, Alypius, asked to see what I had read: I showed him; and he looked even further than I had read, and I knew not what followed. This followed, him that is weak in the faith, receive; which he applied to himself, and disclosed to me. And by this admonition was he strengthened; and by a good resolution and purpose, and most corresponding to his character, wherein he did always very far differ from me, for the better, without any turbulent delay he joined me. Then we go in to my mother; we tell her; she rejoices: we relate in order how it took place; she leaps for joy, and triumphs, and blesses You, Who are able to do above that which we ask or think; for she perceived that You had given her more for me, than she was wont to beg by her pitiful and most sorrowful groanings. For You converted me to Yourself, so that I sought neither wife, nor any hope of this world, standing in that rule of faith, where You had shown me to her in a vision, so many years before. And You did convert her mourning into joy, much more plentiful than she had desired, and in a much more precious and purer way than she before required, by having grandchildren of my body.

DR. RONDA'S CONTEMPORARY APPLICATIONS AND PERSONAL REFLECTIONS

The *Confessions* are regarded as the first full scale autobiography ever written. This may be, some surmise, because there is such an emphasis in Christianity on being called to conversion personally by God. A contemporary application for us could be the dynamic impact of witness stories for evangelization of unbelievers and also for motivation of believers.

Augustine's frank descriptions of the moral evils he fell into as a youth and also as a young adult certainly resonate with our times. Even though there are certainly some teens and older people who never experiment or indulge chronically in sexual sins, theft, gang activities, or cult-like practices, many do. Reading of Augustine's conversion is, therefore, a proof that God's grace can change the life of such sinners and bring them to a life of holiness.

A specific contemporary application involves the movement loosely called "New Age." In a book of mine, *Battle for the 20th Century Mind*, I describe elements of this movement. What is important for this chapter is how Augustine, after his conversion, manifests the same basic Catholic philosophy of life we have now. Just as Augustine had to find his way out of the maze of Gnostic ideas of his time, we need to see how the same Catholic philosophy contrasts to the New Age beliefs so much in vogue in our times.

In the 1980's the term New Age became the name for any mixture of astrology, clairvoyance, prophecy, and meditation with the common belief in a cosmic convergence of light. Many New Agers thought that the year 2000 would bring radical changes in the universe, perhaps even a unification of intelligences from other planets with our earth's sages. Often New Agers included elements of classical Christianity, especially communication with angels, but also with Jesus. The Jesus of most New Agers, however, is different from the Jesus worshiped by Christians in the past. In New Age movements, Jesus is generally seen as only one of many great sources of light. He is on a par with Buddha, Krishna or with contemporary gurus such as Sai Baba, an alleged worker of miracles in India.

It is characteristic of the New Age movement to take elements from many sources, sometimes even demonic, to create a personal synthesis. New Agers usually take some ideas from one system and some from other systems. By contrast, Catholics and other Christians study Scripture, tradition and the writings of the great Christian masters for formation. Even though loyal Catholics are open to truths of other traditions, they will be careful to avoid anything coming from the occult.

Whereas New Agers hold to individual religious experience, even when it is contrary to classical Christian belief, Catholics see their spirituality as a response to the persons of the Trinity and as an exemplification of dogmatic truth.

Most New Agers believe the Divine is within the soul instead of above and beyond the self. By contrast, believers in revealed religion, such as Catholics, Jews, Moslems, and non-Catholic Christians know God as beyond the universe yet, also, being present within it.

Many New Agers overcome emotions of loneliness and alienation by immersing themselves in meditation on the oneness of everything in the universe. They seek an ultimate unity where their own selfhood would be fused into the divine. On the contrary, Catholics and others belonging to Western religions believe that the unique self will never disappear since it is created in love by God for the purpose of uniting in love to God, other persons and all other beings of the universe.

It is characteristic of many New Age systems to emphasize ignorance as the main source of suffering in the world. Accordingly, an enlightened person chooses good not so much out of love, but out of desire to avoid the consequences of wrong choices for oneself such as turbulence, anxiety, and emotional enslavement. Catholics and others of Judeo-Christian or Moslem background know that moral evil and the sufferings that follow come from the deliberate choice of evil called sin.

Many New Agers come from Jewish or Christian families where God was seen as a harsh authority figure, perhaps in the image of their own, often unreasonable, human fathers. As a result these seekers and others who simply cannot accept traditional religious authority, find comfort in the belief that no one can enforce anything upon them against their own judgment and will. By contrast, Catholics and others coming from a revealed religion will see God's authority as absolutely binding. In a difference of opinion how could the absolute omniscient God be wrong, and limited puny-minded I be right?

Because many New Agers reject the concept of creation by God at a given moment in time, they tend to think of time in the most common Eastern way as an everlasting cycle. Since they see God as the divine within, there is no God to judge the soul. Instead the soul evolves from ignorance to enlightenment through a series of incarnations in different bodies. Classical Judeo-Christian thought accepts God's revelation of a beginning and end of time with the soul being judged after one lifetime.

Generally speaking, most New Agers reject laboring for justice on this earth in terms of righting wrongs or alleviating physical suffering. This is because such seekers think that spiritual solutions are more important. Such a dualistic philosophy is contrary to the Christian insistence that spiritual growth is normally expressed in works of justice and compassion.

For me, St. Augustine's writings are most important as manifesting that spirituality can be passionate rather than sedate and sort of "safe." Whereas the liturgy has to be formal to bind people together in public prayer, personal prayer can be as full of passionate yearning as fits a person's specific need or mood. Even though I love the rosary, mercy chaplet, and liturgy of the hours, with set words, I also love to just heave my heart up to Jesus and beg Him to help me understand, or help me to love better, or help me to endure heavy crosses. Augustine style, I heave all this up to God in prayer.

Augustine goes back and forth between writing to the God within and the God beyond. This is called immanence vs. transcendence. I think it is good for us to go back and forth between these realms. If we think of God only as utterly beyond us, we have to "stand on tippy-toe" to pray. But if we think of God only as within us, we can make Him into a sort of "pocket God" to take out and tell Him what to do from time to time each day!

Augustine writes of life on this earth as a kind of "living death." Does he mean there are no joys in life? I don't think so. However, in terms of the four temperaments I would place him more among the melancholic, very serious, long-suffering types than among those who find life mainly delightful, with tragedies the exception.

St. Augustine

KATHLEEN'S CONTEMPORARY APPLICATIONS AND PERSONAL REFLECTIONS

One of the most wonderful things about exploring the lives and experiences of the saints is that, no matter what our own struggles and difficulties, we can always find someone who has experienced them before. Their journeys can often help us on our way. In our own time, when so much emphasis is placed on experimentation, be it scientific, philosophical, chemical, sexual or whatever other type, the life of St. Augustine is completely relevant.

Turning his back on the faith of his mother, he followed the teaching of nearly every school of thought of his time. Each new idea, no matter how heretical, was food for thought for him, and worth trying on for size. He wanted to enjoy life with no responsibility and to do things his way, much to the heartache of his mother, St. Monica. Even when he began to pray, he asked God for chastity, "but not yet." He was having too much fun.

Being a professor of rhetoric, Augustine was accustomed to expressing his views, and using his persuasion on others. He likely would have been completely at home with YouTube, Facebook and Twitter. Today, many of us experience the same thing. So many are observing life online that they do not know how to live it. It is increasingly difficult to foster relationship when our eyes are constantly on some form of technology. We even text the person beside us!

But eventually the emptiness of Augustine's life took a toll on him and he began to earnestly seek truth. He found it in the Catholic faith. The philosophies of his time were for the elite and well-educated. In Christianity, Augustine found truth for everyone, and a way to live it. In Christ he found standards coupled with mercy. It was the mercy that made Christianity different and attractive.

Although he lived in the fourth century, there could not be a more perfect saint for our times than Augustine. With civilization crumbling around us like the Roman Empire around Augustine, we are in need of a moral compass, of truth, and most assuredly of mercy. Maybe all we need to do is follow St. Augustine through his *Confessions* to find the answers we seek.

The story of Augustine's conversion touches me because my own conversion to the faith was pretty dramatic. After having spent my youth as an Episcopalian with many perfect attendance bars on my Sunday School pin, I spent most of my teen years as a doubter. How could a good and merciful God allow all the suffering in the world, especially among innocent children? I sometimes thought leaving this world would be the answer and am sure the only reason I did not act on such thoughts was because of pride coupled with fear that in death I would cease to exist altogether.

In terms of the seeking and conversion, however, I know it began early in my life with musings and wonderings about what was "out there." I recall in fourth grade walking home from a friend's house and wondering as I went what had been in that place before. When had these houses been built, what was there before them, and before that, and before that? I brought my thoughts, without then realizing what I was doing, to the first cause. I brought my thoughts?

Or God brought my thoughts? Like St. Augustine, I do see that He has put within our hearts knowledge of Him and His law, yearning for Him, and thoughts and questions that will lead us to Him.

After the birth of our daughter, I began to fear that people would hurt her in the future, and that we had brought her into a world where there was no justice. I saw so much lack of responsibility and accountability that I needed to know there was hope of some ultimate authority Who was just, and yet somehow loving and merciful. There was an absolute craving to know there was someone or something in ultimate control.

Divine Providence brought into my life a very faith-filled Catholic woman. She did not set out to convert me, but I had no intention of going back to my old faith. The Catholic Church had always intrigued me, but when she tried to guide me to Our Lady, I told her that I had no belief in God and, therefore, none in His mother. She posed an interesting question to me. "If you go to Our Lady and get no answer, are you any worse off than you are now?" I had to admit I would not be. "If, on the other hand, you go to Our Lady and get an answer – and you will get an answer because she always answers – then what?" She admonished me to, "get on your knees and call her dear Lady and speak with respect."

That night I got down on my knees. I said, "Dear Lady, if you are there and if you hear me, I need to know that there is a God and that there is hope for the future. I need you to send me a sign, a scapular." I had no idea what a scapular was. I had just heard my new friend talking about one. I knew that if I heard from Mary all would be well. I somehow knew that if she helped me, her Son must be God.

Shortly thereafter, I visited another Catholic friend and told her of my fears. She said she had something for me. She had just returned from a trip to Rome and gave me a small plastic envelope containing a green scapular. She said it had been blessed by the Pope, and that she wanted me to have it. I put it around my neck that night and went to bed.

Waking around midnight, I sat straight up in bed, grasping the scapular around my neck and sobbing, "O my God, this is my sign!!!" For days I held that scapular in my hand and walked around as if I were a dog taking myself for a walk on my new leash. I kissed the scapular and held it to my cheek often. It was my lifeline, my tangible "proof" that someone had heard my prayer!

But God did even more than answer me through His Mother. At the time of my conversion my uncle was dying of Hodgkin's Disease. He was not yet 40. He was given 24-48 hours to live, and I was going to visit him.

Before my husband and I left the hospital that night, I took the Green Scapular from my neck and slipped it under my uncle's pillow. I didn't need it anymore. The next day, I called to see how he was doing and my mother told me that he was awake, sitting up, and feeding himself. Without hesitation I said, "That's my Lady!"

Some weeks later, Uncle Pat was again near death. I went to visit and pray for him. It was Sunday, March 13th. As no one was there with him then but me, I asked St. Joseph, Patron of a happy death, to pray that he would not die alone. My Dad called that evening to see how my visit had gone. Instantly I said, "He's going to die Thursday." My dad replied, sounding slightly amused, "On St. Patrick's Day?"

At 4 p.m. on Thursday, I was putting towels away in the linen closet and prayed, "St. Patrick, today is your feast day. Please look down on your namesake and ask God to take him Home if he isn't going to get better." That night my mother called at 7:00 p.m. to tell me Uncle Pat had died—at 4:30 p.m. He did not die alone. God used death, the very thing of which I was most frightened, to give me my faith.

It is said that converts make the best Catholics. Perhaps that is because, as St. Augustine observed, being away from God makes finding Him all the more precious. As he wrote in Book VIII, "For the enemy is more overcome in one, of whom he hath more hold; by whom he hath hold of more."

FOR PERSONAL REFLECTION AND GROUP SHARING

1. St. Augustine certainly felt personally called to conversion. Have you felt so called as a convert or a revert? If so, describe your story.

2. In the *Confessions* we read how Augustine mingles his yearning for truth with constant prayer. Do you believe that this is relevant for our own time? How can someone else's faith jour-

ney help you with yours?

3. What questions has God put in your heart to help you seek Him?

4. Do you experience God within you or more above and without—by your side or in the realities you experience outside yourself?

5. Augustine was critical of the education methods of his time. What aspects of his critique would you think of as defects in education today?

6. In Book VIII Augustine shares his conversion with his convert friend. Have stories of converts ever moved you?

7. St. Augustine certainly felt personally called to conversion. Have you felt so called as a convert or a revert? If so, describe your story.

8. In the *Confessions* we read how Augustine mingles his yearning for truth with constant prayer. Do you believe that this is relevant for our own time? How can someone else's faith journey help you with yours?

9. What questions has God put in your heart to help you seek Him?

10. If you wish, write a prayer – for yourself or others – inspired by this reading.

ST. BENEDICT (480–547)
ST. BENEDICT'S RULE

Benedict, son of a noble family, spent his youth studying in Rome. As a young adult, he discerned that living the Gospel was contrary to the world around him. He left Rome and sought the company of men who had withdrawn from the temptations of the culture of the age. After some time, however, he began to seek even greater solitude and poverty in the town of Subiaco. He became a hermit, living in a cave. A group of monks begged him to be their leader. He did so reluctantly, thinking they were not sincere. It is important to know that these monks tried to poison him. Otherwise, when we read his Rule we may think he was being harsh in his estimation of what might be hidden in the hearts of men – even those withdrawn from the world.

Because of the miracles attributed to him, many looked to St. Benedict for spiritual advice. From these disciples came many monasteries. It was for these that St. Benedict wrote his famous Rule.

Saint Benedict is most well known as the founder of monasticism in the West. Aside from parish priests at the time, there were many hermits but none living together under a detailed rule. St. Benedict founded twelve communities for monks at Subiaco. There were also what we would call boarding schools established for youth sent by their parents to be trained in Christian virtue. Later he founded Monte Cassino in the mountains of southern Italy. St. Benedict's Rule influenced not only members of the order but also educators, rulers, and heads of families. It is still followed by monks and nuns in our times, and is characterized by a spirit of balance. The rule is, however, demanding because it admonishes us to watch our every thought, word, and deed.

Excerpts from The Rule Of St. Benedict[1]

[As you read this document you will see that some of it relates best to monks, but you will also see that much of it is good for the spiritual growth of any person trying to be a follower of Christ. You might highlight portions of relevance to your own state of life. Dr. Ronda has added in brackets brief explanations of words or concepts that might puzzle you.]

Prologue

Listen, O my son, to the precepts of your master, and incline the ear of your heart, and cheerfully receive and faithfully execute

---

1 Boniface Verheyen, O.S.B., *The Rule of St. Benedict,* at CCEL, http://www.ccel.org/ccel/benedict/rule.html (Common Domain)

the admonitions of your loving Father, that by the toil of obedience you may return to Him from whom by the sloth of disobedience you have gone away.

To you, therefore, my speech is now directed, who, giving up your own will, take up the strong and most excellent arms of obedience, to do battle for Christ the Lord, the true King.

In the first place, beg of Him by most earnest prayer, that He perfect whatever good you begin, in order that He who has been pleased to count us in the number of His children, need never be grieved at our evil deeds. For we ought at all times so to serve Him with the good things which He has given us, that He may not, like an angry father, disinherit his children, nor, like a dread lord, enraged at our evil deeds, hand us over to everlasting punishment as most wicked servants, who would not follow Him to glory.

Let us then rise at length, since the Scripture arouses us, saying: "It is now the hour for us to rise from sleep" (Rom 13:11); and having opened our eyes to the deifying light, let us hear with awe-struck ears what the divine voice, crying out daily, admonishing us, saying: "Today, if you shall hear his voice, harden not your hearts" (Ps 94[95]:8). And again: "He that has ears to hear let him hear what the Spirit says to the churches" (Rev 2:7). And what does He say?—"Come, children, listen to me, I will teach you the fear of the Lord" (Ps 33[34]:12). "Run while you have the light of life, that the darkness of death overtake you not" (Jn 12:35).

And the Lord seeking His workman in the multitude of the people, to whom He proclaims these words, says again: "Who is the man that desires life and loves to see good days" (Ps 33[34]:13)? If hearing this you answer, "I am he," God says to you: "If you will have true and everlasting life, keep your tongue from evil, and your lips from speaking guile; turn away from evil and do good; seek after peace and pursue it" (Ps 33[34]:14-15). And when you shall have done these things, my eyes shall be upon you, and my ears to your prayers. And before you shall call upon me I will say: "Behold, I am here" (Is 58:9).

Chapter 2 - What Kind of Man the Abbot Ought to Be

The Abbot who is worthy to be over a monastery, ought always to be mindful of what he is called, and make his works square with his name of Superior. For he is believed to hold the place of Christ in the monastery, when he is called by his name, according to the saying of the Apostle: "You have received the spirit of adoption of sons, whereby we cry Abba (Father)" (Rom 8:15). Therefore, the Abbot should never teach, prescribe, or command (which God forbid) anything contrary to the laws of the Lord; but his commands and teaching should be instilled like a leaven of divine justice into the minds of his disciples.

Let the Abbot always bear in mind that he must give an account in the dread judgment of God of both his own teaching and of the obedience of his disciples. And let the Abbot know that whatever lack of profit the master of the house shall find in the sheep, will be laid to the blame of the shepherd. On the other hand he will be blameless, if he gave all a shepherd's care to his restless and unruly flock...

When, therefore, anyone takes the name of Abbot he should govern his disciples by a twofold teaching; namely, he should show them all that is good and holy by his deeds more than by his words; explain the commandments of God to intelligent disciples by words, but show the divine precepts to the dull and simple by his works. And let him show by his actions, that whatever he teaches his disciples as being contrary to the law of God must not be done, "lest perhaps when he has preached to others, he himself should become a castaway" (1 Cor 9:27)...

The Abbot ought always to remember what he is and what he is called, and to know that to whom much has been entrusted, from him much will be required; and let him understand what a difficult and arduous task he assumes in governing souls and accommodating himself to a variety of characters. Let him so adjust and adapt himself to everyone—to one gentleness of speech, to another by reproofs, and to still another by entreaties, to each one according to his bent and understanding—that he not only suffer no loss in his flock, but may rejoice in the increase of a worthy fold...

Chapter 4 - The Instruments of Good Works

1. In the first place to love the Lord God with the whole heart, the whole soul, the whole strength...
2. Then, one's neighbor as one's self (cf Mt 22:37-39; Mk 12:30-31; Lk 10:27).

3. Then, not to kill...

4. Not to commit adultery...

5. Not to steal...

6. Not to covet (cf Rom 13:9).

7. Not to bear false witness (cf Mt 19:18; Mk 10:19; Lk 18:20).

8. To honor all men (cf 1 Pt 2:17).

9. And what one would not have done to himself, not to do to another (cf Tob 4:16; Mt 7:12; Lk 6:31).

10. To deny one's self in order to follow Christ (cf Mt 16:24; Lk 9:23).

11. To deny earthly pleasures (cf 1 Cor 9:27).

12. Not to seek after pleasures.

13. To love fasting.

14. To relieve the poor.

15. To clothe the naked...

16. To visit the sick (cf Mt 25:36).

17. To bury the dead.

18. To help in trouble.

19. To console the sorrowing.

20. To hold one's self aloof from worldly ways.

21. To prefer nothing to the love of Christ.

22. Not to give way to anger.

23. Not to foster a desire for revenge.

24. Not to entertain deceit in the heart.

25. Not to make a false peace.

26. Not to forsake charity.

27. Not to swear, lest perchance one swear falsely.

28. To speak the truth with heart and tongue.

29. Not to return evil for evil (cf 1 Thes 5:15; 1 Pt 3:9).

30. To do no injury, yea, even patiently to bear the injury done us.

31. To love one's enemies (cf Mt 5:44; Lk 6:27).

32. Not to curse them that curse us, but rather to bless them.

33. To bear persecution for justice sake (cf Mt 5:10).

34. Not to be proud...

35. Not to be given to wine (cf Ti 1:7; 1 Tm 3:3).

36. Not to be a great eater.

37. Not to be drowsy.

38. Not to be slothful (cf Rom 12:11).

39. Not to be a complainer.

40. Not to be a detractor.

41. To put one's trust in God.

42. To refer what good one sees in himself, not to self, but to God.

43. But as to any evil in himself, let him be convinced that it is his own and charge it to himself.

44. To fear the day of judgment.

45. To be in dread of hell.

46. To desire eternal life with all spiritual longing.

47. To keep death before one's eyes daily.

48. To keep a constant watch over the actions of our life.

49. To hold as certain that God sees us everywhere.

50. To dash at once against Christ the evil thoughts which rise in one's heart.

51. And to disclose them to our spiritual father.

52. To guard one's tongue against bad and wicked speech.

53. Not to love much speaking.

54. Not to speak useless words and such as provoke laughter.

55. Not to love much or boisterous laughter.

56. To listen willingly to holy reading.

57. To apply one's self often to prayer.

58. To confess one's past sins to God daily in prayer with sighs and tears, and to amend them for the future.

59. Not to fulfill the desires of the flesh (cf Gal 5:16).

60. To hate one's own will.

61. To obey the commands of the Abbot in all things, even though he himself (which Heaven forbid) act otherwise, mindful of that precept of the Lord: "What they say, do; what they do, do

not" (Mt 23:3).

62. Not to desire to be called holy before one is; but to be holy first, that one may be truly so called.

63. To fulfill daily the commandments of God by works.

64. To love chastity.

65. To hate no one.

66. Not to be jealous; not to entertain envy.

67. Not to love strife.

68. Not to love pride.

69. To honor the aged.

70. To love the younger.

71. To pray for one's enemies in the love of Christ.

72. To make peace with an adversary before the setting of the sun.

73. And never to despair of God's mercy.

Behold, these are the instruments of the spiritual art, which, if they have been applied without ceasing day and night and approved on judgment day, will merit for us from the Lord that reward which He has promised: "The eye has not seen, nor the ear heard, neither has it entered into the heart of man, what things God has prepared for them that love Him" (1 Cor 2:9). But the workshop in which we perform all these works with diligence is the enclosure of the monastery, and stability in the community.

Chapter 5 - Of Obedience

…This obedience, however, will be acceptable to God and agreeable to men then only, if what is commanded is done without hesitation, delay, lukewarmness, grumbling or complaint, because the obedience which is rendered to Superiors is rendered to God. For He Himself has said: "He that hears you hears Me" (Lk 10:16)…

Chapter 6 - Of Silence

Let us do what the Prophet says: "I said, I will take heed of my ways, that I sin not with my tongue: I have set a guard to my mouth, I was dumb, and was humbled, and kept silence even from good things" (Ps 38[39]:2-3). Here the prophet shows that, if at times we ought to refrain from useful speech for the sake of silence, how much more ought we to abstain from evil words on account of the punishment due to sin…

Chapter 7 - Of Humility

Brethren, the Holy Scripture cries to us saying: "Every one that exalts himself shall be humbled; and he that humbles himself shall be exalted" (Lk 14:11; 18:14). Since, therefore, it says this, it shows us that every exaltation is a kind of pride…

The first degree of humility, then, is that a man always have the fear of God before his eyes (cf Ps 35[36]:2)…and that he be ever mindful of all that God has commanded…and that life everlasting is prepared for those who fear God. And whilst he guards himself evermore against sin and vices of thought, word, deed, and self-will, let him also hasten to cut off the desires of the flesh...

The second degree of humility is, when a man loves not his own will, nor is pleased to fulfill his own desires but by his deeds carries out that word of the Lord which says: "I came not to do My own will but the will of Him that sent Me" (Jn 6:38). It is likewise said: "Self-will has its punishment, but necessity wins the crown."

The third degree of humility is, that for the love of God a man subject himself to a Superior in all obedience, imitating the Lord, of whom the Apostle says: "He became obedient to death" (Phil 2:8).

The fourth degree of humility is, that, if hard and distasteful things are commanded, nay, even though injuries are inflicted, he accept them with patience and even temper, and not grow weary or give up, but hold out, as the Scripture says: "He that shall persevere to the end shall be saved" (Mt 10:22)...

(Note from Dr. Ronda Chervin: The next chapters up to chapter 20 detail the hours for liturgical prayer. In our times these have been adjusted but most monks do arise very early in the morning for Office of Readings and then go to bed early keeping the grand silence through the night. All the monks participate in Holy Mass, morning prayer, evening prayer and night prayer spoken or chanted together. Since the language describing these hours in this translation is archaic, I will skip ahead. I will also skip many other chapters of lesser general importance.)

Chapter 20 - Of Reverence at Prayer

If we do not venture to approach men who are in power, except with humility and reverence, when we wish to ask a favor, how much must we beseech the Lord God of all things with all humility and purity of devotion? And let us be assured that it is not in many words, but in the purity of heart and tears of compunction that we are heard. For this reason prayer ought to be short and pure, unless, perhaps it is lengthened by the inspiration of divine grace. At the community exercises, however, let the prayer always be short, and the sign having been given by the Superior, let all rise together.

Chapter 40 - Of the Quantity of Drink

"Everyone has his proper gift from God, one after this manner and another after that" (1 Cor 7:7). It is with some hesitation, therefore, that we determine the measure of nourishment for others. However, making allowance for the weakness of the infirm, we think one hemina of wine a day [about 10 ounces] is sufficient for each one. But to whom God grants the endurance of abstinence, let them know that they will have their special reward. If the circumstances of the place, or the work, or the summer's heat should require more, let that depend on the judgment of the Superior, who must above all things see to it, that excess or drunkenness do not creep in.

Although we read that wine is not at all proper for monks, yet, because monks in our times cannot be persuaded of this, let us agree to this, at least, that we do not drink to satiety, but sparingly; because "wine makes even wise men fall off" (Sir 19:2). But where the poverty of the place will not permit the aforesaid measure to be had, but much less, or none at all, let those who live there bless God and complain not. This we charge above all things, that they live without complaining.

Chapter 48 - Of the Daily Work

Idleness is the enemy of the soul; and therefore the brethren ought to be employed in manual labor at certain times, at others, in devout reading...

If, however, the needs of the place, or poverty should require that they do the work of gathering the harvest themselves, let them not be downcast, for then are they monks in truth, if they live by the work of their hands, as did also our forefathers and the Apostles...let all things be done with moderation...

Above all, let one or two of the seniors be appointed to go about the monastery during the time that the brethren devote to reading and take notice, lest perhaps a slothful brother be found who gives himself up to idleness or vain talk, and does not attend to his reading, and is unprofitable, not only to himself, but disturbs also others.

Chapter 49 - On the Keeping of Lent

The life of a monk ought always to be a Lenten observance.

However, since such virtue is that of few, we advise that during these days of Lent he guard his life with all purity and at the same time wash away during these holy days all the shortcomings of other times. This will then be worthily done, if we restrain ourselves from all vices. Let us devote ourselves to tearful prayers, to reading and compunction of heart, and to abstinence.

During these days, therefore, let us add something to the usual amount of our service, special prayers, abstinence from food and drink, that each one offer to God "with the joy of the Holy Ghost" (1 Thes 1:6), of his own accord, something above his prescribed measure; namely, let him withdraw from his body somewhat of food, drink, sleep, speech, merriment, and with the gladness of spiritual desire await Holy Easter.

Let each one, however, make known to his Abbot what he offers and let it be done with his approval and blessing; because what is done without permission of the spiritual father will be imputed to presumption and vain glory, and not to merit. Therefore, let all be done with the approval of the Abbot.

Chapter 52 - Of the Oratory of the Monastery

Let the oratory be what it is called, and let nothing else be done or stored there. When the Work of God is finished, let all go out with the deepest silence, and let reverence be shown to God; that a brother who perhaps desires to pray especially by himself is not prevented by another's misconduct. But if perhaps another desires to pray alone in private, let him enter with simplicity and pray, not with a loud voice, but with tears and fervor of heart. Therefore, let him who does not say his prayers in this way, not be permitted to stay in the oratory after the Work of God is finished, as we said, that another may not be disturbed.

Chapter 52 - Of the Reception of Guests

Let all guests who arrive be received as Christ, because He will say: "I was a stranger and you took Me in" (Mt 25:35). And let due honor be shown to all, especially to those "of the household of the faith" (Gal 6:10) and to wayfarers...

Chapter 72 - Of the Virtuous Zeal Which the Monks Ought to Have

As there is a harsh and evil zeal which separates from God and leads to hell, so there is a virtuous zeal which separates from vice and leads to God and life everlasting.

"Therefore, practice this zeal with most ardent love; namely, that in honor they forerun one another" (cf Rom 12:10). Let them bear their infirmities, whether of body or mind, with the utmost patience; let them vie with one another in obedience. Let no one follow what he thinks useful to himself, but rather to another. Let them practice fraternal charity with a chaste love.

Let them fear God...with sincere and humble affection; let them prefer nothing whatever to Christ, and my He lead us all together to life everlasting.

DR. RONDA'S CONTEMPORARY APPLICATIONS AND PERSONAL REFLECTIONS

From the very start of St. Benedict's Rule there is an emphasis on obedience. Some of the readers of this book of excerpts belong to communities where rules of obedience are carefully spelled out. The Church provides rules for all of her members involving liturgy and also morality. Family life and work life depend on obedience.

In our 21st century culture there is probably more rebellion against obedience than in any other time. We might ponder why this is so and also what the consequences are of disobedience. Perhaps our consciousness of the evils of obedience to illegitimate authority in the case of totalitarian countries of the 20th and 21st centuries has influenced us to be wary of obedience. What about reaction against rigid authority in certain Church groups leading to wariness toward good forms of authority? Have we pushed individualism to a ridiculous degree? Some obvious good consequences of obedience to legitimate authority would be order, peace, self-control, just to mention a few. How does a pride, detrimental to holiness, come into play in the area of disobedience?

The description of the Abbot includes seeking counsel even of the youngest. This seems to me to be an early sign of a democratic vs. a monarchic view of community life. Being the leader is not an inherited role but is subject to election.

In chapter 4 St. Benedict provides a long list of approved and disapproved attitudes and acts. It is noteworthy that some of these are generally accepted as necessary for peaceful community living whether belief in God is in play or not, but others of these ways can usually be embraced by those who believe in God and in eternal rewards and punishments. Examples from St. Benedict's chapter would be love of enemies, avoidance of revenge, to deny one's self in order to follow Christ, to chastise the body [self-denial], not to seek after pleasures [he doesn't mean not having any pleasures, but not looking for them and certainly not being what we would call addicted to them], to love fasting…to hold one's self aloof from worldly way [think of forms of entertainment, for example, that promote sin], to prefer nothing to the love of Christ; to do no injury, yea, even patiently to bear the injury done us; not to be proud [he doesn't mean to have low self-esteem but to attribute to God rather than oneself whatever we do that is good]; to put one's trust in God; to fear the day of judgment; to be in dread of hell; to desire eternal life with all spiritual longing; to keep death before one's eyes daily; to hold as certain that God sees us everywhere; to dash at once against Christ the evil thoughts which rise in one's heart and to disclose them to our spiritual father [note that this is different from repression]; to confess one's past sins to God daily in prayer with sighs and tears, and to amend them for the future…; to hate one's own will [that is, not to always work for the fulfillment of all one's own needs instead of for the common good]; to hate no one; to make peace with an adversary before the setting of the sun, and never to despair of God's mercy.

I tend to find the sober admonitions of this Rule a little daunting. I would like to think there is a short-cut to communal life where love and joy could come without so much self-control. However, my experience is that when there is plenty of love of God and love of neighbor but without the kind of prudence and justice described in Benedict's Rule, instead of joy there often comes unbearable injustices, conflicts, and discontent.

On the degrees of humility, I notice that many times I don't see that I am doing things others find annoying because I am self-centered. My actions sometimes don't take into account the needs of others, so that it seems as if I were saying "I count and you don't." An example would be interrupting others in conversation or in their tasks to insist they listen to me or help me. Dietrich Von Hildebrand had a related teaching. He called it not being too attached to "the immanent logic of an activity." This is what he meant. You are doing something good such as cooking dinner. Someone calls from another room to ask you to help with something. What is asked is more important in itself, but the immanent logic of your activity is to put the spices in the stew right after throwing the vegetables and meat into the pot. So, you put the person who needs you off, and finish your activity first. This example is trivial, but much less trivial would be when you finish all your e-mails while on the cell phone with a friend who needs your full attention about his/her problems. The immanent logic of finishing the e-mails should not dictate my choices, but rather what is the most loving thing to do at this time.

Most readers find Benedict's admonitions against levity extreme. I think, however, that sometimes I indulge in humor inappropriately out of a kind of nervousness where others would prefer to continue a more serious conversation. And, certainly some of the humor on TV or in books I read is not wholesome but ridiculing or making light of sin.

I find St. Benedict's insistence on telling others one's sins and problems, especially a spiritual director and/or confessor, extremely relevant to our times. Catholic therapists warn against stuffing emotions, what was previously called repression. When I try to do that I get angry at myself or others, and then depressed, but the minute I tell what I am feeling or my sins in confession I feel relief and readiness for a new start.

I always find the parts about hospitality in Benedict's Rule challenging. Even though I greatly benefit from those virtues of hospitality when I am the recipient, I find housework boring. I need to realize that the goal of life is not exciting projects but love and that little deeds of love are just as important as big ventures.

KATHLEEN'S CONTEMPORARY APPLICATIONS AND PERSONAL REFLECTIONS

We come from all walks of life to this study of spiritual classics. At first glance it may seem that at best St. Benedict's Rule is applicable only to those in religious life, or at worst is completely outdated and irrelevant. But if we look at it with a truly open heart and mind, it is more likely we will come to find in it a wisdom that is easily and readily adapted to every kind of life.

We spend so many hundreds and thousands of dollars on counseling these days. There are life coaches, motivational speakers, family counselors, marriage counselors, career counselors, self-help books, and all manner of advice-givers. Every talk show host gives advice on how to nourish our spirits or fulfill our dreams, how to vote, how to think. Everyone is an expert on political correctness.

The trouble with all of this is that it is based on varied perceptions and changing schools of thought. The advice or guidance that seems good today can be completely contradicted tomorrow, often leaving us confused and lost.

In The Rule of St. Benedict, however, we find sound wisdom based on unchanging, eternal truth, according to the natural law of God written in our hearts. He gives us guidelines to help us become our best selves while also encouraging the common good. What applies to communal life in the monastery can also be applied to each individual, to relationships, to marriages and families, to parishes, teams, towns, states, nations – every type of community.

How different the world would be if we still lived according to this kind of wisdom! The selfishness, entitlement, and anything-goes outlooks that result in our acquisitive hearts and "what about me" attitudes are producing the bullying, broken marriages and families, and win-at-any-cost priorities that are the norm today. We are desperately in need of individual responsibility, respect for legitimate authority (both in those who lead and in those who follow), commitment, self-control, honesty, humility, and contrition. Having written the first rule of its kind for the first communities of their kind, St.

Benedict offers us an insight and guidance that we would do well to follow today as well!

What speaks to me most in St. Benedict's introduction are the admonitions about tongue and lips and words. I have, half-jokingly and half in fear, often thought that my purgatory will be 4,000 years with my tongue on fire. I do believe my mouth is my greatest source of sin. Of course, the mouth only reflects what is in the mind and heart. He has also inspired me to take my evil thoughts and "dash them against the rock, which is Christ." What a wonderful habit to develop, God help me!

The prominent thing the Lord seems to be doing in me these days is to remind me again and again that it is not about me. It's about Him. So, St. Benedict's urging to remember that we must not become "puffed up" but, rather, give the glory to God is also striking to me. My job is not to do well, it is to be well.

Chapter 4 of the Rule is simple and yet complex. It is simple in that all we really need to do is the first point: "First of all, to love the Lord thy God with all thy heart, with all thy soul, and with all thy strength." Truly, if we do that we must, by definition, do all the points that follow.

But the Rule is complex in that all the points are necessary in order to make it clear to us imperfect, still-learning humans how to do point one! Number 30 is especially hard for me: "To do no wrong to anyone, but to bear patiently any wrong done to oneself." Although I fail, I do try to do no wrong to anyone. The harder part, for me, although I am also working on this, is to bear patiently any wrong done to me. I don't instantly think, "Let me be silent and offer this to Jesus." I usually think, "Why is this happening to me?" I usually say, "Lord, do you see this? Did you hear that?" After some time I may, by the prompting of God through my Guardian Angel, finally get around to thinking, "Oh, yeah, let me offer this up to God." But I have such a long way to go on this one point alone that I cannot imagine I will ever achieve living it readily.

Lord Jesus, St. Benedict quotes at the end of his Rule the reading I use so often with my students: "Eye has not seen, ear has not heard, nor has it so much as dawned on man what God has prepared for those who love Him." Help me, with your grace, to love you—really love you—with all my heart and with all my soul and with all my strength, so that one day where you are I also may be. Amen.

FOR PERSONAL REFLECTION AND GROUP SHARING

1. Where do you see a greater need for obedience in our society? In the church?

2. Read Chapter 4 of St. Benedict's Rule slowly and see what the Holy Spirit might be telling you.

3. Do people consider you to be humble or proud, or to use more contemporary language do they think you are often self-centered?

4. Did any of the admonitions in the rule seem to you to be excessive? Did any seem realistic and necessary even if, in our times, we would tend to be more lax even in a monastery?

5. In Chapter 40 St. Benedict writes about drink. What experience do you have yourself or with others, if you wish to share, concerning social drinking becoming excessive?

6. While the Rule of St. Benedict is directed toward religious life in a monastery, do you see ways of applying it to life in society that can be of benefit?

7. If you wish, compose your own prayer to integrate a truth in the readings into your life.

ST. BERNARD OF CLAIRVAUX (1090-1153) SERMONS ON THE SONG OF SONGS

St. Bernard of Clairvaux (1090-1153) was a Frenchman born to a noble family. He had a wonderful education in literature and theology. As a young adult he became a monk, followed eventually by all his brothers, his widower father, and his sister who, after being married, became a nun with her husband's consent. Bernard entered the Cistercian Order in Citeaux but then founded a new one in Clairvaux. Though an Abbot, he also preached outside the monastery and became a famous inspirer of the Crusades. St. Bernard was responsible for the founding of more than sixty-eight monasteries. He wrote many treatises of which the most famous is the one from which I have excerpted on the Song of Songs. Because these were originally talks he gave to his monks, I have included the charming way he ends each one with remarks about their other duties. (To understand these sermons it would be well to first read the Song of Songs in the Old Testament.)

It should be noted that in the tradition of Old Testament commentaries by Jewish rabbis, the Song of Song, was always considered to be an allegory of union with God vs. simply a beautiful, passionate, love song.

Excerpts from St. Bernard's Sermons on the Song of Songs[1]

Sermon 1

1. The instructions that I address to you, my brothers, will differ from those I should deliver to people in the world, at least the manner will be different. The preacher who desires to follow St. Paul's method of teaching will give them milk to drink rather than solid food, and will serve a more nourishing diet to those who are spiritually enlightened: "We teach," he said, "not in the way philosophy is taught, but in the way that the Spirit teaches us: we teach spiritual things spiritually." And again: "We have a wisdom to offer those who have reached maturity," in whose company, I feel assured, you are to be found, unless in vain have you prolonged your study of divine teaching, mortified your senses, and meditated day and night on God's law. Be ready then to feed on bread rather than milk. Solomon has bread to give that is splendid and delicious, the bread of that book called "The Song of Songs." Let us bring it forth then if you please,

---

[1] Wright, Darrell (etext arrangement), St. Bernard of Clairvoux, *Commentary on the Song of Songs*, at http://www.archive.org/details/StBernardsCommentaryOnTheSongOfSongs (The version from which excerpts have been taken is in common domain and the language modernized)

and break it.

3. ...Before the flesh has been tamed and the spirit set free by zeal for truth, before the world's glamour and entanglements have been firmly repudiated, it is a rash enterprise on any man's part to presume to study spiritual doctrines... "an unspiritual person cannot accept anything of the Spirit of God..."

7. ...The title is not simply the word "Song," but "Song of Songs," a detail not without significance. For though I have read many songs in the Scriptures, I cannot recall any that bear such a name. Israel chanted a song to Yahweh celebrating his escape from the sword and the tyranny of Pharaoh, and the twofold good fortune that simultaneously liberated and avenged him in the Red Sea. Yet even though chanted, this has not been called a "Song of Songs"; Scripture...introduces it with the words: "Israel sang this song in honor of Yahweh." Song poured from the lips of Deborah, of Judith, of the mother of Samuel, of several of the prophets, yet none of these songs is styled a "Song of Songs." You will find that all of them... were inspired to song because of favors to themselves or to their people, songs for a victory won, for an escape from danger or the gaining of a boon long sought. They would not be found ungrateful for the divine beneficence, so all sang for reasons proper to each ... But King Solomon himself, unique as he was in wisdom, renowned above all men, abounding in wealth, secure in his peace, stood in no need of any particular benefit that would have inspired him to sing those songs...

8. We must conclude then it was a special divine impulse that

inspired these songs of his that now celebrate the praises of Christ and his Church, the gift of holy love, the sacrament of endless union with God. Here too are expressed the mounting desires of the soul, its marriage song, an exultation of spirit poured forth in figurative language…I consider this nuptial song to be well deserving of the title… the Song of Songs, just as he in whose honor it is sung is uniquely proclaimed King of kings and Lord of lords.

9. Furthermore if you look back on your own experience, is it not in that victory by which your faith overcomes the world…that you yourselves sing a new song to the Lord for all the marvels he has performed? Again, when he purposed to "settle your feet on a rock and to direct your steps," then too, I feel certain, a new song was sounding on your lips, a song to our God for his gracious renewal of your life. When you repented he not only forgave your sins but even promised rewards, so that rejoicing in the hope of benefits to come, you sing of the Lord's ways: how great is the glory of the Lord!…

11. But there is that other song which…excels all those I have mentioned and any others there might be…the Song of Songs… For it is not a melody that resounds abroad but the very music of the heart, not a trilling on the lips but an inward pulsing of delight, a harmony not of voices but of wills. It is a tune you will not hear in the streets, these notes do not sound where crowds assemble; only the singer hears it and the one to whom he sings—the lover and the beloved. It is preeminently a marriage song telling of chaste souls in loving embrace, of their wills in sweet concord, of the mutual exchange of the heart's affections.

St. Bernard of Clairvaux

Various Meanings of the Kiss

Sermon 2

1. During my frequent ponderings on the burning desire with which the patriarchs longed for the incarnation of Christ, I am stung with sorrow and shame. Even now I can scarcely restrain my tears, so filled with shame am I by the lukewarmness, the frigid unconcern of these miserable times. For which of us does the consummation of that event fill with as much joy as the mere promise of it inflamed the desires of the holy men of pre-Christian times? Very soon now there will be great rejoicing as we celebrate the feast of Christ's birth. But how I wish it were inspired by his birth! All the more therefore do I pray that the intense longing of those men of old, their heartfelt expectation, may be enkindled in me by these words: "Let him kiss me with the kiss of his mouth."…

3. I must ask you to try to give your whole attention here. The… kiss…takes its being both from the giver and the receiver, a person… none other than "the one mediator between God and mankind, himself a man, Christ Jesus."… A fertile kiss therefore, a marvel of stupendous self-abasement that is not a mere pressing of mouth upon mouth; it is the uniting of God with man. Normally the touch of lip on lip is the sign of the loving embrace of hearts, but this conjoining of natures brings together the human and divine, shows God reconciling "to himself all things, whether on earth or in heaven. For he is the peace between us, and has made the two into one."…

4. …Even the holy men who lived before the coming of Christ understood that God had in mind plans of peace for the human race… What he did reveal however was obscure to many. For in those days faith was a rare thing on the earth, and hope but a faint impulse in the heart even of many of those who looked forward to the deliverance of Israel. Those indeed who foreknew also proclaimed that Christ would come as man, and with him, peace. One of them actually said: "He himself will be peace in our land when he comes." Enlightened from above they confidently spread abroad the message that through him men would be restored to the favor of God. John, the fore-runner of the Lord, recognizing the fulfillment of that prophecy in his own time, declared: "Grace and truth have come through Jesus Christ." In our time every Christian can discover by experience that this is true…

7. We should by now have come to understand how the discontent of our ancestors displayed a need for this sacrosanct kiss, that is, the mystery of the incarnate word, for faith…was ever on the point of failing…Therefore because Christ was late in coming, and the whole human race in danger of being lost in despair…those good men whose faith remained strong eagerly longed for the more powerful assurance that only his human presence could convey. They prayed intensely for a sign that the covenant was about to be restored for the sake of a spiritless, faithless people…

Sermon 3

1. Today the text we are to study is the book of our own experi-

ence. You must therefore turn your attention inwards, each one must take note of his own particular awareness of the things I am about to discuss. I am attempting to discover if any of you has been privileged to say from his heart: "Let him kiss me with the kiss of his mouth." Those to whom it is given to utter these words sincerely are comparatively few, but anyone who has received this mystical kiss from the mouth of Christ at least once, seeks again that intimate experience, and eagerly looks for its frequent renewal. I think that nobody can grasp what it is except the one who receives it...

2. I should like however to point out to persons...still attached to sin that there is an appropriate place for them on the way of salvation. They may not rashly aspire to the lips of a most benign Bridegroom...Like the publican full of misgiving, they must turn their eyes to the earth rather than up to heaven. Eyes that are accustomed only to darkness will be dazzled by the brightness of the spiritual world, overpowered by its splendor, repulsed by its peerless radiance and whelmed again in a gloom more dense than before.

All you who are conscious of sin, do not regard as unworthy and despicable that position where the holy sinner laid down her sins, and put on the garment of holiness... You may ask what skill enabled her to accomplish this change, or on what grounds did she merit it? I can tell you in a few words. She wept bitterly, she sighed deeply from her heart, she sobbed with a repentance that shook her very being, till the evil that inflamed her passions was cleansed away...

It is up to you, wretched sinner; to humble yourself as this happy penitent did so that you may be rid of your wretchedness.

Prostrate yourself on the ground, take hold of his feet, soothe them with kisses, sprinkle them with your tears and so wash not them but yourself...

3. Though you have made a beginning by kissing the feet, you may not presume to rise at once by impulse to the kiss of the mouth; there is a step to be surmounted in between, an intervening kiss on the hand... He... who gave me the grace to repent, must also give me the power to persevere, lest by repeating my sins I should end up by being worse than I was before. Woe to me then, repentant though I be, if he without whom I can do nothing should suddenly withdraw his supporting hand. I really mean nothing; of myself I can achieve neither repentance nor perseverance...

4. I am now able to see what I must seek for and receive before I may hope to attain to a higher and holier state... On receiving such a grace then, you must kiss his hand, that is, you must give glory to his name, not to yourself...

5. Once you have had this twofold experience of God's benevolence in these two kisses (the kiss of the feet and of the hand) you need no longer feel abashed in aspiring to a holier intimacy. Growth in grace brings expansion of confidence you will love with greater ardor, and knock on the door with greater assurance, in order to gain what you perceive to be still wanting to you. "The one who knocks will always have the door opened to him."...

Sermon 6 - on The Song of Songs

9. I myself, however wretched I may be, have been occasion-

ally privileged to sit at the feet of the Lord Jesus, and to the extent that his merciful love allowed, have embraced with all my heart, now one, now the other, of these feet... of mercy and judgment I will sing to you, O Lord. I shall never forget your precepts, mercy and judgment will be the theme of my songs in the house of my pilgrimage, until one day when mercy triumphs over judgment, my wretchedness will cease to smart, and my heart, silent no longer, will sing to you. It will be the end of sorrow.

Intimacies of the Love of God

Sermon 7

2. "Let him kiss me with the kiss of his mouth," she said. Now who is this "she"? The bride. But why bride? Because she is the soul thirsting for God. In order to clarify for you the characteristics of the bride, I shall deal briefly with the diverse affective relationships between persons. Fear motivates a slave's attitude to his master, gain that of wage-earner to his employer, the learner is attentive to his teacher, the son is respectful to his father. But the one who asks for a kiss, she is a lover.

Among all the natural endowments of man love holds first place, especially when it is directed to God, who is the source...No sweeter names can be found to embody that sweet interflow of affections between the Word and the soul, than bridegroom and bride. Between these all things are equally shared, there are no selfish reservations, nothing that causes division. They share the same inheritance, the same table, the same home, the same marriage-bed, they are flesh of each other's flesh. "This is why a man leaves his father and mother and joins himself to his wife, and they become one body." The bride for her part is bidden to "forget her nation and her ancestral home," so that the bridegroom may fall in love with her beauty.

Therefore if a love relationship is the special and outstanding characteristic of the bride and groom, it is not unfitting to call the soul that loves God a bride. Now one who asks for a kiss is in love. It is not for liberty that she asks, nor for an award, not for an inheritance nor even knowledge, but for a kiss. It is obviously the request of a bride who is chaste, who breathes forth a love that is holy, a love whose ardor she cannot entirely disguise...but with a spontaneous outburst from the abundance of her heart, direct even to the point of boldness, she says: "Let him kiss me with the kiss of his mouth."...

8. ...Her desire is to be kissed, she asks for what she desires; but she doesn't call her lover by name, she is certain that they know him because he has been so often the subject of her conversation with them. Accordingly she does not say: "Let this one or that one kiss me;" but simply: "let him kiss me." This was the way Mary Magdalene behaved; she did not mention the name of the person she sought when she spoke to the man whom she took to be the gardener: "Sir, if you have taken him away..." Who is this "him"? She names no name, she takes for granted that what her own heart could not forget, even for a moment, must be plain to all. And so the bride's

words to the Bridegroom's companions imply that they know her secret, that her inward state is manifest to them, and no name passes her lips in that impulsive pleading about her beloved: "Let him kiss me with the kiss of his mouth." ...

Sermon 9

2. ..."I cannot rest," she said, "unless he kisses me with the kiss of his mouth. I thank him for the kiss of the feet, I thank him too for the kiss of the hand; but if he has genuine regard for me, let him kiss me with the kiss of his mouth. There is no question of ingratitude on my part, it is simply that I am in love. The favors I have received are far above what I deserve, but they are less than what I long for... My shame indeed rebukes me, but love is stronger than all. I am well aware that he is a king who loves justice; but headlong love does not wait for judgment...I implore; let him kiss me with the kiss of his mouth.

"Don't you see that by his grace I have been for many years now careful to lead a chaste and sober life, I concentrate on spiritual studies, resist vices, pray often; I am watchful against temptations, I recount all my years in the bitterness of my soul. As far as I can judge I have lived among the brethren without quarrels. I have been submissive to authority...Yet in all these practices there is evidence only of my fidelity, nothing of enjoyment...I obey the commandments, to the best of my ability I hope, but in doing so my soul thirsts like a parched land. If therefore he is to find my holocaust acceptable, let him kiss me, I entreat, with the kiss of his mouth."...

The Kind of Shepherd by which the Bride Says She was Found and the Love of Truth Which She Has Learned From Them

Sermon 77

...Holy Mother Church...Your guardians do not slumber or sleep. Your guardians are the holy angels, your watchmen are the spirits and souls of the righteous. Anyone is correct in feeling that you have been found by both alike, and by both alike you are guarded. And they each have their special care for you: the saints because they will not themselves be made perfect without you; the angels because without you their full number cannot be restored...Be sure then that it is your voice which says in the Psalm, "The just wait for me, until you reward me."

5. ...And so it was; she sought the bridegroom, and this was not hidden from him, for he himself had urged her on to seek him, and given her the desire to fulfill his commands and follow his way of life. But there must be someone to instruct her and teach her the way of prudence. Therefore he sent out, as it were, gardeners to cultivate and water his garden, to train and strengthen her in all truth, that is, to teach her and give her sure tidings of her beloved, since he is himself the truth which she seeks and which her soul truly loves. Indeed, who is the faithful and true lover of the soul if not he through whom the truth is loved? I am endowed with reason; I am capable of

receiving truth, but this would be vain if I lacked the love of truth. He is the fruit of this vine, and I am the root. I am not safe from the axe if I am found apart from him. It is doubtless by nature's endowment that the divine likeness shines forth, and in this I am superior to all living creatures. Therefore my soul ventures to respond to the chaste embraces of truth, and so to rest in the complete assurance of his love and sweetness, provided that it finds favor in the eyes of so great a bridegroom, and that he accounts it worthy to attain to his glory, and even presents it to himself as a bride without spot or wrinkle or anything of that kind...

6. But now the Bride does not find him whom she sought, but is found by those whom she did not seek. Let this be a warning to those who are not afraid to enter the paths of life without anyone to guide and teach them, but act as their own pupils as well as their own teachers in the spiritual life. Nor are they satisfied with this; they even collect disciples, the blind leading the blind. How many have we seen wander from the right path, to their great peril, as a result of this? For their ignorance of the wiles and tricks of Satan brings it about that those who began in the spirit finish in the flesh. They are led seriously astray and fall damnably. Such men should see that they walk carefully and take warning from the Bride, who could not reach her beloved until she was met by those whose ministry she used to gain knowledge of her beloved, to learn the fear of the Lord...The man who sends his sheep to pasture without a guardian is a shepherd not of sheep but of wolves...

How God, the Angelic Host, and Man Work Together

Book 86 - The Modesty of the Bride

3. ...Anyone who wishes to pray must choose not only the right place but also the right time. A time of leisure is best and most convenient, the deep silence when others are asleep is particularly suitable, for prayer will then be freer and purer. "Arise at the first watch of the night, and pour out your heart like water before the face of the Lord, your God." How secretly prayer goes up in the night, witnessed only by God and the holy angel who receives it to present it at the heavenly altar! How pleasing, how unclouded it is, colored with the blush of modesty! How serene, how calm, free from noise and interruption! How pure it is, how sincere, unsullied by the dust of earthly care, untouched by ostentation or human flattery! Therefore the Bride, as modest as she is cautious, when she desired to pray, that is, to seek the Word—for they are the same—sought the privacy of her bed at night. You will not pray aright, if in your prayers you seek anything but the Word, or seek him for the sake of anything but the Word; for in him are all things. In him is healing for your wounds, help in your need, restoration for your faults, resources for your further growth; in him is all that men should ask or desire, all they need, all that will profit them. There is no reason therefore to ask anything else of the Word, for he is all. Even if we seem sometimes to ask for material things, providing that we do so for the sake of the Word, as we should, it is not the things themselves that we are asking for, but him

for whose sake we ask them. ...

(Bernard of Clairvaux died in 1153, not having completed his commentary on The Song of Songs.)

DR. RONDA'S CONTEMPORARY APPLICATIONS AND PERSONAL REFLECTIONS

To understand St. Bernard's writings, it is good to know of the traditional three stages of the spiritual life dating from the time of the 5th-6th centuries. These three stages are called the purgative way, the illuminative way, and the unitive way. Essentially, the purgative way is the period in an individual's spiritual life where he or she is being purged of all kind of sins, mortal and venial. In the illuminative way, the person of prayer receives many grace-filled insights from the Holy Spirit. In the final, unitive way, that precedes life in eternity, the mind is quiet and the heart is usually at peace. Christ lives in such a person's soul and His love overflows from it to others.

The Sermons on the Song of Songs is primarily an exhortation to St. Bernard's monks to courageously pass through the purgative way, to be illumined by the Holy Spirit and to long for and savor union with God. These stages are not shut off from each other for there are elements of each in all our lives until the joys of heaven. Most spiritual directors think that the three stages are universal in the sense that most devoted Christians will go through them.

In my own experience, maybe because I was a convert from an

atheistic background, I think the illuminative stage was given to me more rapidly than usual, as an accompaniment to much purgation. I had none of the basics of Catholic theology given in catechism to born-Catholics to help my understanding. Maybe, also, because of being such an analytic philosopher, in love with concepts, it was very hard for me to make the transition from the illuminative to the beginnings of the unitive stage where God chose to come to me more in silence than with beautiful new ideas.

Some of you may feel that the language of St. Bernard is too emotional. Myself, more a person of the mind and will than of the heart, I also have that problem with St. Bernard's way of writing. However, I love to read it so that I can give my heart more room to grow! In the course of prayer once I wrote these words. I think they were a gift from the Holy Spirit because they are much more lovely than my usual style!

Love is not loved.

(During Eucharistic Adoration, I was crouched in my alcove praying the Office of Readings. I was gazing at the famous face of Christ painted by El Greco on the cover of my prayer book. The words I heard him speaking in my heart as I looked at that Spanish face were those of St. Bernard from a song he wrote: "Love is not loved."

When I, Ronda, stare into Your sad eyes, my Jesus, those words "Love is not loved!" come to me not as a general statement but as directed to me. It seems that You want me to know just how wounding it is for You that I will not trust the love that went to such lengths to prove itself. Staring at the pure whiteness of Your presence in the host in the monstrance and, then, down at Your face in the painting I try to respond.

I could produce many reasons why I don't love Love enough:
- is it easier for me to love You as truth because truth is strong and love is vulnerable?
- is it easier for me to love You as beauty because beauty is sublime and love is messy?
- is it easier for me to love You as mercy because mercy is balm and love is strenuous?

When I look into Your tragic eyes, my Jesus, I think the reason might be deeper still. Terror of surrender to Your Divine heart whose beat is so loud I could no longer hear my own? Fear that after diving into Your waves You might cast me out on the shore even more helpless to survive?

Or, still more simply, that I could refuse You nothing, no matter how painful, if I was close enough to know You wanted it!

I hear You telling me that I cannot experience the fullness of Your love for me if I am afraid to come closer. 'Perfect love casts out fear.' Surrender!

Yet a perfect unison of heartbeat with Jesus would be you, Mother Mary. You certainly did not emerge from your surrender to the Holy Spirit as a dead fish. No! Rather as Queen of Apostles!

Another term in spiritual theology of describing St. Bernard's writings is Bridal Mysticism. This term, in German, "Braut Mystique", means experiencing the soul as the beloved of Christ. It has quite a different flavor than, say, mostly seeing Jesus as a friend walking beside someone to give them advice! You will find lots of bridal mysticism not only in St. Bernard but in other writers in our anthology. If the experience is a bit foreign to you, still, open your heart to the possibility of surprises.

KATHLEEN'S CONTEMPORARY APPLICATIONS AND PERSONAL REFLECTIONS

Nearly 1,000 years ago St. Bernard lamented in Sermon 2 Paragraph 1, "Very soon now there will be great rejoicing as we celebrate the feast of Christ's birth. But how I wish it were inspired by his birth!" Although we may perceive his time as having been holier and more God-centered than our own, his words might have been written today. So many of us struggle to "keep Christ in Christmas" and to retain the wish for a "Merry Christmas," when the majority of people seem to settle for the generic and Christ-less "Happy Holidays."

The lesson that I find extremely pertinent today in the sermons of St. Bernard is the glorious demonstration and example of love between God and His people. We are given a clearer understanding of how God loves us, but equally as important is the guideline for us to love God. If we think of God at all these days, it is usually to ask Him for blessings. We seem to imagine Him as some sort of genie sitting up in heaven granting wishes, or some benevolent, aging grandfather kindly and patiently showing us the way and giving us treats, waiting for us to have time to visit.

St. Bernard's reminder to put our focus on God where it belongs, to respond to Him and to give Him the love and worship due Him is critical. Once we see this, however, we can also apply these lessons of love to other areas of life. It seems to me the greatest need for this today is in two places: our marriages and families, and in the priesthood.

The need to be fulfilled and happy has been so ingrained in us that we have lost our sense of commitment and giving. Instead of asking how we can contribute to the success and well-being of those around us, we are more likely to ask, "What about me?"

The Sermons on The Song of Songs, however, offer us a new way to look at things. Whether we are in marriage or in priesthood, the image of the Bridegroom and His Bride, The Church, gives us an example of loving and giving no matter what. We are shown how to give of ourselves not of "stuff," not to be overindulgent, but to give what matters: our time and attention – our love. If we spent more time loving each other, and less time criticizing, demanding, and acquiring, how different things would be.

St. Bernard writes about my favorite image of Christ: the Bridegroom. In researching a paper on *The Songs of Songs*, I fell in love with Origen's commentary on this book of Scripture and that exquisite image of the love between Christ and His Bride, the Church. The depth of the significance of this image is infinite: Christ loving us to His death, grooming us for heaven, filling us with all we need through His sacraments, and directly giving an example to married couples of the total self-giving and infinite forgiveness that is required in marriage. This is the consummate representation of Jesus not only telling us what to do, but also doing it first Himself, giving us His own example.

We are made in the image and likeness of God and are to become as much like Christ as we can. We are given everything we need to achieve that: the Ten Commandments tell us what God expects of us, the Incarnation and Paschal Mystery redeem our souls and reunite us to God *in* His Son, and the Sacraments of the Church give us His own life and love in the grace we receive, enabling us to do and be what He wants us to do and be.

Origen adds that the oils, the spices, and fragrances of the Groom are graces and love that cannot help but cover the Bride as He unites in love with her. Here is God's grace covering us and changing us, and making us fit for heaven. We reflect Him. His odor of sanctity is our odor of sanctity. He is the anointed One and we are transformed by His anointing.

St. Bernard talks about the love between the Bridegroom and the Bride. He makes it quite clear that love is the only way in which we respond in likeness to God in our relationship with Him. He points out that we do not judge God as He judges us, nor do we save Him as He saves us. It is only in responding to His love with our own that we act in like manner to Him, although we do not love perfectly as does our God.

This image of Christ and His Bride, the Church, is so overwhelming to me that I truly believe it is the single most powerful image in the whole spiritual tradition. The meaning and interpretations contained in it are so far-reaching that I believe it answers every possible question and is the most perfect example to us. More importantly, it gives great hope that we can, in fact, make marriages work, be self-giving priests, be cleansed of every stain of sin, be strengthened against temptation, and finally arrive at union with God, who loves us unto goodness.

FOR PERSONAL REFLECTION AND GROUP SHARING

1. St. Bernard displays in his writings what is called Bridal Mysticism. Do you find this idea and the style of St. Bernard too "feminine," or can you appropriate it to understanding your own soul as bride?

2. Can you apply this image of love to your own relationships or your own ability to give or receive love?

3. What do you see of value in St. Bernard's lesson about having proper guides along our way?

ST. HILDEGARD OF BINGEN (11TH C – 1170)

Hildegard was born in 1098, the tenth child of a noble family in Germany. In early childhood, her parents placed her with a visionary named Jutta. In their cell, connected to a Benedictine monastery, there was probably prayer, meditation, scripture reading, and handwork. Others joined them and, at the age of 15, Hildegard became a Benedictine nun.

Following Jutta's death in 1136, Hildegard became her successor in the community. In search of greater poverty, she moved to Rupertsberg. In 1165, with the community continuing to grow, she founded a second monastery at Eibingen.

Considered the first German Mystic, Hildegard began having visions when she was three. She revealed that her experience of God came through her five senses. When she was 42, she believed God instructed her to write her experiences but she was hesitant to do so. Finally, with the approval of the Pope, she wrote of her visions as revelations given her by the Holy Spirit.

Hildegard wrote an extensive collection of music based on Gregorian Chant, and was also known for her ability to heal using herbs, precious stones, and minerals. She was sensitive to the natural world around her and noted that God put everything here for the use of mankind.

A popular and gifted speaker, Hildegard addressed clergy and laity, particularly unusual for a woman of her times. She died in 1170 and was canonized in 2012 as a Doctor of the Church.

Quotations from St. Hildegard of Bingen

Letter to the Monk Guibert, 1175[1]

Just as a mirror, which reflects all things, is set in its own container, so too the rational soul is placed in the fragile container of the body. In this way, the body is governed in its earthly life by the soul, and the soul contemplates heavenly things through faith.

Letter to the Abbot, c. 1166 [2]

Like hairs on the head, mortal man is joined to Jesus Christ, the head of all, but they are full of transgressions and sins because of man's delight in the flesh. But the Church regenerates and purifies these from the unclean stench and filth of sin by penitence and confession, just as hair is cleansed from dew and drops, and as dust is

---

1 *The Letters of Hildegard of Bingen* : Volume II, Volume 2, page 22
2 *The Letters of Hildegard of Bingen* : Volume II, Volume 2, page 90

shaken out and cleansed from wool.

Letter to the Monk Guibert, 1176[3]

May the Holy Spirit enkindle you with the fire of His Love so that you may persevere, unfailingly, in the love of His service. Thus you may merit to become, at last, a living stone in the celestial Jerusalem.

"Quia ergo femina"[4]

> For since a woman drew up death,
> a virgin gleaming dashed it down,
> and therefore is the highest blessing found
> in woman's form
> before all other creatures.
> For God was made a human
> in the blessed Virgin sweet.

"Soul Weavings"[5]

The marvels of God are not brought forth from one's self.

---

3 The Letters of Hildegard of Bingen : Volume II, Volume 2, page 41
4 http://www.hildegard-society.org/2014/09/quia-ergo-femina-antiphon.html Latin collated from the transcription of Beverly Lomer and the edition of Barbara Newman; translation by Nathaniel M. Campbell
5 *Swallow's Nest: A Feminine Reading of the Psalms* By Marchiene Vroon Rienstra

Rather, it is more like a chord, a sound that is played.
The tone does not come out of the chord itself, but rather, through the touch of the Musician.
I am, of course, the lyre and harp of God's kindness.

Letter to Elisabeth of Schönau[6]

...Man is a vessel which God has fashioned for himself, and which He has imbued with His inspiration so that He might complete all His works in him...

...For although God gave him (man) great knowledge, man elevated himself in his own spirit, and turned away from God. God had looked on man to perfect all His works in him, but the ancient evil deluded him, and through the delight of an unseasonable wind tainted him with the sin of disobedience when he sought for more than he should have.

"Caritas Abundat"[7]

Love abounds in all things,
excels from the depths to beyond the stars,
is lovingly disposed to all things.
She has given the king on high
the kiss of peace.

---

6 *The Personal Correspondence of Hildegard of Bingen*, edited by Joseph L. Baird, Page 103-104
7 *Selected Writings* Hildegard of Bingen Penguin UK, 2005

St. Hildegard of Bingen

Letter to the Abbot, c. 1166[8]

The devil keeps man from good with a thousand machinations spewed from his belly, so that when a person sighs to do good, he pierces him with his shafts; and when he desires to embrace God with his whole heart in love, he subjects him to poisonous tribulations, seeking to pervert good work before God. And when a person seeks virtue, the devil tells him that he does not know what he is doing, and he teaches him that he can set his own law for himself.

Quotes with Book Citations

The soul is a breath of living spirit, that with excellent sensitivity, permeates the entire body to give it life. Just so, the breath of the air makes the earth fruitful. Thus the air is the soul of the earth, moistening it, greening it.[9]

I, the fiery life of divine wisdom, I ignite the beauty of the plains, I sparkle the waters, I burn in the sun, and the moon, and the stars.[10]

The earth which sustains humanity must not be injured, it must not be destroyed.[11]

---

8 The Letters of Hildegard of Bingen : Volume II, Volume 2, page 90
9 Meditations with Hildegard of Bingen By Hildegard von Bingen pg 61
10 Hildegard of Bingen: An Integrated Vision By Anne H. King-Lenzmeie Pg 65
11 Personal Pilgrimage: One Day Soul Journeys for Busy People By Viki Hurst pg 176

Quotes with Web Citation[12]

Every element has a sound, an original sound from the order of God; all those sounds unite like the harmony from harps and zithers.

There is the Music of Heaven in all things and we have forgotten how to hear it until we sing.

Underneath all the texts, all the sacred psalms and canticles, these watery varieties of sounds and silences, terrifying, mysterious, whirling and sometimes gestating and gentle must somehow be felt in the pulse, ebb, and flow of the music that sings in me. My new song must float like a feather on the breath of God.

When the words come, they are merely empty shells without the music. They live as they are sung, for the words are the body and the music the spirit.

Symphony of the Blessed (From Vision Thirteen/Death for Martyrs)[13]

Then I saw the lucent sky, in which I heard different kinds of music, marvelously embodying all the meanings I had heard before. I heard the praises of the joyous citizens of Heaven, steadfastly preserving in the ways of Truth: and laments calling people back to those praises and joys; and the exhortations of the virtues, spurring one another on to secure the salvation of the peoples ensnared by the Devil. And the virtues destroyed the snares, so that the faithful at last

---

12 http://www.humanitiesweb.org/spa/ccq/ID/3
13 Adrienne Nater, "Hildegard of Bingen, *Scivias,* 1141," *Death, Dying, Grief and Mourning in Western Literature,* at www.deathdyinggriefandmourning.com/. Permission received from Adrienne Nater to reprint this.

St. Hildegard of Bingen

through repentance passed out of their sins and into Heaven.

And their song, like the voice of the multitude, making music in harmony praising the ranks of Heaven, had these words:

To the Martyrs

O ye who have poured out your blood in triumph,
And conquered a share in the blood of the Lamb who perished,
Feasting upon the slain calf's sacrifice,
And so built the Church, what a great reward is yours!
Alive, you followed the Lamb, and despised your bodies,
Adorned His pains, and so recaptured your portions.

O rose blossoms, blessed in the joy of your blood's effusion!
Your fragrant blood flowed forth from the inner counsel
Of Him Who has been always, without beginning,
And planned before time began His great redemption.

Your company is honor, whose blood abounded

To build the church in the stream from your noble wounds.

Ave Generosa – *Hymn to the Virgin*[14]

In the pupil of chastity's eye
I beheld you
untouched.
Generous maid! Know that it's God
who broods over you.

---

14 *Symphonia: A Critical Edition of the Symphonia Armonie Celestium ...* By Saint Hildegard, Trans. Barbara Newman pg 123

For heaven flooded you like
unbodied speech
and you gave it a tongue.

Glistening
lily: before all worlds
you lured the supernal one.

How he reveled
in your charms! How your beauty
warmed to his caresses
till you gave your breast to his child.

And your womb held joy when heaven's
harmonies rang from you,
a maiden with child by God,
for in God your chastity blazed.

Yes your flesh held joy like the grass
when the dew falls, when heaven
freshens its green: O mother
of gladness, verdure of spring.
Ecclesia, flush with rapture! Sing
for Mary's sake, sing
for the maiden, sing
for God's mother. Sing!

St. Hildegard of Bingen

Antiphon for the Trinity[15]

To the Trinity be praise!
God is music,
God is life
that nurtures every creature in its kind.
Our God is the song of the angel throng
and the splendor of secret ways
hid from all humankind,
But God, our life is the life of all.

Antiphon for God the Father[16]

Father,
Great is our need and we beg,
we beg with a word that was
fullness within us:
look again.
It is fitting—let your word
look again that we fail not,
that your name be not
darkened within us.
Tell us your name again
lest we forget.

---

15 *Symphonia: A Critical Edition of the Symphonia Armonie Celestium ... By Saint Hildegard*, Trans. Barbara Newman pg. 142
16 *Symphonia: A Critical Edition of the Symphonia Armonie Celestium ... By Saint Hildegard*, Trans. Barbara Newman pg. 105

Antiphon for Patriarchs and Prophets[17]

    Spectacular men! you see
    with the spirit's eyes,
    piercing the veil.
    In a luminous shade you proclaim
    a sharp living brightness
    that buds from a branch
    that blossomed alone
    when the radical light took root.

    Holy ones of old! you foretold
    deliverance for the souls
    of exiles
    slumped in the dead lands.

    Like wheels you
    spun round in wonder as you spoke
    of the mysterious mountain
    at the brink of heaven
    that stills many waters, sailing
    over the waves.

    And a shining lamp
    burned in the midst of you!

---

17 *Symphonia: A Critical Edition of the Symphonia Armonie Celestium ...* By Saint Hildegard ,Trans. Barbara Newman pg. 159

Pointing,

he runs to the mountain.

DR. RONDA'S CONTEMPORARY APPLICATIONS AND PERSONAL REFLECTIONS

In the history of the Church we see how the Church baptizes (makes Catholic) things in cultures that, at first, seem inimical to truth. Examples would be Augustine baptizing Neo-Platonic ideas, or Aquinas baptizing Aristotle. The ideas of St. Hildegard have been used by movements such as New Age and Ecology. Now that no less a thinker than Pope Benedict has sealed with approval the basic concepts of St. Hildegard in naming her a Doctor of the Church, we would do well to use those ideas as a way to transform what is true in ecology as part of our own synthesis.

KATHLEEN'S CONTEMPORARY APPLICATIONS AND PERSONAL REFLECTIONS

How beautiful these teachings and insights of St. Hildegard! She is able to take the most profound musings and make them so simple for us. She sees all creation as a great symphony in which glory is given to God and, because of His great mercy, each of us is a part of it!

I love the way these visions, inspirations, and writings of St. Hildegard make clear that each of us is a vessel God fills with His glory, to be reflected to others and back to Him. It's such a beautiful image. Each of us is to reflect the glory of God in our own place and time. How very sad that we have lost sight of this. We spend so much time chasing after "stuff" and trying to achieve what others perceive as success, that we have no time left to contemplate this glorious creation God has given us, or our part in HIS plan for its fulfillment.

We spend so much time moaning and whining about how hard life is and asking, "Why me?" Perhaps if we spent less time trying to do things our way and more time reflecting on God's way, things would come together as He intends or, at least, we would be able to see that there is a reason for the struggle. Suffering is redemptive. We are to endure what comes with love for the salvation of souls.

St. Hildegard reminds us that when we try to get close to God, the enemy will attack us. We seldom think the enemy is at work. Very often, we think God is punishing us for something, or we ask why all these things happen to us when we are trying to please Him. The answer is, that the enemy does not want us to be close to God, or to please Him, or to even believe in Him. Hasn't he done a wonderful job of distracting us from the glory meant to be reflected in us, or to be shared by us?!

St. Hildegard is given to see that God has designed this creation. It is not some accidental explosion with random results. There is a plan here. When we focus on God, apply the guidance He has given us in His Word, and the strength He provides in His Sacraments, we are purified of our sin and the result is a beautiful symphony glorifying God. We have the hope to share in that glory.

But St. Hildegard says we cannot bring forth God's marvels on our own. My favorite line in St. Hildegard's writing *Symphony of the Blessed/Vision Thirteen* is, "And the virtues destroyed the snares, so that the faithful at last through repentance passed out of their sins and into Heaven." If only we would submit ourselves to the divine Musician, as St. Hildegard calls Him. If only we would play His tune under His divine direction, we might be quite surprised at how much music there is in us—and in the whole creation around us!

FOR PERSONAL REFLECTION AND GROUP SHARING

1. Do you think that St. Hildegard writes in a more feminine manner than, say, St. Augustine, or St. Benedict? In what way?

2. What part of St. Hildegard's writings helps you to see God's plan for creation in a different way than you have before?

3. What part of her writings helps you to see God's plan for you in a different way?

4. Does St. Hildegard's reminder of the work of the enemy change your perspective at all?

5. Does the image of music speak to you?

ST. FRANCIS OF ASSISI (1182-1225)
THE LITTLE FLOWERS

St. Francis, originally named Giovanni, was born in 1181 or 1182 to a wealthy family in Assisi. His father was a cloth merchant who changed his infant son's name to Francesco, possibly following a business trip to France. Francis was a spoiled boy, intent on having fun. He was not an exceptional student, although he was good at events in the competitions between the young nobles of his time. Despite his penchant for flashy clothes and merry songs, he was surprisingly compassionate to the poor, even in his youth.

Shortly after his teen years, Francis went off to fight the Perugians. He was captured and held prisoner for a year, during which time he was sick with a fever that left him weak and unable to do much of anything but think. He began to consider his lifestyle and how he might spend eternity. As his health returned, however, so did his thirst for merriment and fortune. He pursued military life, having had a dream about armor marked with the sign of the cross. A voice told him these were "for your soldiers." Francis went off, expecting to become great.

But again Francis took ill, and again he heard the voice. This time, it told him to go back to Assisi. He did so in 1205 and his friends began to notice a change in their companion. He spent some time in prayer and reflection and began to embrace poverty. While riding on horseback, Francis came upon a leper. The sight made him turn away, but he thought better of it and returned to embrace the man and give him all the money he had.

Praying at St. Damiano, a small unkempt chapel, Francis heard a voice tell him, "Francis, repair my house which, as you see, is falling into ruin." Francis was determined to do so, resulting in his renouncing his inheritance, removing the very clothes from his back and determining to call only God his father. He spent the rest of his life rebuilding the Church, serving Christ in the poorest of the poor, especially lepers.

Gradually, others joined Francis living in total poverty, begging, preaching, and praying in the forests. They became the Order of St. Francis. Clare followed Francis also and started the Order of St. Clare.

The glorious confessor of Christ, Saint Francis, passed away from this life in the year of our Lord 1226, on the fourth day of October, being Saturday, and was buried on the Sunday.

[Note from Dr. Ronda: *The Little Flowers of St. Francis of Assisi* is a controversial spiritual reading because it is thought that legend was mixed in with historical narrative in such a way that it is hard to know what is really true and what is fictional. However, the

St. Francis

Giotto Sermon to the Birds

book is such a classic in the form it was read in Italian and then in translations that I consider that reading it as it has been read through the centuries is more important than sifting any edition for literal truth. Just the same, we are only excerpting here the stories in *The Little Flowers* that also appear in more scholarly works.]

Excerpts from *The Little Flowers of St. Francis*[1]

Chapter I

In the name of our Lord Jesus Christ the Crucified and of his Virgin Mother Mary. In this book are found certain little Flowers, Miracles and devout examples of the glorious poor little one of Christ, Saint Francis, and of his holy Companions, to the praise of Jesus Christ. Amen.

First, we must consider how in all the acts of Francis his life conformed to Christ the blessed: how even as Christ in the beginning of His preaching chose out twelve Apostles, to condemn all earthly things, to follow him in poverty and other virtues; so Saint Francis in the beginning chose out for the founding of the Order twelve companions, possessors of the deepest poverty... These most holy companions of Saint Francis were men of such sanctity that, from the time of the Apostles until now, the world never saw men so marvelous and so saintly. One of them was caught up into the third heaven, like Saint Paul, and this was Brother Giles. One of them, Brother Philip Lungo, was touched on the lips by an angel with a coal of fire, as was Isaiah the prophet. One of them, and he was Brother Silvester, spoke with God, as one friend does with another, even as Moses did. One through subtlety of intellect flew up even to the light of the divine Wisdom, like the eagle, John the Evangelist, and this was the

---

[1] Israel Gollancz, M.A. (ed), *The Little Flowers of St. Francis*, trans T. W. Arnold (London, J. M. Dent and Co., 1900).[In common domain but archaic words and phrases changed to contemporary language.].

most humble Brother Bernard, who set forth clearly the deep things of Scripture. One of them was sanctified of God and canonized in heaven, being yet alive in the world, and he was Brother Ruffino, a gentleman of Assisi. They were all favored with singular marks of sanctity, as is set forth hereafter…

Chapter VIII

As Saint Francis and Brother Leo were going by the way, he explained to him what things were perfect joy.

When as Saint Francis was going one day from Perugia to Saint Mary of the Angels with Brother Leo in the spring tide, and the very bitter cold grievously tormented him, he called to Brother Leo that was going on before and said this, "Brother Leo, though the Brothers…throughout all the world were great examples of sanctity and true edification, nevertheless write it down and take heed diligently that not there is perfect joy."

And going on a little further, Saint Francis called a second time, "O Brother Leo, albeit the Brothers Minor should give sight to the blind, make straight the crooked, cast out devils, make the deaf to hear, the lame to walk, the dumb to speak, and (greater still) should raise them that have been dead four days that not there is perfect joy."

And going on a little, he cried aloud, "O Brother Leo, if the Brother Minor should know all tongues and all sciences and all the Scriptures, so that he could prophesy and reveal not only things to come but also the secrets of consciences and souls, write that not there is perfect joy."

Going on yet a little further, Saint Francis called aloud once more, "O Brother Leo, little sheep of God, albeit the Brother Minor should speak with the tongue of angels, and know the courses of the stars and the virtues of herbs, and though all the treasures of the earth were revealed to him and he understood the virtues of birds, and of fishes, and of all animals, and of men, and of trees, and of stones, and of roots, and of waters, write that not there is perfect joy."

And going on a little further, Saint Francis cried aloud, "O Brother Leo, albeit the Brother Minor could preach so well as to turn all the infidels to the faith of Christ, write that not there is perfect joy."

And this manner of speech continuing for full two miles, Brother Leo with much marvel besought him, saying, "Father, I pray in the name of God that you tell me, where is perfect joy."

And Saint Francis made this answer, "When we come to Saint Mary of the Angels, all soaked as we are with rain and numbed with cold and besmirched with mud and tormented with hunger, and knock at the door, and the porter comes in anger and says, 'Who are you?' and we say, 'We are two of your brethren;' and he says, 'You are no true men; no, you are two rogues that gad about deceiving the world and robbing the alms of the poor. Get away,' and then he shuts the door and makes us stand without in the snow and the rain, cold and hungry, till nightfall; if we patiently endure such wrong and such cruelty and such rebuffs without being disquieted and without complaining against him; and with humbleness and charity think that this porter knows us full well and that God makes him to speak against us; O Brother Leo, write that here is perfect joy.

"And if we are insistent in knocking and he comes out full of wrath and drives us away as importunate knaves, with insults and buffetings, saying, 'Get away already, vilest of thieves, be gone to the alms-house, for here you shall find neither food nor lodging,' If we suffer this with patience and with gladness and with love, O Brother Leo, write that here is perfect joy.

"And if we still constrained by hunger, cold and night, knock yet again and shout and with much weeping pray him for the love of God that he will but open and let us in; and he yet more enraged should say, 'These are importunate knaves, I will pay them well as they deserve,' and should rush out with a knotty stick and taking us by the hood, throw us upon the ground and send us rolling in the snow and beat us with all the knots of that stick. If with patience and with gladness we suffer all these things, thinking on the pains of the blessed Christ and how we ought to suffer for the love of Him, O Brother Leo, write that here is perfect joy. Then hear the conclusion of the whole matter, Brother Leo. Above all graces and gifts of the Holy Spirit that Christ grants to His beloved, is to overcome oneself, and to willingly, for the love of Christ, endure pains and insults and shame and want. Inasmuch as in all other gifts of God we may not glory, since they are not ours but God's, for the Apostle said, "What have you that you have not received of God? And if you have received it of Him, why do you boast of yourself as if you had it of yourself? But in the cross of tribulation and affliction we may boast, since this is ours," and therefore, said the Apostle, "I would not that I should glory save in the cross of our Lord Jesus Christ."

Chapter XVI

How... Saint Francis... founded the third Order, and preached to the birds, and made the swallows hold their peace.

... Saint Francis was ready to preach, but first he bade the swallows that were twittering around to keep silence till such time as he had done the third preaching. The swallows were obedient to his word, and he preached there with such fervor that all the men and women of that town wanted through their devotion to come after him and leave the town. Saint Francis did not tolerate them, saying, "Do not be hasty and leave your homes, and I will ordain for you what you should do for the salvation of your souls," and he resolved to found the third Order, for the salvation of the entire world. And so leaving them much comforted and with minds firmly set on penitence, he departed...

And as with great fervor he was going on the way, he lifted up his eyes and beheld some trees near by the road whereon sat a great company of birds nearly without number. At this Saint Francis marveled, and said to his companions, "You shall wait for me here upon the way and I will go to preach to my little sisters, the birds."

And he went to the field and began to preach to the birds that were on the ground. Immediately those that were on the trees flew down to him, and all of them remained still and quiet together, until Saint Francis made an end of preaching. Not even then did they depart, until he had given them his blessing. And according to what

Brother Masseo afterwards related unto Brother Jacques da Massa, Saint Francis went among them touching them with his cloak, nevertheless none moved from out of his place.

He preached to the birds, "Much obliged are you to God, your Creator, and always in every place ought you to praise Him, for He has given you liberty to fly about everywhere, and has also given you double and triple raiment. Moreover He preserved your seed in the ark of Noah, so that your race might not perish out of the world. Still more are you obliged to Him for the element of the air which He has appointed for you. Beyond all this, you do not sow, neither do you reap, and God feeds you, and gives you the streams and fountains for your drink, the mountains and the valleys for your refuge and the high trees whereon to make your nests. Because you do not know how to spin or sew, God clothes you, you and your children. Therefore your Creator loves you much, seeing that He bestowed on you so many benefits, and therefore, my little sisters, beware of the sin of ingratitude, and try always to give praises to God."

As Saint Francis spoke these words to them, all of those birds began to open their beaks, and stretch their necks, and spread their wings, and reverently bend their heads down to the ground, and by their acts and by their songs to show that the holy Father gave them exceedingly great joy…

Having ended the preaching, Saint Francis made over them the sign of the cross, and gave them leave to go away. Then all the birds with wondrous singing rose up in the air, and then, in the fashion of the cross that Saint Francis had made over them, divided themselves into four parts. One part flew toward the East, and the other towards the West, and the other towards the South, and the fourth towards the North, and each flight went on its way singing wondrous songs, signifying that Saint Francis, the standard-bearer of the Cross of Christ, had preached to them, and made over them the sign of the cross, after the pattern of which they separated themselves to the four parts of the world. Just like this, the preaching of the Cross of Christ, renewed by Saint Francis, would be carried by him and the brothers throughout the entire world. The brothers, after the fashion of the birds, possessing nothing of their own in this world, commit their lives wholly to the providence of God…

Chapter XXI

Of the most holy miracle that Saint Francis wrought when he converted the fierce wolf of Gubbio

When Saint Francis resided in the city of Agobio (usually called Gubbio in later times), there appeared in the country of Agobio an exceedingly great wolf, terrible and fierce, which not only devoured animals, but also men. So much that all the city folk stood in great fear, since he often came near to the city, and all men when they went out arrayed themselves in arms as it were for the battle, and yet were not able to defend themselves against him whenever any chanced on him alone. For fear of this wolf they were come to such a pass that none went forth from that place.

For this matter, Saint Francis having compassion on the people of that land, wished to go to that wolf, albeit the townsfolk all gave counsel against it. Making the sign of the most holy cross he went forth from that place with his companions, putting all his trust in God. And the others doubting whether to go further, Saint Francis took the road to the place where the wolf lay.

And in the sight of many of the townsfolk that had come out to see this miracle, Saint Francis went up to the open-mouthed wolf and made over him the sign of the most holy cross, and called him to him, and told him this, "Come here, brother wolf: I command you in the name of Christ that you do no harm, to me or to anyone."

O wondrous thing! As Saint Francis made the sign of the cross, the terrible wolf shut his jaws and stayed his running, and when he was bid, came gently as a lamb and lay down at the feet of Saint Francis.

Then Saint Francis told him, "Brother wolf, much harm have you wrought in these parts and done grievous ill, spoiling and slaying the creatures of God, without His leave. And not alone have you slain and devoured the brute beasts, but have dared to slay men, made in the image of God. For this, you are deserving of the gallows as a thief and a most base murderer. All men cry out and complain against you and all this land is your enemy. But I would, brother, make peace between you and these, so you may no more offend them, and they may forgive you all your past offences, and neither men nor dogs pursue you anymore."

At these words the wolf with movements of body, tail, and eyes, and by the bending of his head, gave sign of his assent to what Saint Francis said, and of his will to abide by it.

Then Saint Francis spoke again, "Brother wolf, since it pleases you to make and hold this peace, I promise you that I will see to it that the folk of this place give you food always so long as you shall live, so that you will not suffer hunger anymore. For I know well that through hunger you have wrought all this ill. But since I win for you this grace, I want, brother wolf, that you promise me to do no hurt anymore, to man or beast. Do you promise me this?"

And the wolf gave clear token by the bowing of his head that he promised.

Then said Saint Francis, "Brother wolf, I want you to give a solemn oath for this promise, that I may trust you full well." Saint Francis stretched forth his hand to take pledge of his loyalty, and the wolf lifted up his right paw before him and laid it gently on the hand of Saint Francis, giving such sign of good faith as he was able.

Then said Saint Francis, "Brother wolf, I bid you in the name of Jesus Christ come now with me, doubting nothing, and let us go establish this peace in God's name." And the wolf obediently set forth with him, in fashion as a gentle lamb. Beholding this the townsfolk made mighty marvel, and straightway the story of it was spread through all the city, so that all the people, men-folk and women-folk, great and small, young and old, went to the market place to see the wolf with Saint Francis. And the people being gathered all together, Saint Francis rose up to preach. Advising them among other matters how for their sins God let such things be, and pestilences also, and how far more precarious is the flame of hell, which must vex the damned eternally, than is the fury of the wolf that can but slay the body. How much then should men fear the jaws of hell, when such a multitude stands so afraid of the jaws of so small a beast? Then turn, beloved, to God, and work out a fit repentance for your sins, and God will set you free from the wolf in this present time, and in time to come from out of the fires of hell…

Then promised all the folk with one accord to give (the wolf) food abidingly…

This act, and the others set forth above, wrought such great joy and marvel in all the people, both through devotion to the saint, and through the newness of the miracle, and through the peace with the wolf, that all began to lift up their voices to heaven praising and blessing God, that had sent Saint Francis to them, who by his merits had set them free from the jaws of the cruel beast.

And thereafter this same wolf lived two years in Agobio and went like a tame beast in and out of the houses, from door to door, without doing hurt to any or any doing hurt to him, and was courteously nourished by the people. As he passed this way through the country and the houses, never did any dog bark at him.

At length, after a two years' space, brother wolf died of old age. At this the townsfolk sorely grieved, since seeing him pass so gently through the city, reminded them the better of the virtue and the sanctity of Saint Francis.

Chapter XXV [2]

How St. Francis Healed Miraculously a Leper Both in His Body and in His Soul, and What the Soul Said to Him on Going up to Heaven

The true disciple of Christ, St. Francis, as long as he lived in this miserable life, endeavored with all his might to follow the example of Christ the perfect Master. It happened often, through the operation of grace, that he healed the soul at the same time as the body, as we read of Jesus Christ himself. Not only did he willingly serve the lepers himself, but he willed that all the brethren of his Order, both when they were traveling about the world and when they were halting on their way, should serve the lepers for the love of Christ, who for our sake was willing to be treated as a leper.

It happened once, that in a convent near the one in which St. Francis then resided there was a hospital for leprosy and other infirmities, served by the brethren. One of the patients was a leper so impatient, so insupportable, and so insolent, that many believed of a certainty that he was possessed of the devil (as indeed he was) for he ill-treated with blows and words all those who served him and, what was worse, he blasphemed so dreadfully our Blessed Lord and his most holy Mother the Blessed Virgin Mary, that none was found who could or would serve him. The brethren, indeed, to gain merit, en-

---

2 Dom Roger Hudleston, *The Little Flowers of Saint Francis of Assisi,* XXV (New York, Heritage Press) at EWTN, www.ewtn.com, (In common domain changed to contemporary language in part.)

deavored to accept with patience the injuries and violence committed against themselves, but their consciences would not allow them to submit to those addressed to Christ and to His Mother, therefore they determined to abandon this leper, but this they would not do so until they had signified their intention to St. Francis, according to the Rule. On learning this, St. Francis, who was not far distant, himself visited this perverse leper, and said to him: "May God give you peace, my beloved brother!" To this the leper answered: "What peace can I look for from God, who has taken from me peace and every other blessing, and made me a putrid and disgusting object?" St. Francis answered: "My son, be patient; for the infirmities of the body are given by God in this world for the salvation of the soul in the next; there is great merit in them when they are patiently endured." The sick man answered: "How can I bear patiently the pain which afflicts me night and day? For not only am I greatly afflicted by my infirmity, but the friars you have sent to serve me make it even worse, for they do not serve me as they ought." Then St. Francis, knowing through divine revelation that the leper was possessed by the malignant spirit, began to pray, interceding most earnestly for him. Having finished his prayer, he returned to the leper and said to him: "My son, I myself will serve you, seeing you are not satisfied with the others." "Willingly," answered the leper; "but what can you do more than they have done?" "Whatsoever you wish I will do for you," answered St. Francis. "I will then," said he, "that you wash me all over; for I am so disgusting that I cannot bear myself." Then St. Francis heated some water, putting in many odoriferous herbs;

he then undressed him, and began to wash him with his own hands, while another brother threw the water upon him, and, by a divine miracle, wherever St. Francis touched him with his holy hands the leprosy disappeared, and his flesh was perfectly healed also. On this the leper, seeing his leprosy beginning to vanish, felt great sorrow and repentance for his sins, and began to weep bitterly. While his body was being purified externally of the leprosy through the cleansing of the water, so his soul internally was purified from sin by the washing of tears and repentance; and feeling himself completely healed both in his body and his soul, he humbly confessed his sins, crying out in a loud voice, with many tears: "Unhappy me! I am worthy of hell for the wickedness of my conduct to the brethren, and the impatience and blasphemy I have uttered against the Lord;" and for fifteen days he ceased not to weep bitterly for his sins, imploring the Lord to have mercy on him, and then made a general confession to a priest. St. Francis, perceiving this evident miracle which the Lord had enabled him to work, returned thanks to God, and set out for a distant country; for out of humility he wished to avoid all glory, and in all his actions he sought only the glory of God, and not his own. It pleased God that the leper, who had been healed both in his body and in his soul, after having done penance for fifteen days, should fall ill of another infirmity; and having received the sacraments of the Church, he died a most holy death. His soul on its way to heaven appeared in the air to St. Francis, who was praying in a forest, and said to him: "Do you know me?" "Who are you?" asked the saint. Said he: "I am that leper whom our Blessed Lord healed through your merits, and today I am going to life eternal, for which I return thanks to God and to you. Blessed by your soul and your body, blessed by your holy words and works, for through you many souls are saved in the world; and know that there is not a single day in which the angels and other saints do not return thanks to God for the holy fruits of your preaching and that of your Order in various parts of the world. Be comforted, then, and thank the Lord, and may his blessing rest on you." Having said these words, he went up to heaven, leaving St. Francis much consoled.

The Canticle of Brother Sun

>Most High, all powerful, good Lord,
>Yours are the praises, the glory, the honor, and all blessing.
>To You alone, Most High, do they belong,
>and no man is worthy to mention Your name.
>Be praised, my Lord, through all your creatures,
>especially through my lord Brother Sun,
>who brings the day; and you give light through him.
>And he is beautiful and radiant in all his splendor!
>Of you, Most High, he bears the likeness.
>Praised be You, my Lord, through Sister Moon
>and the stars, in heaven you formed them
>clear and precious and beautiful.
>Praised be You, my Lord, through Brother Wind,
>and through the air, cloudy and serene,
>and every kind of weather through which

You give sustenance to Your creatures.
Praised be You, my Lord, through Sister Water,
which is very useful and humble and precious and chaste.
Praised be You, my Lord, through Brother Fire,
through whom you light the night and he is beautiful
and playful and robust and strong.
Praised be You, my Lord, through Sister Mother Earth,
who sustains us and governs us and who produces
varied fruits with colored flowers and herbs.
Praised be You, my Lord,
through those who give pardon for Your love,
and bear infirmity and tribulation.
Blessed are those who endure in peace
for by You, Most High, they shall be crowned.
Praised be You, my Lord,
through our Sister Bodily Death,
from whom no living man can escape.
Woe to those who die in mortal sin.
Blessed are those whom death will
find in Your most holy will,
for the second death shall do them no harm.
Praise and bless my Lord,
and give Him thanks
and serve Him with great humility.
AMEN

Chapter 50 - On the Stigmata

Then Saint Francis sent for the other brothers and told them how he wanted to keep the forty days' fast of Saint Michael in that lonely place; and therefore he asked them to make him a little cell there, so that no cry of his could be heard by them. And when the cell was made, Saint Francis said to them: "Go to your own place, and leave me here alone, for, with the help of God, I want to keep the fast here, without disturbance or distraction, and therefore let none of you come to me, nor tolerate any lay folk to come to me. But, Brother Leo, you alone shall come to me, once a day, with a little bread and water, and at night once again at the hour of Matins; and then you shall come to me in silence, and when you are at the bridgehead, you shall say; "Domine, labia mea aperies;" and if I answer you, cross over and come to the cell, and we will say Matins together; and if I do not answer you, then depart straightway...

During this time St. Francis began to think on the immeasurable glory and joy of the blessed in the life eternal; and began to pray to God to grant him the grace of tasting a little of that joy. And as he continued in this thought, suddenly there appeared to him an Angel with exceedingly great splendor, having a viol in his left hand and in his right the bow; and as Saint Francis stood all amazed at the sight of him, the Angel drew the bow once across the viol; and straightway Saint Francis was aware of such sweet melody that his soul melted away for very sweetness and was lifted up above all bodily feeling; insomuch that, as he afterwards told his companions, he doubted that, if the Angel had drawn the bow a second time across the strings, his mind would have left his body for the all too utter sweetness thereof. ...

And from that time forth, Saint Francis began more plenteously to taste and feel the sweetness of divine contemplation and of the divine visitings. Among which he had one that was an immediate preparation for the imprinting of the most holy Stigmata, and it was after this manner. On the day before the feast of the most holy Cross, in the month of September, as Saint Francis was praying in secret in his cell, there appeared to him the Angel of God, and told him in the name of God: "I am come to comfort and admonish you, that you make yourself ready and set yourself in order, humbly with all patience to receive whatsoever God will give to you and work in you."

Replied Saint Francis: "I am ready to endure with patience all things whatsoever my Lord may will to do to me:" and this said, the angel was away. So the next day came, the day of the most holy Cross: and early in the morning before dawn, Saint Francis fell on his knees in prayer in front of the entrance to his cell, and turning his face towards the East, prayed in this manner: "Oh my Lord Jesus Christ, I pray You grant me two graces, before I die: the first, that in my lifetime I may feel in my soul and in my vision and in my body, so far as may be, the pain that You, sweet Lord, did bear in the hour of Your most bitter passion; the second is, that I may feel in my heart, as far as may be, that exceeding love, by which You, O Son of God, were kindled to willingly endure such agony for us sinners."...

And as he was this way set on fire in this contemplation, on that same morn he saw descend from heaven a Seraph with six wings resplendent and aflame, and as with swift flight the Seraph drew near to Saint Francis, so that he could discern him, he clearly saw that he bore in him the image of a man crucified: and his wings were in such guise displayed, that two wings were spread above his head, two were spread out to fly, and the other two covered all his body...

Then the whole mount of Alverna appeared as though it burned with bright-shining flames, that lit up all the mountains and valleys round as though it had been the sun upon the earth; whereby the shepherds, that were keeping watch in those parts, seeing the mountain aflame and so great a light around, had exceedingly great fear, according as they afterwards told the brothers, declaring that this flame rested upon the mount of Alverna for the space of an hour and more. In like manner, at the bright shining of this light, which through the windows lit up the hostels of the country round, certain muleteers that were going into Romagna, arose, believing that the day had dawned, and saddled and laded their beasts: and going on their way, they saw the said light die out and the material sun arise.

In the said seraphic apparition, Christ, who appeared to him, spoke to Saint Francis certain high and secret things, which Saint Francis in his life-time desired not to reveal to any man: but after his life was done, Francis did reveal them, as is set forth below; and the words were these: "Know you," said Christ, "what it is that I have done to you? I have given you the Stigmata, that are the signs of my passion, to the end that you may be my standard-bearer."...

Then this marvelous vision vanishing away, after long space

and secret converse, left in the heart of Saint Francis an exceeding ardor and flame of love divine: and in his flesh a marvelous image and copy of the passion of Christ. For straightway in the hands and feet of Saint Francis began to appear the marks of the nails, in such wise as he had seen them in the body of Jesus Christ, the Crucified, who had shown Himself to him in the likeness of a Seraph: and thus his hands and feet appeared to be pierced through the middle with nails, and the heads of them were in the palms of his hands and the soles of his feet outside the flesh, and their points came out on the back of his hands and of his feet, so that they seemed bent back and riveted in such fashion that under the bend and riveting, which all stood out above the flesh, might easily be put a finger of the hand, as in a ring: and the heads of the nails were round and black. Likewise in the right side appeared an image of a wound made by a lance, unhealed, and red and bleeding, which afterwards often dropped blood from the sacred breast of Saint Francis, and stained with blood his tunic and his hose.

St. Bonaventure (1221-1274) was one of the greatest Franciscan Saints and a Doctor of the Church. Here is a selection. You might want to follow up by reading the Journey of the Mind to God, which is considered by many to be a masterpiece of late medieval philosophy and metaphysics, in keeping with the teaching of St. Augustine and Neo-Platonism. In it, Bonaventure considers what we know and how we know it. For him, knowledge of the hierarchy of being is a way to God, moving us from ideas to reality. He moves us from the vision of the Seraph that St. Francis had, through philosophical and metaphysical considerations, to find God in the order we see in creation, and from what we see to mystic experience.

St. Bonaventure, Doctor of the Church, was born in 1221. Little is known of his childhood, but Bonaventure made it known that it was through the intercession of St. Francis that he was saved from death at an early age. In his youth, probably around 1238, Bonaventure entered the Friars Minor and was elected Minister General before he was 36.

A wonderful preacher and teacher, Bonaventure labored for unity among the Order and spent his life for the glory of God. It is well known that St. Thomas Aquinas found Bonaventure in his cell in ecstasy during the time he was working on his biography of St. Francis. Because many miracles were wrought through his intercession and because of his well-respected character, the people greatly desired his canonization upon his death on July 16, 1274.

This reading on mystical (contemplative) prayer, taken from St. Bonaventure's *Journey of the Mind to God* (Cap. 7,1 2.4.6: Opera Omnia, 5, 312-313), is used in the Roman Office of Readings for the Feast (liturgical memorial) of St. Bonaventure on July 15.

Christ is both the way and the door. Christ is the staircase and the vehicle, like the throne of mercy over the Ark of the Covenant, and the mystery hidden from the ages. A man should turn his full attention to this throne of mercy, and should gaze at him hanging on the cross, full of faith, hope and charity, devoted, full of wonder and joy, marked by gratitude, and open to praise and jubilation. Then such a man will make with Christ a pasch, that is, a passing-over. Through the branches of the cross he will pass over the Red Sea, leaving Egypt and entering the desert. There he will taste the hidden manna, and rest with Christ in the sepulchre, as if he were dead to things outside. He will experience, as much as is possible for one who is still living, what was promised to the thief who hung beside Christ: Today you will be with me in paradise.

For this passover to be perfect, we must suspend all the operations of the mind and we must transform the peak of our affections, directing them to God alone. This is a sacred mystical experience. It cannot be comprehended by anyone unless he surrenders himself to it; nor can he surrender himself to it unless he longs for it; nor can he long for it unless the Holy Spirit, whom Christ sent into the world, should come and inflame his innermost soul. Hence the Apostle says that this mystical wisdom is revealed by the Holy Spirit.

If you ask how such things can occur, seek the answer in God's grace, not in doctrine; in the longing of the will, not in the understanding; in the sighs of prayer, not in research; seek the bridegroom not the teacher; God and not man; darkness not daylight; and look not to the light but rather to the raging fire that carries the soul to God with intense fervor and glowing love. The fire is God, and the furnace is in Jerusalem, fired by Christ in the ardor of his loving passion. Only he understood this who said: My soul chose hanging and my bones death. Anyone who cherishes this kind of death can see God, for it is certainly true that: No man can look upon me and live.

Let us die, then, and enter into the darkness, silencing our anxieties, our passions and all the fantasies of our imagination. Let us pass over with the crucified Christ from this world to the Father, so that, when the Father has shown himself to us, we can say with Philip: It is enough. We may hear with Paul: My grace is sufficient for you; and we can rejoice with David, saying: My flesh and my heart fail me, but God is the strength of my heart and my heritage forever. Blessed be the Lord forever, and let all the people say: Amen. Amen!

DR. RONDA'S CONTEMPORARY APPLICATIONS AND PERSONAL REFLECTIONS

In this section I will emphasize applications concerning simplicity of life. The best recent writing about simplicity of life for lay people in our times I believe to be Thomas Dubay's *Happy are You Poor: The Simple Life and Spiritual Freedom* (San Francisco: Ignatius Press, 1981) I will here summarize some of the main concepts in this book.

Gospel poverty is not the same as destitution: malnutrition, ragged clothing…absence of necessities for a decent human life. In Scriptures there are numerous references to the blessedness of poverty in the sense of not having things that are not needed (a computer is needed for a writer; a piano for a pianist; shelter for a family) and giving what is not needed of money and things to the poor. It is not enough to give to the poor but still have a superfluity of goods.

I like to challenge people this way: if you have so much you can't even find what you need in your closets, how can that be simplicity. Or, if you could actually see the really starving vs. beggars you may rightly think are using donations for addictions, would you want to buy more than you need or give it to the poor through trustworthy charities such as the Missionaries of Charity of Mother Teresa who feed the starving throughout the world and in some places don't even have toilet paper for themselves!

According to Dubay, simplicity of life must be understood in the context that Jesus taught that happiness is not found in things but in persons, especially Divine Persons. The earth is not our true home. We are pilgrims. Having many unnecessary possessions distracts us from prayer. Pulled by the lure of diversions, we cannot be pulled to God. "To the extent that things are important to a person, love diminishes. Men and women in love scarcely give a thought to things." (p. 163)

I first found out about St. Francis on a Catholic Art Tour in 1958. I was utterly charmed by Assisi and what was told to me about this saint. I read *The Little Flowers*. I first wanted to imitate his love of the beauty of nature. It was not until years after my conversion to the Catholic faith that I became eager to copy his simplicity of life. Here is how it happened. My twin sister, a dancer, became a Catholic. She met a man called Paul from the Catholic Worker movement who asked her to teach him how to dance the Gospels. This led to leading people to enter into sacred dance on the steps of a Church in New York City. Then, they set off together to dance the gospels from town to town without carrying any money but counting on passers-by to give them food and lodging. Since this was before the drug era got really underway, they were accepted as beautiful missionaries. Carla De Sola, my sister, continued after their 6-month pilgrimage, to live much more simply than I did as a married woman with children. But, later, when I heard of Mother Teresa of Calcutta living like St. Francis, it sparked in me a passion for never wasting money on luxuries and giving the saved money to the starving through Mother Teresa's Sisters all over the world.

KATHLEEN'S CONTEMPORARY APPLICATIONS AND PERSONAL REFLECTIONS

The most incredible thing about St. Francis for me is his simple humility. In every chapter, regardless of the other persons or animals involved, St. Francis is humble and faithful. He courageously and wisely speaks the truth without compromise, and sees himself and his shortcomings even as he preaches to others on how to attain holiness.

I am so touched by Chapter VIII in *The Little Flowers of St. Francis*, regarding his talk to Brother Leo on perfect joy. It is so hard for me to endure with humility whatever comes. I vacillate between being a victim pointing out to the Lord the injustice I am suffering, and being a doormat failing to see in myself the dignity of having been made in the image and likeness of God. As I wrote in the assignment on St. Benedict's Rule, by the time I get around to saying, "Let me grasp this opportunity for grace and offer it to God," there is nothing left worth offering because I have let the grace of the moment slip away in self-pity or righteous indignation.

I have so much more to learn in terms of self-discipline, taking up my cross, and following the Master. I sometimes wonder if I will ever instantly accept what comes. Will I learn to accept that what has been said or done to me is accurate at the very least, and an opportunity to share in the suffering of Christ at the very best? Will I ever just naturally offer it to God in reparation for my sins and for the salvation of souls?

The short excerpt by St. Bonaventure is so powerful to me. Early in my Catholic life a priest once told me in Confession that I had it "in here" (pointing to his head) but now needed to get it "in here" (pointing to his heart). I can expound on doctrine and write papers connecting the dots in our faith – the old and the new, the Sacraments and our journey to heaven, the pre-figurements of the Lord. I have courage, understanding, knowledge and reverence. Where, oh where, is my kindness, gentleness, patience, WISDOM????? Where is my humble surrender to the Bridegroom who loves me and seeks to perfect me in preparation for His Kingdom? I have passion – that is the single most-used word when people describe me and my work. Where is my <u>com</u>passion??? I like Christ. I am not, however, Christ-like. I need, in the darkness of surrender, to find that fire of which St.

Bonaventure writes, so that I can truly love Him.

So seldom do I sit quietly in the Presence of the Lord and just let Him work in me. I say the prayers I want to say, ask for the graces I want for myself and my family, intercede for others, praise Him, thank Him, read, pray the rosary—and almost NEVER allow myself to just BE in His Presence. While there is no question in my mind that He has much to tell me, it would be hard for Him to get a word, much less The Word, in edgewise. Lord Jesus, have mercy on me.

I do love the liturgy of the Church. Those few times when the Lord has been able to reach me have been during the Mass. Oftentimes the Lord has spoken to me in an especially beautiful and well-thought-out homily. There are many times when the reading of the day will be directly related to something about which I am praying or teaching, or with which I am struggling.

Sometimes I "see" the Lord's Most Holy Face in the stones on a wall in the Church, or on the front of the tabernacle as the shades of light shine on it in just the right way to make the image of a face emerge. As a daily communicant, I have to say that there have been many times over the years in various churches where I have seen the Lord's Face on the tabernacle. I just seem to be given the grace to see His Face on tabernacles, not as a portrait or vision, but as people see pictures in the clouds.

I sometimes wonder if it is because the tabernacle is so precious to me, and my belief in the Real Presence so central to my Catholic faith, that Jesus will from time to time allow me this grace. It almost never happens because I am looking for it. Usually, it just jumps out at me. But it does always surprise me and make me smile when I see it.

Possibly the most important way in which the words of the liturgy inspire me is when I am confronted by those who dismiss the Real Presence of the Lord in the Blessed Sacrament. I always quote Jesus' words at the Last Supper, "This is my Body, which is given up for you. This is the cup of my Blood." He does not say, "This represents" or, "This symbolizes" or, "Let's pretend." He, Who can never deceive or be deceived, says, "This is."

It's the most important thing in my life.

FOR PERSONAL REFLECTION AND GROUP SHARING

1. What aspects of St. Francis' life and spirituality resonate most with your own desires?

2. Try going through a whole day calling everything "brother" or "sister".

3. Who are the "lepers" in your life you need to kiss?

4. If you wanted to live more simply what would be the minimum of things you would need to fulfill what you feel called to: state of life (single, married, parent); occupation?

5. What do you need to die to in order to live in God?

6. What did you want to remember from the St. Bonaventure readings?

ST. GERTRUDE THE GREAT (C. 1256-1302)

Gertrude was given to a Benedictine monastery at Helfta, Germany when she was 5 years old, as was a custom among Catholic families in those days. It was a monastery influenced by Cistercian spirituality. Gertrude joined the order as a young woman, spending most of her time in studies of Latin and rhetoric. In 1281, as a young woman she had a spiritual experience which convinced her to spend the rest of her life on religious studies. She was a renowned and loved counselor of other nuns. She became highly influential because of her autobiographical writings, especially because of the way her spirituality is permeated by the liturgy of the hours, and, even more so, because of her experience of the Sacred Heart.

Excerpts from *The Revelations of St. Gertrude*[1]

...I was in the twenty-sixth year of my age when...You the

---

[1] *The Life and Revelations of St. Gertrude* (London: Burns Oates and Washbourne LTD, 1870) at Open Library, www.openlibrary.org – (In common domain but archaic language changed to more contemporary language.)

true Light, who are clearer than any light, and yet deeper than any recess... sweetly and gently commenced my conversion...and... showed me Your salvation.

...On raising my head I beheld You, my most loving Love, and my Redeemer, surpassing in beauty the children of men, under the form of a youth of sixteen years, beautiful and amiable, and attracting my heart and my eyes by the infinite light of Your glory...and standing before me, You uttered these words, full of tenderness and sweetness: "Your salvation is at hand; why are you consumed with grief? Have you no counselor, that you are so changed by sadness?" When you had spoken this, ...I heard these words: " I will save you, I will deliver you; fear not;" and after I had heard them, I saw You place Your right hand in mine, as if to ratify Your promise.

Then I heard You speak this: "You have licked the dust with My enemies, and you have sucked honey amidst thorns; but return now to Me I will receive you, and inebriate you with the torrent of My celestial delights." When You said these words, my soul melted within me...Then I paused to weep over my faults and crimes, which... divided us...You took me by the hand, and placed me near You instantly, without difficulty, so that, casting my eyes upon the precious Hand which You had extended to me as a pledge of Your promises, I recognized, O sweet Jesus, Your radiant wounds...

By these and other illuminations You enlightened and softened my mind, detaching me powerfully... from an inordinate love of literature and from all my vanities, so that...You alone were pleasing to my soul. And I praise, bless, adore, and thank from my inmost soul, as far as I am able, but not as far as I ought, Your wise mercy and Your merciful wisdom...

Chapter 2

Hail, Salvation and Light of my soul! ...After the infusion of Your most sweet light, I saw many things in my heart which offended Your purity...Nevertheless, my most loving Jesus, neither all these defects, nor all my unworthiness, prevented You from honoring me with Your visible presence nearly every day that I received the life-giving nourishment of Your Body and Your Blood, although I only beheld You indistinctly, as one who sees at dawn: You endeavored...to attract my soul, so that it might be entirely united to You, and that I might know You better and enjoy You more fully.

But since it is not possible for me to describe in what manner You visited me, Orient from on high...permit me, O Giver of gifts, to immolate a sacrifice of Thanksgiving to You on the altar of my heart, in order to obtain for myself and for all Your elect the blessedness of experiencing frequently this union of sweetness and this sweetness of union, which before this time was utterly unknown to me...

You gave me from henceforward a more clear knowledge of Yourself, which was such that the sweetness of Your love led me to correct my faults far more than the fear of the punishments...But I do not remember ever to have enjoyed so great happiness at any other time as during these days of which I speak, in which You invited me to the delights of Your royal table...

Chapter 3

While You did act so lovingly towards me, and did not cease to draw my soul from vanity and to Yourself, it happened on a certain day, between the Festival of the Resurrection and Ascension, that I... seated myself near the fountain, and I began to consider the beauty of the place, which charmed me on account of the clear and flowing stream, the verdure of the trees which surrounded it, and the flight of the birds, and particularly of the doves, above all, the sweet calm, apart from all, and considering within myself what would make this place most useful to me, I thought that it would be the friendship of a wise and intimate companion, who would sweeten my solitude or render it useful to others, when You, my Lord and my God after having inspired me...with the thought that if by continual gratitude I return Your graces to You, as a stream returns to its source; if, increasing in the love of virtue, I put forth, like the trees, the flowers of good works... if, despising the things of earth, I fly upwards, freely, like the birds, and thus free my senses from the distraction of exterior things, my soul would then be empty, and my heart would be an agreeable abode for You. As I was occupied with the recollection of these things...this passage of the Gospel came suddenly to my mind: "If any man love Me, he will keep My word, and My Father will love him, and "We will come to him and will make Our abode with him" (John 14:23)...

The excess of Your goodness obliges me to believe that...although my mind takes pleasure in wandering after and in distracting itself with perishable things, yet, after some hours, after some days, and...after whole weeks, when I return into my heart, I find You there, so that I cannot complain that You left me even for a moment, from that time until this year, which is the ninth since I received this grace, except once, when I perceived that You left me for the space of eleven days, before the Feast of St. John Baptist...and Your absence lasted until the Vigil of St. John...Then Your sweetest humanity and Your stupendous charity moved You to seek me...

I cannot now be sufficiently amazed at the mania which possessed my soul, unless, indeed, it was, that You desired me to know by my own experience what St. Bernard said: "When we fly from You, You pursue us; when we turn our backs, You present Yourself before us; when we despise You, You entreat us...laboring unweariedly to bring us to the attainment of that which eye has not seen, nor ear heard, and which the heart of man cannot comprehend."

Chapter 4

...But my unworthiness had not yet exhausted the abyss of Your mercy; for I received...this remarkable gift that each time during the day in which I endeavored to apply myself in spirit to those adorable Wounds, saying five verses of the Psalm Benedice, anima mea, Domino (Ps. 102), I never failed to receive some new favor. At the first verse, "Bless the Lord, O my soul" I deposited all the rust of my sins...at the Wounds of Your blessed Feet; at the second verse, "Bless the Lord, and never forget all He has done for You," I washed away all the stains of carnal...pleasures in the sweet bath of Blood and Water which You poured forth for me; at the third verse, "Who forgives all Your iniquities," I reposed my spirit in the Wound of Your Left Hand...at the fourth verse, "Who redeems Your life from destruction," I approached Your Right Hand, and took...all that I needed for my perfection in virtue and...passed to the fifth verse, "Who satisfies Your desire with good things," that I might be purified from all the defilement of sin, so that I might become worthy of Your presence...and might merit the joy of Your chaste embraces...

Chapter 5

Seven years after, a little before Advent...I engaged a certain person to say this prayer every day for me before a crucifix, " O most loving Lord, by Your pierced Heart, pierce her heart with the arrow of Your love, so that nothing earthly may remain therein, and that it may be entirely filled with the strength of Your Divinity." Being moved, as I believe, by these prayers, on the Sunday when they sang the Mass Gaudete in Domino, having permitted me...to approach the Communion of Your adorable Body and Blood, You infused a desire in me when I approached It, which broke forth in these words: "Lord, I am not worthy to receive the least of Your gifts; but I beseech You, by the merits and prayers of all here present, to pierce my heart with the arrow of Your love." I soon perceived that my words had reached Your Divine Heart...and...You showed me in the image of Your crucifixion. After I had received the Sacrament of life, and had retired to the place where I pray, it seemed to me that I saw a ray of light like an arrow coming forth from the wound of the right side of the crucifix, which was in an elevated place, and it continued...for some time, sweetly attracting my cold affections. But my desire was not entirely satisfied with these things until the following Wednesday, when, after the Mass, the faithful meditated on Your adorable Incarnation and Annunciation... And, behold, You... imprinted a wound in my heart, saying these words: "May the full tide of your affections flow hither, so that all your pleasure, your hope, your joy, your grief, your fear, and every other feeling may be sustained by My love!"...

Chapter 6

...It was on that most sacred night in which the sweet dew of Divine grace fell on all the world, and the heavens dropped sweetness...my soul beheld before it suddenly a delicate Child, but just born, in whom were concealed the greatest gifts of perfection. I imagined that I received this precious deposit in my bosom with the tenderest affection. As I possessed it within me, it seemed to me that all at once I was changed into the color of this Divine Infant, if we may be permitted to call that color which cannot be compared to anything visible.

Then I understood the meaning contained in those sweet... words: "God will (erit) be all in all" (1 Cor. xv. 28); and my soul, which was enriched by the presence of my Beloved, soon knew, by its transports of joy, that it possessed the presence of its Spouse. Then it received these words...: "As I am the figure of the substance of God, My Father, in His Divinity, so also you shall be the figure of My substance in My Humanity, receiving in your deified soul the infusions of My Divinity, as the air receives the brightness of the solar rays, that these rays may penetrate you so intimately as to prepare you for the closest union with Me." ...

Chapter 7

The day of the most holy Purification, as I was confined to bed after a severe illness...fearing that my corporal infirmity would deprive me of the Divine visit with which I had been so often consoled, on the same day...the Mother of God the true Mediator, consoled me by these words: "As you never remember to have endured more severe corporal sufferings than those caused by your illness, know also that you have never received from my Son more noble gifts than those which will now be given to you, and for which your sufferings have prepared you."

This consoled me exceedingly; and having received the Food which gives life immediately after the Procession, I thought only of God and myself; and I beheld my soul, under the similitude of wax softened by the fire, impressed like a seal upon the bosom of the Lord; and immediately I beheld it surrounding and partly drawn into this treasure house, where the ever-peaceful Trinity abides corporally in the plenitude of the Divinity, and resplendent with its glorious impression...

Chapter 8

... But since we may understand the invisible things of God, in some measure, by those which are visible...I saw...that the part of His blessed Heart where the Lord received my soul on the Feast of the Purification...was...dropping a sweat...This sacred reservoir attracted these drops to itself with surprising force...one saw evidently that love...had an absolute power in this place, where it discovered secrets which were so great, so hidden, and so impenetrable...

Chapter 9

Soon after, during the fast when I was confined to bed for the second time by a severe sickness...the Lord, who never abandons those who are deprived of human consolation, came to verify these words of the prophet: "I am with him in tribulation" (Ps. 90:15). He turned His right Side towards me, and there came forth from His blessed and inmost Heart a pure and solid stream, like crystal; and on His Breast there was a precious ornament, like a necklace, which seemed to alternate between gold and rose color. Then our Lord said to me: "This sickness which you suffer will sanctify your soul; so that each time you go forth from Me, like the stream which I have shown you, for the good of your neighbor, either in thought, word, or act, even then, as the purity of the crystal renders the color of the gold and the rose more brilliant, so the cooperation of the precious gold of My Divinity, and the rose of the perfect patience of My Humanity, will render your works always agreeable to Me by the purity of your intention."...

Chapter 10

I considered it so unsuitable for me to publish these writings that my conscience would not consent to do so; therefore I deferred doing it until the Feast of the Exaltation of the Holy Cross. On that day... the Lord conquered the repugnance of my reason by these words: "Be assured that you will not be released from the prison of the flesh until you have paid this debt which still binds you." And as I reflected that I had already employed the gifts of God for the advancement of my neighbor, if not by my writing at least by my words, He brought forward these words which I had heard used at the preceding Matins: "If the Lord had willed to teach His doctrine only to those who were present, He would have taught by word only, not by writing. But now they are written for the salvation of many." He added further: "I desire your writings to be an indisputable evidence of My Divine goodness in these latter times, in which I purpose to do good to many."

...I inquired what would be the advantage of these writings; and Your goodness, my God, solaced my trouble with Your usual sweetness, refreshing my soul by this reply: "Since this deluge appears useless to you, behold, I will now approach you to My Divine Heart, that your words may be gentle and sweet, according to the capabilities of your mind." Which promise, my Lord and my God, You most faithfully fulfilled. And for four days, at a convenient hour each morning, You suggested with so much clearness and sweetness what I composed, that I have been able to write it without difficulty and without reflection, even as if I had learned it by heart long before; with this limitation...as the Scripture teaches: "Let none so apply himself to action as to omit contemplation."...

Chapter 11

...On one occasion, when I assisted at a Mass at which I was to communicate (Note from Dr. Ronda: For many centuries daily communion was rare. Even consecrated religious thought that they should receive only seldom and that it was a kind of spiritual bravado to receive Jesus in the Eucharist frequently. In our times we understand the Eucharist not as something for the holy but more as balm for the wounded.), I perceived that You were present, by an admirable condescension, and that You used this similitude to instruct me, by appearing as if parched with thirst, and desiring that I should give You to drink; and while I was troubled thereat, and could not even force a tear from my eyes, I beheld You presenting me with a golden cup with Your own Hand. When I took it, my heart immediately melted into a torrent of fervent tears. Then I saw a certain despicable creature at my right hand, who was secretly putting something bitter and venomous into it, and inciting me to put it in this cup. But as this was followed by an instant motion of vainglory I easily understood that it was a stratagem of that ancient enemy, who turns against us all his rage when he sees us enriched with Your gifts...

You taught me also, on another occasion, that to yield easily to the enemy makes him insolent in attacking us again on the same subject; therefore Your justice requires that You should sometimes conceal the greatness of Your mercy in pardoning our negligence, because we resist evil more certainly, more usefully, more efficaciously, and more happily, when we resist it with all our might...

Chapter 14

The Sunday before Lent, while they chanted the Esto mihi, You made me understand by the words of this introit, O only Object of my love, that, being wearied by the persecutions and outrages which so many persons inflict on You, You asked for my heart, that You might repose therein...

Chapter 15

The day of Your adorable Nativity, I took You from the crib, wrapped in swathing-clothes, like a little infant newly born, and placed You in my heart...on the same day, the following year, as the Mass Dominus dixit was said, I received You, coming forth from the virginal womb of Your Mother as a feeble and delicate Infant, and carried You for some time in my arms. It seemed to me that the compassion which I had shown before the Feast, by some special prayers for a person in affliction, had obtained this favor for me...

Chapter 16

On the Feast of the Purification, at the Procession...when these words of the Gospel were read, "... (be with us in) our walking, advancement in virtue; the lights we carry, Christ, the true Light," Your spotless Mother presented You to me with her pure hands. And You… endeavored to embrace me with all Your might; I, though utterly unworthy, received You, and You put Your little arms round my neck, exhaling on me from Your mouth a breath so full of sweetness, that I was nourished and abundantly satisfied…For this, O Lord my God, may my soul and all that is within me adore and bless Your Holy Name! And when Your Blessed Mother sought to wrap You in Your swathing-clothes, I desired to be wrapped up in them also, for fear of losing the company of One whose smiles and favors exceed the sweetness of honey and the honeycomb…

Chapter 19

I give thanks to Your loving mercy and to Your merciful love, most loving Lord, for the revelation by which Your goodness satisfied my weak and wavering soul when I so ardently desired to be released from the chains of the flesh: not that I might suffer less, but that I might release Your goodness…When…I desired to be dissolved, You, my God, who are the honor and glory of heaven, appeared to me, descending from the royal throne of Your majesty, and approaching to sinners by a most obliging and favorable condescension; and then certain streams of precious liquor seemed to flow through heaven, before which all the saints prostrated themselves in thanksgiving; and having satisfied their thirst with joy in this torrent of delights, broke forth in canticles of praise for all Your mercy towards sinners. While these things happened I heard these words:

"Consider how agreeable this concert of praise is, not only to My ears, but even to My most loving Heart; and beware for the future how you desire...to be separated from the body, merely for the sake of being delivered from the flesh, in which I pour forth so freely the gifts of My grace; for the more unworthy they are...the more I merit to be glorified...by all creatures."...

Chapter 22

...during a certain Lent...on the second Sunday, as they sang at Mass before the procession, the response which commences Vidi Dominum fade adfaciem...When You displayed Your most adorable Face...embracing me, unworthy, a light of inestimable sweetness passed through Your...eyes into mine, passing through my inmost being, operating in all my members with admirable power and sweetness: first, it appeared as if the marrow were taken from my bones; then, my flesh and bones appeared annihilated; so much so, that it seemed as if my substance no longer had any consciousness save of that Divine splendor...Oh, what shall I say further of this most sweet vision...? For all the eloquence in the world...could never convince me that I should behold You more clearly even in glory, my God...if You had not taught me by experience. I will dare to say that if anything, human or Divine, can exceed the blessedness of Your embrace in this vision...the soul would never remain in the body after a momentary taste of this blessedness. I render thanks to You, through the union of mutual love which reigns in the adorable Trinity...that You deigned to favor me with Your caresses...while I sat meditating, or reading the Canonical Hours, or saying the Office of the Dead, You often, during a single Psalm, embraced my soul many times with a kiss…and…You looked on me favorably in the…caresses You gave to my soul. But though all these things were filled with an extreme sweetness…nothing touched me so much as this majestic look of which I have spoken...

Chapter 23

You have given me Your sweetest Mother, the Blessed Virgin, for my advocate, and You have lovingly recommended me to her many times with the same ardor as a faithful bridegroom would recommend his beloved bride to his own mother. You have also often sent the princes of Your court to minister to me, not only from the choirs of angels and archangels, but even those of higher rank, as Your kindness, my God, judged it expedient for my advancement in spiritual exercises…and, as I ought to declare with tears in my eyes, sometimes pretending not to understand Your will, lest the reproaches of my conscience should oblige me to obey it.

I have also despised the aid of Your most glorious Mother, and that of the blessed spirits whom You have sent to me; and I have been so unhappy as to prove an obstacle even to my earthly friends, on whom I have leant, instead of relying on You alone…

Chapter 24

Behold, O loving Lord…I desire also that You should be praised for those who, reading these things, are charmed with the sweetness of Your charity, and inwardly drawn to desire the same; and also for those who, studying them as students…led by the perusal of these things…to search for the hidden manna, which increases the hunger of those who partake of it…

Therefore, since You, the Almighty Dispenser of all good things, vouchsafe to pasture us during our exile until, "beholding the glory of the Lord with unveiled countenance, we are transformed into His image, and from glory to glory by the power of the spirit of love" (2Cor 3:18)…

DR. RONDA'S CONTEMPORARY APPLICATIONS AND PERSONAL REFLECTIONS

Catholics, for whom the Eucharist is the center of our spirituality, often wonder that so many of the writings of the saints of the past have so little mention of the Real Presence of God. It is thought that they were so steeped in the Holy Mass along with the other Catholics of their time that it was not something to write about as a theme. But in the writings of St. Gertrude we find the Liturgy of the Mass and of the Hours chanted by the nuns to be absolutely central.

Reading St. Gertrude always reminds me of the central theme of Dietrich Von Hildebrand's book *Liturgy and Personality* (Baltimore: Helicon Press, 1960). His concept was that growth in virtue does not take place only through our efforts and personal prayers, but also from the way the rhythm of the great truths of our salvation permeates the words of the Mass and the themes in the Liturgy of the Hours. An example would be the way we come into the church for Holy Mass blessing ourselves with holy water, or open our Liturgy of the Hours prayer books in a disgruntled, negative mood. But words such as "we lift our hearts up to the Lord" waft us out of this transient mood into the exalted reality of our access to the God of glory.

Having been brought into the Church at age 21 by daily Mass Catholics, the liturgy and the Eucharist have always been central to my spirituality. Of course there are those who could not possibly go to daily Mass because of their work hours or family obligations, but for those who can it is a great, great blessing. In cities where there are more Catholic churches and more daily Masses, workers can be found in large numbers at early morning or early evening daily liturgies. And in retirement areas, it is the joy of the devout elderly to be able to come to this Feast every day.

I was struck by St. Gertrude's description of the youthful Jesus who came to her in visions. I often have graces of words in the heart (locutions) but in the visions I have received Jesus is always a young adult. As a widow I had one such vision where Jesus was dressed like a modern bridegroom so I would recognize He wanted to be my second bridegroom in my widowhood.

I associate the image of the Sacred Heart with my transition from relating to God more as truth than love, because of my being so philosophical. Reading Von Hildebrand's book *The Heart*, now once more in print, helped me to understand the depth of what human love can be and even more so that of Jesus. St. Gertrude's writings about being ravished by the love of Jesus correspond to graces I received in less profusion. These graces helped me to experience the intimate way that God loves me as an individual.

Since she knew herself to be so sinful, St. Gertrude had scruples about writing about her supernatural experiences. The fact that she overcame these scruples under obedience helps me to see that I should share such experiences also. (See www.rondachervin.com – books—free e-books—*One Foot in Eternity*.)

KATHLEEN'S CONTEMPORARY APPLICATIONS AND PERSONAL REFLECTIONS

In this time when many of our churches around the globe are so sadly nearly empty, when many parents send their children to Religious Education (if there is any connection to the Church at all) but do not bring them to Mass, when our own individual will is so much more the focal point of our lives than is God's will, when we feel entitled rather than grateful and appreciative, The Revelations of St. Gertrude offer us so much on which to reflect.

Connecting the parts of the Mass or the Liturgy of the Hours to momentous occasions in her spiritual life was very significant. Not only did she notice the graces and gifts given her by God's mercy and generosity, she remembered when they happened, what she was praying at the time, how it connected to her participation in the liturgy.

While most of us do not have St. Gertrude's type of encounters with Our Lord, He does speak to us: in His Word, in others, through His saints, in the beauty of creation. Are we listening? I remember questioning the Scripture passage in which a woman says, "Blessed is the womb that bore you and the breasts that nursed you," and Jesus replies, "Rather, blessed are those who hear the word of God and keep it" (Lk 11:27-28). I wondered why He would dismiss this reference to His Mother and seem to be disrespectful. Hearing this reading at Mass one Sunday, it occurred to me that Jesus was not dismissing the reference to His Mother. He was clarifying it. She was blessed because of her faithfulness to the Word of God. She became His Mother because of her devotion to God's will over her own. It was as if Jesus was saying, "Mary is not holy because she is my mother, she was chosen to be My Mother because she is holy."

Now each time I hear that Scripture, I remember how the Holy Spirit gave me the gift of understanding during that Mass. He also gave me hope, because we can be holy too! While I do not have a multitude of such experiences to recount, I do try to notice what God is saying in His Word, how the Old Testament reading points to Jesus, and how in the New Testament reading Jesus is the fulfillment of the Old Testament reading.

But how many times has the Lord tried to speak to me when I wasn't listening? How many blessings have there been of which I am not even conscious? How many times has he tried to correct or change me and I haven't noticed or, worse, have ignored it? St. Gertrude writes in Chapter 23 of the need to relate with tears in her eyes the times she has pretended not to understand God's will for her. Can there be enough tears for me to shed in the same regard? How many times have I pretended not to understand God's will for me?

How many times have I "rattled on like the pagans do" (Mt 6:7) thinking I will be heard for "the sheer multiplication of words"? How often have I spent time telling God all the reasons He should answer my prayers?

For me, St. Gertrude offers us a great example of reflection, of gratitude, of humility, of recognizing how unworthy we are of the graces and blessings God bestows on us, and how very much we need to notice what we have been given by an almighty God who, but for His goodness, mercy, and great love, could have just as easily condemned us all to hell.

It seems to me that the times in which we live call for a great effort on our part to remember that we are made in God's image and likeness, and that we are to serve and glorify Him, not vice versa. St. Gertrude offers us a great insight into the way to do that.

FOR PERSONAL REFLECTION AND GROUP SHARING

1. What are the highlights of St. Gertrude's writing for you?
2. When are you particularly aware of God's grace?
3. Has there been a time you are willing to share when you received a revelation or some special grace at Mass or praying

the Liturgy of the Hours?

4. Has there been a time you are willing to share when you became aware of God's goodness and/or your ingratitude or preoccupation?

5. What can you learn, if anything, from St. Gertrude's encounters with the Lord? Can you apply them to your own spiritual journey?

BL. JULIAN(A) OF NORWICH (C.1342 – C.1416)
REVELATIONS OF DIVINE LOVE

(Note from Dr. Ronda: I have long believed that there is a special manner in which mystical writings are received when they are written originally in the language of the reader. For most readers of this anthology that will be English and this will be the first set of excerpts that is from an English person.)

In the Catholic Church Julian is called Blessed Julian. The name Julian, however, may have been taken from the Church where she was a walled-in anchorite rather than being her birth name. For this reason some later editors prefer to call her Julianna, Julianne, or in this older manuscript Lady Julian to signify that she was a woman.

There is no evidence external to her own autobiographical work about the facts of her life. From her own account, she was born around 1342 and became an anchoress in the year 1373. During an illness that threatened her life she tells that she received a series of visions and revelations. She was still living in the year 1413.

Since many of the excerpts contain words that are not familiar to 21st century readers, the Ethereal Library included a Glossary at the end of the work. We have chosen to include those notes, instead, within the manuscript as bracketed definitions or synonyms, sometimes with the easier to understand word later and sometimes before the older word for the same meaning. Also in brackets are other words we thought it helpful to define in more modern English.

Excerpts from *Revelations of Divine Love*[1]

These Revelations were shown to a simple creature…the year of our Lord 1373, the Thirteenth day of May. This creature [had]… desired three gifts of God. The First was to experience His Passion; the Second was bodily sickness in youth, at thirty years of age; the Third was to have of God's gift three wounds. As to the First, I thought I had some feeling in the Passion of Christ, but yet I desired more by the grace of God…so that I might have more knowledge of the bodily pains of our Savior and of the compassion of our Lady and of all His true lovers that saw…His pains. For I would be one of them and suffer with Him…that…I should have a truer understanding of the Passion of Christ. The Second came to my mind with contrition…that I might in that sickness receive all my rites of Holy Church…In this sickness I desired to have all manner of

---

1 Julian of Norwich, *Revelations of Divine Love,* trans. Grace Warrack (London: 1901), at Christian Classics Ethereal Library at Calvin College, www.ccel.org. (In common domain but archaic language changed to more contemporary language.)

pains bodily and spiritual that I should have if I should die...[that] I would be purged, by the mercy of God, and afterward live more in the worship of God because of that sickness...These two desires of the Passion and the sickness I desired with a condition, saying this: "Lord, You know what I wish,—if it be Your will that I have it"... For the Third [petition], by the grace of God and teaching of Holy Church I conceived a mighty desire to receive three wounds in my life: that is to say, the wound of real contrition, the wound of kind compassion, [natural] and the wound of steadfast longing toward God. [For these wounds] And all this last petition I asked without any condition.

CHAPTER III

"I desired to suffer with Him" and when I was thirty years old and a half, God sent me a bodily sickness, in which I lay three days and three nights; and on the fourth night I took all my rites of Holy Church, and thought not to have lived till day... And being in youth as yet, I thought it great sorrow to die... nothing that was in earth that I wanted to live for... for no pain that I had fear of: for I trusted in God of His mercy. But it was to have lived that I might have loved God better, and longer time, that I might have the more knowing and loving of God in bliss of Heaven...

Then came suddenly to my mind that I should desire the second wound of our Lord's gracious gift: that my body might be fulfilled with mind and feeling of His blessed Passion. For I would that His pains were my pains... therefore I desired to suffer with Him.

CHAPTER IV

...I saw the red blood trickle down from under the Garland hot and freshly and plenteously, as it were in the time of His Passion when the Garland of thorns was pressed on His blessed head who was both God and Man...that suffered this for me...And in the same Apparition suddenly the Trinity fulfilled my heart most of joy. And so I understood it shall be in heaven without end to all that shall come there. For the Trinity is God: God is the Trinity; the Trinity is our Maker and Keeper, the Trinity is our everlasting love and everlasting joy and bliss, by our Lord Jesus Christ...Through this sight of the blessed Passion, with the Godhead that I saw...I knew well that it was strength enough for me...and for all creatures living, against all the fiends of hell and spiritual temptation. In this [Apparition] He brought our blessed Lady to my understanding. I saw her spiritually, in bodily likeness: a simple maid and a meek, young of age...in the stature that she was when she conceived. Also God showed in part the wisdom and the truth of her soul: so that I understood the reverent beholding in which she beheld her God and Maker, marveling with great reverence that He would be born of her... a simple creature of His making. And this wisdom and truth: knowing the greatness of her Maker and the littleness of herself...caused her to say...meekly to Gabriel: Behold me, God's handmaid! In this sight I understood... that she is more than all that God made...in worthiness and grace; for above her is nothing that is made but the blessed Manhood...

"God, of Your Goodness, give me Yourself—only in You I have

all"... I saw that He is to us everything that is good and comfortable for us: He is our clothing that for love wraps us, clasps us, and all encloses us for tender love, that He may never leave us; being to us everything that is good...Also in this He showed me a little thing, the quantity of an hazelnut, in the palm of my hand; and it was as round as a ball. I looked at it with the eye of my understanding, and thought: What may this be? And it was answered generally this: It is all that is made...In this Little Thing I saw three properties. The first is that God made it, the second is that God loves it, the third, that God keeps it...

For this is the cause why we are not all in ease of heart and soul: that we seek here rest in...things that are so little...and know not our God that is All-mighty, All-wise, All-good...God wills to be known, and it pleases Him that we rest in Him...And this is the cause why that no soul is rested till it is... willingly made naught for love, to have Him that is all, then is it able to receive spiritual rest...

CHAPTER VI

...For our soul is so specially loved of Him that is highest, that...there is no creature that is made that may [fully] know how much and how sweetly and how tenderly our Maker loves us. And therefore we may with grace and His help stand in spiritual beholding, with everlasting marvel of this high...[unmeasurable] Love that Almighty God has for us...And therefore we may ask of our Lover with reverence all that we will...For He wills that we be occupied in knowing and loving till the time that we shall be fulfilled in Heaven;

and therefore was this lesson of Love shown…

CHAPTER IX

For…I am, I hope, in oneness of charity with all my fellow Christians. For in this oneness stands the life of all mankind that shall be saved. For God is all that is good…and God has made all that is made, and God loves all that He has made…for God, he loves all that is…But in all things I believe as Holy Church believes, preaches, and teaches…

CHAPTER XIII

"The Enemy is overcome by the blessed Passion and Death of our Lord Jesus Christ."

Then He, without voice and opening of lips, formed in my soul these words: Here is the Fiend overcome…

On this showed our Lord that the Passion of Him is the overcoming of the Fiend. God showed that the Fiend has now the same malice that he had before the Incarnation. And…he sees that all souls of salvation escape him … by the virtue of Christ's precious Passion. And that is his sorrow…for his might is all taken [locked] into God's hand…

CHAPTER XIV

…God showed three degrees of bliss that every soul shall have in Heaven that willingly served God in any degree in earth. The first is the worshipful thanks of our Lord God…when he is delivered of pain. The second is that all the blessed creatures that are in Heaven shall see that worshipful thanking…The third is, that as new and as gladdening as it is received in that time…so shall it last without end…

CHAPTER XXV

… (Regarding Blessed Juliana's desire to see Our Lady) Oftentimes I prayed this, and I thought to have seen her in bodily presence, but I saw her not so. And Jesus in that word showed me spiritual sight of her: right as I had seen her before little and simple, so He showed her then high and noble and glorious, and pleasing to Him above all creatures. And He wills that it be known; that [so] all those that please them in Him should please them in her, and in the pleasure that He has in her and she in Him…

…And her He showed three times. The first was as she was with Child; the second was as she was in her sorrows under the Cross; the third is as she is now in pleasing, worship, and joy.

CHAPTER XXVII

"Often I wondered why by the great foreseeing wisdom of God the beginning of sin was not hindered: for then, I thought, all should have been well." "Sin plays a needful part—but all shall be well." After this the Lord brought to my mind the longing that I had to

Him before. And I saw that nothing [stopped] me but sin. And so I looked, generally, upon us all, and I thought: If sin had not been, we should all have been clean and like to our Lord, as He made us.

...Pain...purges, and makes us to know ourselves and to ask mercy. For the Passion of our Lord is comfort to us against all this, and so is His blessed will.

And for the tender love that our good Lord has to all that shall be saved, He comforts readily and sweetly, signifying this...that sin is cause of all this pain; but all shall be well, and all shall be well, and all manner [of] thing shall be well.

These words were said very tenderly, showing no manner of blame to me nor to any that shall be saved. Then were it a great unkindness...to blame...God for my sin, since He blames not me for sin.

CHAPTER XXIX

...Our blessed Lord...showed that Adam's sin was the most harm that ever was done, or ever shall be, to the world's end; and also He showed that this [sin] is openly known in all Holy Church on earth. Furthermore He taught that I should behold the glorious Satisfaction [fulfillment]: for this Amends-making is more pleasing to God and more worshipful, without comparison, than ever was the sin of Adam harmful...

CHAPTER XXXIV

...God showed full great pleasure that He has in all men and women that mightily and meekly and with all their will take the preaching and teaching of Holy Church. For it is His Holy Church: He is the Ground, He is the Substance, He is the Teaching, He is the Teacher, He is the End, He is the [reward]...

CHAPTER XXXIX

"Sin is the sharpest scourge. . . . By contrition we are made clean, by compassion we are made ready, and by true longing towards God we are made worthy."

Sin is the sharpest scourge that any chosen soul may be smitten with...till [that time] when contrition takes him by touching of the Holy Spirit, and turns the bitterness into hopes of God's mercy.... By contrition we are made clean, by compassion we are made ready, and by true longing toward God we are made worthy. These are three means, as I understand, whereby that all souls come to heaven: that is to say, that have been sinners in earth and shall be saved: for by these three medicines...every soul be healed...And so on the contrary-wise, as we be punished here with sorrow and penance, we shall be rewarded in heaven by the courteous love of our Lord God Almighty...

CHAPTER LXXIV

For I understand [that there be] four manner of dreads. One is the dread of an affright that comes to a man suddenly by frailty. This dread does good, for it helps to purge man, as does bodily sickness or such other pain as is not sin. For all such pains help man if they be patiently taken. The second is dread of pain, whereby man is stirred and wakened from sleep of sin. He is not able for the time to perceive the soft comfort of the Holy Spirit, till he have understanding of this dread of pain, of bodily death, of spiritual enemies; and this dread stirs us to seek comfort and mercy of God, and thus this dread helps us, and enables us to have contrition by the blissful touching of the Holy Spirit. The third is doubtful dread. Doubtful dread in as much as it draws to despair, God will have it turned in us into love by the knowing of love: that is to say, that the bitterness of doubt be turned into the sweetness of natural love by grace. For it may never please our Lord that His servants doubt in His Goodness. The fourth is reverent dread: for there is no dread that fully pleases God in us but reverent dread...

...Desire we of our Lord God to dread Him reverently, to love Him meekly, to trust in Him mightily; for when we dread Him reverently and love Him meekly our trust is never in vain. For the more that we trust, and the more mightily, the more we please and worship our Lord... And if we fail in this reverent dread and meek love (as God forbid we should!), our trust shall soon be misruled for the time. And therefore...pray our Lord of grace that we may have this reverent dread and meek love...in heart and in work. For without this, no man may please God.

DR. RONDA'S CONTEMPORARY APPLICATIONS AND PERSONAL REFLECTIONS

Julian(a)'s famous phrase, "All will be well" has been greatly misunderstood. Some who believe in universal salvation, i.e. that everyone will be saved in the end and there will be no hell, claim Julian(a) as proof that blessed Catholic mystics agree there is no hell.

It is true that Blessed Julian(a) writes that God can bring good out of sin, especially in Chapter XIII and following. However, in the Catechism you will find it stated clearly that Satan and all demons are damned eternally. We are not to judge who might be in hell now or in the future, but we cannot as Catholics claim that universal salvation is inevitable. In fact in the same Chapter XIII, Julian(a) refers to "any that shall be saved," not to an idea that "all shall be well" means that all shall be saved. But, she adds in Chapter XIV that we are not to try to determine the fate of others, which is part of the Lord's private counsel (see CCC 1033 - 1041).

In Chapter VI Juliana writes that "If any man or woman (fails) to love any of his (brothers and sisters) he loves really no one, for he loves not all. And so at that time he is not safe, for he is not in peace." This seems clearly false. Why couldn't you love some people in Christ and others find too evil or upsetting to love? But if we are to love in grace, then we must have merciful love for all even as we hate their sins, and our own. As I often put it, a holy person has nothing but love in his/her heart. We feel how unloving our harsh judgments are in the nasty knot we have within us whenever we treat someone either openly badly or in a disparaging way in our thoughts. We feel peaceless until we beg for the grace to love them rightly even if we are upset with their sins. And this includes self-hatred as well.

In Chapter IX there is a famous passage about how part of our heavenly reward will be to be thanked by God for all we have done for Him. This might strike some of us as seeming to be demanding gratitude. But I think it is a lovely promise to encourage us on our arduous journey.

KATHLEEN'S CONTEMPORARY APPLICATIONS AND PERSONAL REFLECTIONS

It seems to me that Blessed Julian(a)'s phrase, "all will be well," refers not to universal salvation, but rather to God's plan and its ultimate end. We know that God is eternal. In Him and for Him there is no past or future and all of His work has already been accomplished. Someone I love very much once described herself to me as "not-a-committed-Catholic." When I ask her if everything is okay with her family, she always answers, "Everything is fine. We just don't know how yet." It's a very Catholic answer. She is, in my mind and without realizing it, paraphrasing Blessed Julian(a).

God's most holy and perfect will has already been achieved. All the things about which we worry and fret have been resolved. We just don't know how each specific thing turns out. We do know that all of us in the Body of Christ are to help each other arrive at that place where all has been resolved and all is "well."

Part of Blessed Julian(a)'s joy is due to her belief that "all will be well." And that belief is based on her own personal and intimate knowledge of God's great love for her and for all He has made. The depth to which God loves us, and the extent to which He goes to show that love and to achieve the ultimate end of His plan, are extremely consoling and encouraging. They are great cause for joy.

His infinite goodness, and His complete sustaining of creation should remove all worry and concern from our minds and hearts. That He is the source of all that is good, and that He covers and "clothes" us with good should be cause for joy. Indeed, if we trust Him and His great love, and His power to fulfill His plan, we should not fear. And yet we do. I do.

Blessed Julian(a) goes on to show us that her joy increased in knowing and understanding that our suffering is transformed in Christ's. He reveals to her that whatever we suffer in this life will be so outweighed by the bliss of heaven that it won't matter anymore. This, too, is great cause for joy.

Blessed Julian(a) expresses such tenderness for the suffering of Christ, and He tells her He would suffer again and again for love of us. But He also says that, while we will not be overcome, we will be tested and we will suffer. We are to endure whatever comes with love and patience, and with great desire for the salvation of souls. Herein lies love and charity. The suffering without the love is fruitless. Our suffering must be in imitation of Christ and His love.

In a surprising and unexpected way, Jesus reveals His Mother to Blessed Julian(a). Instead of seeing her bodily, Blessed Julian(a) is given to understand Our Lady's virtue, which is what makes her so pleasing in the sight of God. By seeing and knowing Our Lady, Blessed Julian(a) is given to see and know herself, her soul, and the goodness of God.

Some have said that a woman is like a teabag. We never know how strong she is until she is thrown in hot water. Similarly, we will never know how virtuous we are until we are tested. Our virtue or vice will reveal its strength in our trials and tribulations, often in relationships with others.

The best way to achieve humility and kindness through these struggles is to offer them, united to the Passion of Christ, for other souls, and our own. We must ask our God to help us discern if He is using others to point out areas of our life and character that need work. This is the hard part for me. I must continue to strive to know God so that I may know myself and then, in humility, love God and neighbor in virtue. St. Bonaventure said we must have the humility to know our place under God, and take it. God help me to do so.

FOR PERSONAL REFLECTION AND GROUP SHARING

1. Blessed Julian(a) is thought to be one of the most joyful of Catholic mystics. Does her famous phrase "all will be well," allegedly from Jesus, mean that there is universal salvation?

2. How did you relate to her reasons for joy?

3. Do you see Mary as simple and glorious both?

4. Do you feel, as Julian(a) did, that God likes you as well as loving you? Did you identify with any of the dreads she describes?

5. Do you ever think, as Julian(a) did, about Jesus' suffering? How does it make you feel?

6. In what ways do you struggle or suffer? How do you accept it and/or deal with it? Do you think it has any value or purpose?

7. Do you judge others? Are you critical? If so, what do you think Jesus may be saying to you about that?

8. Do you see in Julian(a)'s writing a cause for hope?

SAINT CATHERINE OF SIENA (1347-1380)
DOCTOR OF THE CHURCH, THE DIALOGUE

"Midway between sky and earth hangs a City Beautiful: Siena...The town seems to have descended as a bride from airy regions, and lightly settled on the summits of three hills which it crowns with domes and clustering towers. As seen from the vineyards which clothe the slopes of the hills or with its crenellated wall and slender-necked Campanile silhouetted against the evening sky from the neighboring heights...the city is familiar to students of the early Italian painters...

"So it happened that Catherine, being arrived at the age of six, went one day with her brother Stephen, who was a little older than herself, to the house of their sister Bonaventura... in order to carry something or give some message from their mother Lapa. Their mother's errand accomplished, while they were on the way back from their sister's house...the holy child, lifting her eyes, saw on the opposite side above the Church of the Preaching Friars... seated, on an imperial throne, Jesus Christ, the Savior of the world, clothed in pontifical vestments, and wearing on His head a papal tiara; with

155

Dominican Church of San Domenico in Siena, photograph, www.drawn-bylove.com, used with permission

Him were the princes of the Apostles, Peter and Paul, and the holy evangelist John. Astounded at such a sight, Catherine stood still, and with fixed and immovable look, gazed, full of love, on her Savior, who, appearing in so marvelous a manner, in order sweetly to gain her love to Himself...with a tender smile lifted over her His right hand, and, making the sign of the Holy Cross in the manner of a bishop, left with her the gift of His eternal benediction...But while the Lord was working these marvels, the child Stephen, leaving her standing still, continued his way down hill, thinking that she was following, but, seeing her immovable in the distance and paying no heed to his calls, he returned and pulled her with his hands, saying: 'What are you doing here? Why do you not come?' Then Catherine, as if waking from a heavy sleep, lowered her eyes and said: 'Oh, if you had seen what I see, you would not distract me from so sweet a vision!' and lifted her eyes again on high; but the vision had entirely disappeared…and she…began with tears to reproach herself for having turned her eyes to earth."…

[Note from Dr. Ronda and Kathleen: It has been written by many of her biographers that St. Catherine's parents wished her to marry. They put much effort into making her attractive, especially styling her hair and placing headpieces on her. It is reported that a priest proposed that she cut her hair to show her parents how serious she was about committing herself to Christ. Her parents put her to much manual labor, hoping to keep her from having any time to pray. But Catherine humbly set about doing her tasks as though she was doing them for Jesus.]

…"Much might be said of the action of Catherine on her generation. Few individuals perhaps have ever led so active a life or have succeeded in leaving so remarkable an imprint of their personality on the events of their time. Catherine the Peacemaker reconciles warring factions of her native city and heals an international feud between Florence and the Holy See. Catherine the Consoler pours the balm of her gentle spirit into the lacerated souls of the suffering wherever she finds them, in the condemned cell or in the hospital ward. She is one of the most voluminous of letter-writers, keeping up a constant correspondence with a band of disciples, male and female, all over Italy, and last, but not least, with the distant Pope at Avignon…

"More and more, people came to look on the Pope as their temporal ruler no less than as their spiritual father. In many cases, indeed, his was the only government they knew. Kings and nobles had conferred much property on the Roman Church.

"By the end of the sixth century the Bishop of Rome held, by the right of such donations to his See, large tracts of country, not only in Italy, but also in Sicily, Corsica, Gaul, and even Asia and Africa. Gregory successfully defended his Italian property against the invaders, and came to the relief of the starving population with corn from Sicily and Africa, thus laying deep in the hearts of the people the foundations of the secular power of the Papacy..."

[Note from Dr. Ronda and Kathleen: It is written by many of St. Catherine's biographers that she was asked by the politicians in Florence to approach Pope Gregory at Avignon in an effort to make peace between Florence and the Papal territories. The Florentines betrayed her, continuing to try to influence those in Italy to be separate from the Pope, and contradicting any effort for peace. The Pope was intent on peace, however, and after meeting with Catherine, he returned to Rome in 1376, ending a seventy-four year exile of Popes from the Holy City. Although Catherine did not have the success she sought in making peace, it is believed by many that she was the influential factor in returning the papacy to Rome.]

St. Catherine of Siena

Excerpts from *The Dialogue of the Seraphic Virgin Catherine of Siena Dictated by Her, While in a State of Ecstasy, While in Dialogue With God the Father to Her Secretaries, and Completed in the Year of Our Lord 1370*[1]

A Treatise Of Divine Providence

"...How the road to Heaven being broken through the disobedience of Adam, God made of His Son a Bridge by which man could pass.

"Therefore I have told you that I have made a Bridge of My Word, of My only-begotten Son, and this is the truth. I wish that you, My children, should know that the road was broken by the sin and disobedience of Adam, in such a way, that no one could arrive at Eternal Life.

---

1 Catherine of Siena, *the Dialogue of the Seraphic Virgin Catherine of Siena Dictated by Her, While in a State of Ecstasy, While in Dialogue With God the Father to Her Secretaries, and Completed in the Year of Our Lord 1370,* trans. Algar Thorold, (London: Kegan Paul, Trench, Trubner & Co., Ltd., 1907) at Christian Classics Ethereal Library, www.ccel.org. (In common domain but archaic language changed to more contemporary language)

"...Men did not render Me glory in the way in which they ought to have, as they did not participate in that Good for which I had created them, and My truth was not fulfilled. This truth is that I have created man to My own image...in order that he might have Eternal Life, and might partake of Me, and taste My supreme and eternal sweetness and goodness. But, after sin had closed Heaven and bolted the doors of mercy, the soul of man produced thorns and prickly brambles, and My creature found in himself rebellion against himself.

"And the flesh immediately began to war against the Spirit... losing the state of innocence...and all created things rebelled against man, whereas they would have been obedient to him, had he remained in the state in which I had placed him...

"And so, wishing to remedy your great evils, I have given you the Bridge of My Son...See, therefore, under what obligations the creature is to Me, and how ignorant he is, not to take the remedy which I have offered..."

"How God induces the soul to look at the greatness of this Bridge, inasmuch as it reaches from earth to Heaven.

"Open, my daughter, the eye of your intellect, and you will see the accepted and the ignorant, the imperfect, and also the perfect who follow Me in truth, so that you may grieve over the damnation of the ignorant, and rejoice over the perfection of My beloved servants...

"So the height of the Divinity...made the Bridge and reformed the road. Why was this done? In order that man might come to his true happiness with the angels. And...it is not enough...that My Son should have made you this Bridge, unless you walk thereon."

"How this soul prays God to show her those who cross by the aforesaid Bridge, and those who do not.

"Then this soul exclaimed with ardent love… 'Who would not be inflamed by such great love? What heart can help breaking at such tenderness? It seems, oh, Abyss of Charity, as if you were mad with love of Your creature, as if You could not live without him, and yet You are our God who have no need of us, Your greatness does not increase through our good, for You are unchangeable, and our evil causes You no harm, for You are the Supreme and Eternal Goodness.

"'What moves You to do us such mercy through pure love…? I see Your Word, Your Son, fastened and nailed to the Cross, of which You have made me a Bridge, as You have shown me,…for which reason my heart is bursting, and yet cannot burst, through the hunger and the desire which it has…towards You.

"'I remember, my Lord, that You were willing to show me… those who go by the Bridge and those who do not…

"'How this Bridge has three steps, which signify the three states of the soul; and how, being lifted on high, yet it is not separated from the earth; and how these words are to be understood: "If I am lifted up from the earth, I will draw all things to Me.'

"Then the Eternal God…said: 'First…I will now explain to you the nature of this Bridge. I have told you, My daughter, that the Bridge reaches from Heaven to earth; this is through the union which I have made with man…

"'Now learn that this Bridge, My only-begotten Son, has three steps,…two were made with the wood of the most Holy Cross, and the third still retains the great bitterness He tasted when He was given gall and vinegar to drink. In these three steps you will recognize three states of the soul, which I will explain to you below.

"'The feet of the soul, signifying her affection, are the first step, for the feet carry the body as the affection carries the soul…these pierced Feet are steps by which you can arrive at His Side [revealing] the secret of His Heart, because the soul…commences to taste the love of His Heart, gazing into that open Heart of My Son…Then the soul is filled with love, seeing herself so much loved. Having passed the second step, the soul reaches out to the third…the Mouth, where she finds peace from the terrible war she has been waging with her sin.

"'On the first step, then, lifting her feet from the affections of the earth, the soul strips herself of vice; on the second she fills herself with love and virtue; and on the third she tastes peace. So the Bridge has three steps, in order that, climbing past the first and the second, you may reach the last…

"'This Bridge is lifted on high, and yet, at the same time, joined to the earth. Do you know when it was lifted on high? When My Son was lifted up on the wood of the most Holy Cross…'

[Note from Dr. Ronda: With this key image of the Bridge in mind, we can now read from the beginning part of the Treatise and understand better why St. Catherine seeks so passionately to do penance for the sins of those who 'choose to walk under the bridge.']

"… So, the soul, wishing to know and follow the truth… addressed four requests to the Supreme and Eternal Father. The first was for herself; the second for the reformation of the Holy Church; the third a general prayer for the whole world, and in particular for the peace of Christians who rebel...against the Holy Church; in the fourth... she besought the Divine Providence to provide for things in general...

"How the desire of this soul grew when God showed her the neediness of the world. This desire was great and continuous, but grew much more, when the First Truth showed her the neediness of the world, and in what a tempest of offense against God it lay...

"All this lighted the fire of her holy desire with grief for the offenses, and with the joy of the lively hope, with which she waited for God to provide against such great evils. And, since the soul seems, in such communion, sweetly to bind herself fast within herself and with God...she desired the arrival of the morning (for the morrow was a feast of Mary) in order to hear Mass.

"(God the Father told her) 'I wish that you should know, that not all the pains that are given to men in this life are given as punishments, but as corrections, in order to chastise a son when he offends...Infinite grief I wish from My creature in two ways: in one way, through her sorrow for her own sins, which she has committed against Me her Creator; in the other way, through her sorrow for the sins which she sees her neighbors commit against Me...

"'No virtue, my daughter, can have life in itself except through charity, and humility... In self-knowledge, then, you will humble yourself, seeing that...through the ineffable love which I had for you...I have washed you, and recreated you in the Blood of My only-begotten Son, spilled with so great a fire of love... to those who dispose themselves humbly and with reverence, to receive the doctrine of My servants...I remit both guilt and penalty...for their sins. So that, by means of prayer, and their desire of serving Me, they receive the fruit of grace...according to the extent of their exercise of virtue and grace in general...

"'Labor, therefore, to increase the fire of your desire, and let not a moment pass without crying to Me with humble voice, or without continual prayers before Me for your neighbors...

"'...Patience cannot be proved in any other way than by suffering, and patience is united with love as has been said. Therefore bear yourselves with manly courage, for, unless you do so, you will not prove yourselves to be spouses of My Truth, and faithful children, nor of the company of those who relish the taste of My honor, and the salvation of souls....

"'How virtues are accomplished by means of our neighbor, and how it is that virtues differ to such an extent in creatures.

"'...Self-love, which destroys charity and affection towards the neighbor, is the principle and foundation of every evil. All scandals, hatred, cruelty, and every sort of trouble proceed from this perverse root of self-love, which has poisoned the entire world, and weakened the mystical body of the Holy Church, and the universal body of the believers in the Christian religion; and, therefore, I said to you, that it was in the neighbor...in the love of him, that all virtues were founded; and...charity gives life to all the virtues, because no virtue can be obtained without charity, which is the pure love of Me.

"'Therefore, when the soul knows herself...she finds humility and...she discovers in herself the bounty of My goodness through the many benefits which she has received from Me...knowing that, by My grace, I have drawn her out of darkness and lifted her up into the light of true knowledge...

"'And it cannot be otherwise, because love of Me and of her neighbor are one and the same thing, and, so far as the soul loves Me, she loves her neighbor, because love towards him issues from Me. This is the means which I have given you, that you may exercise and prove your virtue...This proves that you possess Me by grace in your soul, producing much fruit for your neighbor and making prayers to Me, seeking...My honor and the salvation of souls. The soul, enamored of My truth, never ceases to serve the whole world...

"'When she has discovered the advantage of this unitive love in Me, by means of which, she truly loves herself, extending her desire for the salvation of the whole world...she strives...to fix her eye on the needs of her neighbor in particular.

"'...When she has discovered...the state of all rational creatures in general, she helps those who are at hand according to the various graces which I have entrusted to her...one she helps with doctrine...with words giving sincere counsel...another with the example of a good life, and this indeed all give to their neighbor, the edification of a holy and honorable life. These are the virtues...too many to enumerate, which are brought forth in the love of the neighbor; but, although I have given them...to one, one virtue, and to another, another, it so happens that it is impossible to have one, without having them all, because all the virtues are bound together.

"'Therefore, learn, that, in many cases I give one virtue, to be as it were the chief of the others…to one I will give principally love, to another justice, to another humility, to one a lively faith, to another prudence or temperance, or patience, to another fortitude. These, and many other virtues, I place, indifferently, in the souls of many creatures; it happens, therefore, that the particular one so placed in the soul becomes the principal object of its virtue; …and, by the effect of this virtue, the soul draws to herself all the other virtues, which, as has been said, are all bound together in the affection of love…

"'…I could easily have created men possessed of all that they should need both for body and soul, but I wish that one should have need of the other, and that they should be My ministers to administer the graces and the gifts that they have received from Me…See then, that I have made men My ministers, and placed them in diverse stations and various ranks, in order that they may make use of the virtue of love.

"'How virtues are proved and fortified by their contraries.

"'… Now I wish to tell you further, that a man proves his patience on his neighbor, when he receives injuries from him.

"'Similarly, he proves his humility on a proud man, his faith on an infidel, his true hope on one who despairs, his justice on the unjust, his kindness on the cruel, his gentleness and benignity on the irascible. Good men produce and prove all their virtues on their neighbor, just as perverse men all their vices; thus, if you consider well, humility is proved on pride in this way. The humble man extinguishes pride, because a proud man can do no harm to a humble one..."'"

DR. RONDA'S CONTEMPORARY APPLICATIONS AND PERSONAL REFLECTIONS

From my many readings of the life of St. Catherine of Siena by Blessed Raymond of Capua and of *The Dialogue* a very simple idea is a standout for me. God tells Catherine how precious are "the little prayers of the faithful." So many Catholics who have never read *The Dialogue* or been graced with mystical experiences, humbly and faithfully pray the rosary and other prayers day after day. Let us never judge such prayer to be "lower" than contemplative flights.

There is quite a bit of controversy in our times about prophetic words allegedly spoken by God into the hearts of Catholics. *The Dialogue* manifests that prophecy, as a gift of the Holy Spirit, does not always mean predictions of the future but can be God's way of speaking to us throughout the centuries in language that touches on our special needs.

The Third Order of St. Dominic is called the Order of Penance (O.P.) and all three parts of the Dominicans (priests/brothers, sisters, and Third Order lay people) traditionally included penance in their charism. How often do you hear the word penance in any sermons nowadays?

I recall some members of a Third Order of St. Dominic, the lay community in New Hope, Kentucky, talking about how wonderful it was to do penance. I was flabbergasted. I was brought into the Church by lay Catholics who emphasized joy and praise, especially through liturgy. Penance seemed to me something medieval, as in accounts of big sinners carrying huge wooden crosses through the streets of their cities or flagellating themselves publicly on Good Friday.

Some spiritual directors tell us that we don't have to do penances, life is so hard for us nowadays. To just take each day as it comes is enough. For me, for example, it would be paradoxically penitential to shoo away chronic worry about the future! However, finally in my old age, I find that many of my greatest woes have no remedy that could come with teaching, writing, and speaking – my favorite apostolic activities. It actually is consoling to me to do tiny voluntary penances, such as household tasks like cleaning the kitty litter box or washing dishes when it is not my "job." I offer such penances for conversions in my family, an end to abortion, and social justice for the poor.

KATHLEEN'S CONTEMPORARY APPLICATIONS AND PERSONAL REFLECTIONS

God, the "First Truth," confirms to St. Catherine of Siena that He has given various strengths and virtues to each one, yet does not give all of them to anyone, in order that we must rely upon each other in the Body of Christ. We are not all intended to "be" or "do" the same.

Nor does this imply that one gift or talent is superior to others – except that we are all called to be perfect as Our Heavenly Father is perfect. He has given us strengths and virtues that complement each other in order for us to help each other to wholeness and holiness. We are to assist one another in attaining heaven. We are to ensure that we build up each member of the Body of Christ.

The "First Truth" makes it abundantly clear to St. Catherine that the most important part of the spiritual life is to know and love God, as well as to know ourselves and the condition of our souls. These two types of knowledge will lead us to love God, and to humility, which is essential for love/charity. She is given to see that we cannot have one type of knowledge without the other.

In these days we are so focused on making sure everyone is "equal" that we often lose perspective. Rather than celebrating our different strengths and admiring/imitating one another's virtues, we often celebrate the kinds of differences that draw us away from God. Surely we must be tolerant and loving, but that does not mean we accept everything and stand up for nothing. Not everything is okay. Admonishing the sinner – in a kind and loving way – is one of the spiritual works of mercy. We are called heroes when we pull people from harm's way, but judgmental hypocrites when we try to pull people from the jaws of an eternal hell.

True self-knowledge and humility should keep us from becoming "holier than thou" and prevent us from being those judgmental hypocrites we are often seen to be. Such knowledge does not come from comparing ourselves to others but, rather, to God. In order to compare ourselves to Him, we need to know Him. When we see Godly character in others, we would do well to imitate <u>that</u> rather than their latest styles, activities, language, or possessions. The example we need to give is not of what we have, but of who we are in Christ.

We have such a wonderful example in St. Catherine, who boldly approached the Holy Father and admonished him to be in Rome where the seat of Peter is. She defended the faith always. She spoke up for injustice, but not to ensure that everything is acceptable. Justice means giving someone what is his/her due under God.

Sometimes, we become our best selves through the suffering God permits in our lives. St. Catherine is given to see that we are not to suffer and do penance for the sake of the suffering. Rather, we are to endure whatever comes with love and patience, and with great desire for the salvation of souls. Herein lies the love and charity. The suffering without the love is fruitless. Our suffering must be in imitation of Christ and His love.

God tells St. Catherine that in love for Him we must love others, that our virtue is seen in our relationship to others. But we cannot love them without first loving Him, and we cannot love Him without first knowing Him, and we cannot know Him without knowing and understanding the condition of our souls. We must humbly seek to atone for our sins by love, and make satisfaction for them through our desire to atone for them.

One of the ways we can come to know God is by spending time alone with Him and allowing Him to reveal Himself. I find that so hard to do – not the spending time alone, the allowing Him in. A powerful part of St. Catherine's story for me is her vision of Jesus when she was a child. Her brother called to her. If she hadn't lowered her eyes, she says, she would not have lost Jesus – and she couldn't bring Him back. It seems that each time I allow myself to practice listening to God, I almost fight getting too close to Him. Whenever I feel myself beginning to surrender, or become aware of a possible Presence, I abruptly think of something else, or look somewhere else and the moment is gone. Why do I do that? What am I afraid of? What am I avoiding? How can I become the holy person I claim I want to be if I don't know God? How can I know Him if I am the one doing all the talking and controlling the encounter?

We seem, in our times especially, to want things our way. We want God to be a wish-granter. We like to blame God for what is wrong and expect Him to make things right in our eyes rather than us working to do what is right in His eyes.

St. Catherine of Siena, help us to seek God, to serve Him, to defend real truth, and to humbly know ourselves so that we can love God and each other as you did.

FOR PERSONAL REFLECTION AND GROUP SHARING

1. Does the image of Jesus as the Bridge to heaven cause you to

see God's plan differently than you have before?

2. What lessons that Jesus gives to St. Catherine about humility were you able to take into your own soul? About suffering for the sins of others?

3. What did you learn about virtue in general or about one specific virtue? Can you draw the parable?

4. A lot of what God tells Catherine is basic doctrine – why do you think God sends it to us through Catherine?

5. How do you suffer for the Church?

6. How does God reveal Himself to you?

7. What struggles do you experience in coming to know God? To know yourself so that you can love God? Have you noticed your progress?

THOMAS A KEMPIS (C. 1379-1471)
THE IMITATION OF CHRIST

Born in Cologne, Germany, Thomas attended the schools of Deventer in Holland when he was only thirteen. The one aim of everyone there was to imitate the lives of the early Christians. Thomas became one of the most notable of the Canons Regular, of whom he was a member for seventy-two years.

Thomas was a particularly kind man, especially to the less fortunate. He often preached in the church at the priory, and also loved reading, writing, or prayer. He was very gifted when speaking about God or the soul. He seems to have sought peace and found it only when he was tucked away in a corner with his books.

The Imitation of Christ was first issued anonymously (1418). However, in 1441 Thomas signed codex 5855-61 containing the four books of *The Imitation* and nine minor treatises. It was held by the Royal Library in Brussels and is still in existence today.

It is judged to be the most popular of all Christian books besides the Bible.

Excerpts from *The Imitation Of Christ*[1]

The First Book

Admonitions Profitable for the Spiritual Life

Chapter I

Of the imitation of Christ, and of contempt of the world and all its vanities He that follow(s) me shall not walk in darkness, (Jn 8:12) says the Lord. These are the words of Christ; and they teach us how far we must imitate His life and character, if we seek true illumination, and deliverance from all blindness of heart. Let it be our most earnest study, therefore, to dwell upon the life of Jesus Christ...

3. What does it profit you to enter into deep discussion concerning the Holy Trinity, if you lack humility, and are thus displeasing to the Trinity? For truly it is not deep words that make a man holy and upright; it is a good life which makes a man dear to God. I had rather feel contrition than be skillful in the definition thereof. If you knew the whole Bible, and the sayings of all the philosophers, what should all this profit you without the love and grace of God? Vanity of vanities, all is vanity, save to love God, and Him only to serve. That is the highest wisdom, to cast the world behind us, and to reach forward to the heavenly kingdom.

---

[1] Thomas a Kempis, *The Imitation of Christ,* trans. Rev. William Benham, (London: J. C. Nimmo, 1886), at Sacred-Texts, www.sacred-texts.com. (In common domain but archaic language changed to more contemporary language).

4. It is vanity then to seek after, and to trust in, the riches that shall perish. It is vanity, too, to covet honors, and to lift up ourselves on high. It is vanity to follow the desires of the flesh and be led by them, for this shall bring misery at the last. It is vanity to desire a long life, and to have little care for a good life. It is vanity to take thought only for the life which now is, and not to look forward to the things which shall be hereafter. It is vanity to love that which quickly passes away, and not to hasten where eternal joy abides....

Chapter II

Of thinking humbly of oneself

There is naturally in every man a desire to know, but what profit is knowledge without the fear of God? ... If I knew all the things that are in the world, and were not in charity, what should it help me before God, who is to judge me according to my deeds?...

4. That is the highest and most profitable lesson, when a man truly knows and judges lowly of himself. To account nothing of one's self, and to think always kindly and highly of others, this is great and perfect wisdom. Even should you see your neighbor sin openly or grievously, yet you ought not to reckon yourself better than he, for you know not how long you shall keep your integrity. All of us are weak and frail; hold...no man more frail than yourself.

Chapter III

...3. The more a man has unity and simplicity in himself, the more things and the deeper things he understands...because he receives the light of understanding from above. The spirit which is pure, sincere, and steadfast, is not distracted though it has many works to do, because it does all things to the honor of God, and strives to be free from all thoughts of self-seeking...Who has a harder battle to fight than he who strives for self-mastery? And this should be our endeavor, even to master self, and thus daily to grow stronger than self, and go on to perfection...

Chapter IV

Of prudence in action...

This is great wisdom, not to be hasty in action, or stubborn in our own opinions. A part of this wisdom also is not to believe every word we hear, nor to tell others all that we hear, even though we believe it. ...

Chapter VI

Of inordinate affections

...The proud and the avaricious men are never at rest; while the poor and lowly of heart abide in the multitude of peace. The man who is not yet wholly dead to self, is soon tempted, and is overcome in small and trifling matters. It is hard for him who is weak in spirit, and still in part…inclined to the pleasures of sense, to withdraw himself altogether from earthly desires. And therefore, when he withdraws himself from these, he is often sad, and easily angered too if any oppose his will.

2.…True peace of heart is to be found in resisting passion, not in yielding to it…

Chapter XI

Of seeking peace of mind and of spiritual progress

We may enjoy abundance of peace if we refrain from busying ourselves with the sayings and doings of others, and things which concern not ourselves. How can he abide long time in peace who occupies himself with other men's matters…

2. How came it to pass that many of the Saints were so perfect, so contemplative of Divine things? Because they steadfastly sought to mortify themselves from all worldly desires, and so were enabled to cling with their whole heart to God, and be free and at leisure for the thought of Him. We are too much occupied with our own affections, and too anxious about transitory things. Seldom, too, do we entirely conquer even a single fault, nor are we zealous for daily growth in grace. And so we remain lukewarm and unspiritual.

3. …When even a little trouble befalls us, too quickly are we cast down, and fly to the world to give us comfort…

6. It is a hard thing to break through a habit, and a yet harder thing to go contrary to our own will. Yet if you overcome not slight

and easy obstacles, how shall you overcome greater ones?...

Chapter XII

Of the uses of adversity

It is good for us that we sometimes have sorrows and adversities, for they often make a man lay to heart that he is only a stranger and sojourner, and may not put his trust in any worldly thing. It is good that we sometimes endure contradictions, and are hardly and unfairly judged, when we do and mean what is good. For these things help us to be humble, and shield us from vain-glory. For then we seek the more earnestly the witness of God, when men speak evil of us falsely, and give us no credit for good.

2. Therefore ought a man to rest wholly upon God, so that he...not seek much comfort at the hand of men. When a man who fears God is afflicted or tried or oppressed with evil thoughts, then he sees that God is the more necessary to him, since without God he can do no good thing...By all this he is taught that in the world there can be no perfect security or fullness of peace.

Chapter XIII

Of resisting temptation

So long as we live in the world, we cannot be without trouble and trial. Therefore it is written in Job, "The life of man upon the earth is a trial" (Job 7:1, Vulgate). And therefore ought each of us to give heed concerning trials and temptations, and watch to prayer, lest the devil find occasion to deceive...No man is so perfect in holiness that he never has temptations, nor can we ever be wholly free from them.

2. Yet, notwithstanding, temptations turn greatly to our profit, even though they be great and hard to bear; for through them we are humbled, purified, instructed. All Saints have passed through much tribulation and temptation, and have profited thereby...

3. ... Many who seek to fly from temptations fall yet more deeply into them. By flight alone we cannot overcome, but by endurance and true humility we are made stronger than all our enemies....

4. Little by little, through patience and longsuffering, you shall conquer by the help of God, rather than by violence and your own strength of will. ...

5. ...Nevertheless, we must watch, especially in the beginnings of temptation; for then is the foe the more easily mastered, when he is not suffered to enter within the mind, but is met outside the door as soon as he has knocked...For first comes to the mind the simple suggestion, then the strong imagination, afterwards pleasure, evil affection, assent. And so little by little the enemy enters in altogether, because he was not resisted at the beginning. And the longer a man delays his resistance, the weaker he grows, and the stronger grows the enemy against him...

7. Therefore we ought not to despair when we are tempted, but the more fervently should cry to God, that He will vouchsafe to help us in all our tribulation; and that He will, as St. Paul said, with the

temptation make a way to escape that we may be able to bear it (1 Cor 10:13). Let us therefore humble ourselves under the mighty hand of God in all temptation and trouble, for He will save and exalt such as are of humble spirit.

8. In temptations and troubles a man is proved, what progress he has made, and there is his reward the greater, and his virtue appears...Some are kept safe from great temptations, but are overtaken in those which are little and common, that the humiliation may teach them not to trust to themselves in great things, being weak in small things.

Chapter XIV

On avoiding rash judgment

Look well on yourself, and beware that you judge not the doings of others. In judging others a man labors in vain; he often errs, and easily falls into sin; but in judging and examining himself he always labors to good purpose....

Chapter XV

Of works of charity

For no worldly good whatsoever, and for the love of no man, must anything be done which is evil...Without charity no work is of benefit, but whatsoever is done in charity, however small and of no reputation it is, brings forth good fruit...

Chapter XVI

Of bearing with the faults of others

Those things which a man cannot amend in himself or in others, he ought patiently to bear, until God shall otherwise ordain.... perhaps it is better for your trial and patience, without which our merits are but little worth...when you find such impediments...beseech God that He would vouchsafe to sustain you, that you be able to bear them with a good will.

2. ...Endeavor to be patient in bearing with other men's faults and infirmities whatsoever they are, for you also have many things which have need to be borne with by others. If you cannot make your own self what you desire, how shall you be able to fashion another to your own liking. We are ready to see others made perfect, and yet we do not amend our own shortcomings...

4. But now has God thus ordained, that we may learn to bear one another's burdens, because none is without defect, none without a burden, none sufficient of himself, none wise enough of himself; but it behooves us to bear with one another, to comfort one another, to help, instruct, admonish one another. How much strength each man has is best proved by occasions of adversity: for such occasions do not make a man frail, but show of what temper he is....

Chapter XX

Of the love of solitude and silence

Seek a suitable time for meditation, and think frequently of the mercies of God. Leave curious questions. Study such matters as bring you sorrow for sin rather than amusement. If you withdraw from trifling conversation...as well as from novelties and gossip, you shall find your time sufficient and apt for good meditation. The greatest saints used to avoid as far as they could the company of men, and chose to live in secret with God.

2. One has said, "As often as I have gone among men, so often have I returned less a man." ...It is easier to remain hidden at home than to keep sufficient guard upon yourself out of doors. He, therefore, that seeks to reach that which is hidden and spiritual, must go with Jesus "apart from the multitude."...

Chapter XXII

On the contemplation of human misery

...Who is he that has everything according to his will? Neither I, nor you, nor any man upon the earth. There is no man in the world free from trouble or anguish, though he were King or Pope. Who is he who has the happiest lot? Even he who is strong to suffer somewhat for God.

2. ...The happiness of man lies not in the abundance of tempo-

ral things but a moderate portion suffices for him. Our life upon the earth is truly wretchedness. The more a man desires to be spiritual, the more bitter does the present life become to him; because he the better understands and sees the defects of human corruption...

3. ...But woe to those who know not their own misery, and yet greater woe to those who love this miserable and corruptible life. For to such a degree do some cling to it (even though by laboring or begging they scarcely procure what is necessary for subsistence) that if they might live here always, they would care nothing for the Kingdom of God...

Chapter XXIII

Of meditation upon death

... You ought in every deed and thought so to order yourself, as if you were to die this day. If you had a good conscience you would not greatly fear death. It is better for you to watch against sin, than to fly from death. If today you are not ready, how shall you be ready tomorrow? Tomorrow is an uncertain day; and how do you know that you shall have a tomorrow?...

3. ...Always be prepared, and live so that death may never find you unprepared. Many die suddenly and unexpectedly. For at such an hour as you think not, the Son of Man comes...

DR. RONDA'S CONTEMPORARY APPLICATIONS AND PERSONAL REFLECTIONS

From the beginning of *The Imitation of Christ*, the author insists that what pleases God is our doing His will, not deep discussion of theological concepts. This is constant theme of spiritual writers. I do not take it to mean that there is no place for theology in our lives as Christians as writers or readers. After all, someone could catch the writer of the Imitation up in a contradiction by saying, "I should be feeding the poor instead of reading your book!" I would put it this way: the human person as a body/soul composite is made up of thoughts, words, feelings, decisions, actions. The goal of our lives as Christians is to grow in love of God and neighbor through all of these facets of our personhood. We should not emphasize any of these facets when the call of the Holy Spirit in our particular vocation and circumstances is one of the other facets. Grieving at a funeral out of love for a family member would not be the time for a doctor at that service to be thinking about all the medical particulars surrounding the person's death. When a poor person needs an emergency loan of money or a loaf of bread we should not be discussing instead all the aspects of the ethics of financial aid vs. helping him find a job. On the other hand, no one should substitute ministry to the poor for studying the teachings of the Church in the form of listening to sermons and spiritual reading.

I am sometimes alarmed at the anxiety of my Christian students concerning grades. I don't see them worrying as much about saying something unloving about another person. Studying a goodly amount before tests or orals is good, but the degree of fear of getting even a "B" grade (B = good) as a sign of not being a "top" student is surely pride. I like the joke with them, "You mean when you get to the pearly gates you think you will be asked what your G.P.A. was at the university?"

Self-seeking is identified as the reason for peaceless distraction rather than "having too much to do" or being "over-extended" as we like to say in our times. Some of us truthfully for absolutely necessary reasons have too much to do such as a parent of many children who is also working outside the home or a middle-aged person working and taking care of an elderly disabled relative in all his/her spare time. But many of us don't organize our time well because we often do first what we like best and leave the necessities until later, then feeling unbearable pressure to finish them. A Kempis believed that when we only do what God wills we can have peace as we accomplish our obligations.

Notice how *The Imitation* in writing about the life of Christ starts with his being the greatest teacher. I find that it helps me to realize this when what He told us stretches us in our humanity. For example, Thomas the doubter asks how he can follow Jesus when he doesn't know where Jesus is going and the response is "I am the Way, the Truth and the Life." Now, "I am the Way" makes sense if we are thinking that the purpose of our lives is to follow Jesus as a teacher. Those who follow famous spiritual leaders in the Buddhist or Hindu traditions don't think that following the teacher means leaving town with him/her. They think it means stretching to follow the spiritual way of the teacher. Much concerned about the future since I am a widow-pilgrim and often can't picture where I will next dwell, I need to stretch to see that the important thing is that I am "on the path" of the truths of Jesus the teacher. Where is less important than who He is and who I am: His child.

The writer of the Imitation tells us never to judge ourselves better than others because we could suddenly fall and they could suddenly change for the better. I find, rather often, that when I have judged someone harshly, the next day, or week, or month, they do something good that I would find it hard to do!

"Fancies about change of place..." Alas! I put it humorously that I will start a group called "Fantasies Anonymous." Many people have no options and resent the fact. But some of us have too many options. This can lead to jumpiness and dissatisfaction as we feel elated about a possibility of a different place to be or people to be close to, but then the fantasy busts after some time in the new place. Of course, the answer is to be dreaming about the joys of heaven that will be ours if we brave our crosses bravely. If new opportunities arise that are clearly good, there is nothing wrong in trying them, but not in the form of feverish desires on a roller-coaster with discouragement. Realistic people are glad for all the good in each situation, never think that anything earthly can be perfect, and therefore pray to always receive the grace of hope in the one who alone can deliver: Our Lord, Jesus Christ.

Thomas a Kempis

KATHLEEN'S CONTEMPORARY APPLICATIONS AND PERSONAL REFLECTIONS

In a sermon at morning Mass, Father explained that vanity, as it is used in the Bible, means "vapor". Thus all the things that are referred to as vanity in the Bible are maybe not so much prideful, self-seeking things (although they can lead to that) as they are puffs of air that disappear because they are not of lasting importance. That image of vapor is prevalent in the readings from *The Imitation of Christ*.

Of particular interest to me, as a catechist, is Chapter IV of *The Imitation*: "This is great wisdom, not to be hasty in action, or stubborn in our own opinions. A part of this wisdom also is not to believe every word we hear, nor to tell others all that we hear, even though we believe it." This follows a chapter about not seeking too much knowledge, and it could also apply to gossip. But it is difficult for me to determine when to speak what I know for the good of my students and their knowledge of the faith, and when I might be telling more than they need to hear just because I do know it. When am I planting seeds for more knowledge and light, and when am I serving my puffed up pride just to show what I know? When am I helping them to understand what the Church teaches and why She teaches it, and when am I going far beyond what they are ready to hear and actually turning them off to the faith or pushing them away? When am I giving them something to chew on, think about and pray about, and when am I putting them in a coma by giving too much information for which they are not ready?

In a sense, this is part of my struggle for self-mastery. Thomas says in Chapter III, "Who hath a harder battle to fight than he who striveth for self-mastery?" Indeed! In paragraph 2 of Chapter VI Thomas writes, "…true peace of heart is to be found in resisting passion, not in yielding to it." Here again, this can be applied to our carnal passions, but I have a passion for the faith. Some may think that passion for the faith is a good thing. I believe it is. But there can be too much of a good thing. Prudence would dictate that I use that passion wisely and cautiously, at the proper time and under the proper conditions. Herein lies my struggle for self-mastery. I am always passionate about the faith. That can turn people off rather than attract them.

I would not suggest compromising the truth, but a wise and prudent application and presentation of it. We surely must concern ourselves more with pleasing God than men, but when we wish to attract others to the faith, it must be done wisely. I am just not good at that. It would be better to give the students less information that they can understand and apply than to give them so much that they shut down and zone out. But then, what of those students who need more and are capable of seeing more?

The priest who taught a class I was taking for catechists told a story of the daughter of a friend of his. She had been in Catholic schools all her life, and left the Church. One weekend while she was home from college, she saw a copy of Fr. John Hardon's book, *A Catholic Catechism* on the coffee table. She picked it up and started to read it. She went to her room and stayed there all weekend. When she came downstairs again, she put the book back on the table and said, "How come no one ever taught me this?" I vowed then that no one would ever say that if they had been in a class of mine. I do not want to face God and have Him ask why I didn't teach the truth – not some watered down version of the truth.

But I have to learn to teach the truth with prudence and wisdom. I need to submit humbly to God, let Him guide me, and just be content to plant the seeds that He or someone in the future will water and bring to fruition. The prideful belief that I can teach the students what they need to know and bring the whole world to conversion must be mastered and tempered. God help me.

FOR PERSONAL REFLECTION AND GROUP SHARING

1. Based on *The Imitation of Christ*, would it be better to be a priest, if God so called you, than to be a famous Christian scholar? Why?

2. Do you think the guidelines in *The Imitation of Christ* are applicable to everyday people, or more to those in a vocation to the priesthood or religious life? Why?

3. Do you imitate Christ? Does this writing help you see how to do so? Does it make you look deeper into yourself, or does it turn you off? Why?

4. Write out lines in the excerpts from *The Imitation of Christ* that you need to remember for yourself or for ministry/teaching.

ST. THOMAS MORE (1478-1535)

St. Thomas More was born in London February 7, 1478. His father, John, was a judge. Thomas studied at St. Anthony's and at Oxford. In his early life he was a page to the Archbishop. Before he was twenty, Thomas began to study the law. He tried the monastic life with the Carthusians, and retained much of that spirituality all his life. Despite his yearning to be a monk, he decided to serve his country and became a member of Parliament in 1504.

He had four children with his first wife, Jane. He loved her very much, but she died in childbirth. Thomas soon married an older woman, Alice, for the convenience of having a mother for his children. Thomas and Alice had no children together, however by the end of his life he would say that he could not tell which of his wives he loved better. There was no doubt that his daughter, Margaret, was especially beloved by St. Thomas. Despite – and probably because of – his great love for her, he forbade her to marry the man she loved when he left the Catholic Church and became Lutheran, calling him a heretic. After some time, however the young man returned to the

Church and he and Margaret were married.

A favorite of King Henry VIII, Thomas became Speaker of the House of Commons and aided Henry in writing *A Defense of the Seven Sacraments* against Luther. Thomas More became the first layman to be Lord Chancellor of England. But he refused to support Henry in his quest to divorce his wife, Katherine, in order to sire a male heir. He would not support Henry when he established the Church of England, or take oaths in opposition to Church teaching as demanded by Henry.

Found guilty of treason, Thomas was held prisoner in the Tower of London for over a year, and beheaded on July 6, 1535. His last words were, "I die the king's good servant, but God's first." Sir Thomas More was beatified in 1886 and became St. Thomas More in 1935.

Excerpts of the Writing of St. Thomas More

"God sends us also such tribulation sometimes, because His pleasure is to have us pray to Him for help. And, therefore, when St. Peter was in prison, the Scripture shows that the whole Church... prayed incessantly for him; and that at their fervent prayer God by miracle delivered him. When the disciples in the tempest stood in fear of drowning, they prayed to Christ and said: 'Save us, Lord, we perish.' And then at their prayer He shortly ceased the tempest... And many a man in his great pain and sickness, by calling upon God, is marvelously made whole. This is God's goodness, that because in wealth we remember Him not, but forget to pray to Him, sends us sorrow and sickness to force us to draw toward Him, and compels us to call upon Him and pray for release of our pain."[1]

If we lay first, for a sure ground, a very fast faith, whereby we believe to be true all that the scripture says (understood truly, as the old holy doctors declare it and as the spirit of God instructs his Catholic church), then shall we consider tribulation as a gracious gift of God, a gift that he specially gave his special friends; a thing that in scripture is highly commended and praised; a thing of which the contrary, long continued, is perilous; a thing which, if God send it not, men have need to put upon themselves and seek by penance; a thing that helps to purge our past sins; a thing that preserves us from sins that otherwise would come; a thing that causes us to set less by the world; a thing that much diminishes our pains in purgatory; a thing that much increases our final reward in heaven; the thing with which all his apostles followed him there; the thing to which our Savior exhorts all men; the thing without which he says we are not his disciples; the thing without which no man can get to heaven.[2]

"How proud are many men of these glistening stones, of which the very brightness…shall never shine half as bright, not show you half so much light, as shall a poor halfpenny candle. How proud is

---

[1] Rev. T. E. Bridgett, C.SS.R (ed), *Wisdom and Wit of Blessed Thomas More* (London: Burns and Oates Ld, 1892). 53.(In common domain but archaic language changed to more contemporary language)

[2] Thomas More, *Dialogue of Comfort Against Tribulation,* online at ccel. org (In common domain but archaic language changed to more contemporary language)

many a man over his neighbor because the wool of his gown is finer, and yet, as fine as it is, a poor sheep wore it on her back before it came on his, and all the time she wore it…she was…but a sheep. And why should he be now better than she by that wool that, though it is his, is yet not so truly his as it was truly hers?"[3]

"Let us every man…mark well when the devil first casts any proud, vain thought into our mind, and let us right away make a cross on our breast, and bless it out by-and-by, and cast it at his head again. For if we gladly take in one such guest of his, he shall not fail to bring in two of his fellows soon after, and every one worse than [the] other."[4]

"Bear malice or evil will to no man living. For, either that man is good or wicked. If he is good, and I hate him, then I am wicked. If he is wicked, either he shall amend and die good and go to God, or remain wicked and die wicked and go to the devil. And then let me remember that, if he shall be saved, he shall not fail, if I am saved too, as I trust to be, to love me very heartily, and I shall then in like-wise love him. And why should I now…hate one for this while, the one which shall hereafter love me for evermore? And why should I be now…enemy to him, with whom I shall in time come to be…in eternal friendship? Or…if he shall continue wicked and be damned, then is there so outrageous eternal sorrow towards him that I may well think myself a deadly cruel wretch if I would not now rather pity his pain than malign his person."[5]

---

3 Bridgett (ed), *Wisdom and Wit*, 56.
4 Bridgett (ed), *Wisdom and Wit*, 57.
5 Bridgett (ed), *Wisdom and Wit*, 62.

"And then what a madness is it, for the poor pleasure of your worldly goods of so few years, to cast yourself both body and soul into the everlasting fire of hell."[6]

In a letter written to Dr. Wilson 1535 from imprisonment in the Tower of London:

"I have, since I came to the Tower, looked once or twice to have died...But I put my trust in God, and in the merits of His bitter passion, and I beseech Him to give me and keep me the mind to look to be out of this world and to be with Him...For I ...trust that who so long to be with Him shall be welcome to Him."[7]

From the poor souls in purgatory:

"The comfort we have here, except our continual hope in our Lord God, comes...from Our Lady, with such glorious saints as either...our own devotion while we lived, or...yours for us since our death have made intercessors for us. And among others...our own good angels; whom when we behold coming with comfort to us... with much confusion and [shamefacedness] consider how little we regarded our good angels, and how seldom we thought upon them while we lived. They carry up your prayers to God and good saints for us, and they bring down from them comfort and consolation to us...how heartily we pray for you...and our prayer must...be profitable: for we stand sure of His grace, and our prayer is for you so fervent, that you can nowhere find any such affection upon earth."[8]

"Our Lord said in the Apocalypse: 'The devil shall send some

---

6 Bridgett (ed), *Wisdom and Wit,* 69.
7 Bridgett (ed), *Wisdom and Wit,* 73.
8 Bridgett (ed), *Wisdom and Wit,* 75-76.

of you to prison to tempt you.' He says not that men shall, but that the devil shall… For, without question, the devil…bring us by temptation with fear…into eternal damnation. And therefore says St. Paul: 'Our wrestling is not against flesh and blood, but against the princes and powers and ghostly enemies that are rulers of these darknesses,' etc. Thus may we see, that in such persecutions it is the midday devil himself that…make us fall for fear. For till we fall, he can never hurt us. And therefore says St. James: 'Stand against the devil, and he shall flee from you.' For he never runs upon a man to seize him with his claws till he see him down on the ground willingly fallen… The devil it is, therefore, that is ready to run upon us and devour us…If he threaten us that we are too weak, let us tell him that our Captain Christ is with us, and that we shall fight with His strength that has vanquished him already…For surely, if we be of the tender, loving mind that our Master was, and not hate them that kill us, but pity them and pray for them with sorrow for the peril they work to themselves; that fire of charity thrown in his face strikes the devil suddenly so blind that he cannot see where to fasten a stroke on us."[9]

"By this Church know we the Scripture and this is that very Church and has begun at Christ, and has had Him for their head, and St. Peter His Vicar after Him the head under Him, and always since the successors of Him continually, and have had His holy faith and His blessed sacraments and His holy Scriptures delivered, kept, and conserved therein by God and His holy Spirit."[10]

---

9 Bridgett (ed), *Wisdom and Wit*, 88-89.
10 Bridgett (ed), *Wisdom and Wit*, 104.

"But we say that God rejoices and delights in the love of man's heart when...man...gladly by fasting and other affliction puts the body to pain for God's sake."[11]

"I would well agree that no temple of stone was so [pleasing to God] as the temple of man's heart. But yet...God will that His Christian people have in ...places...temples and churches to which they should...assemble solemnly and resort in company to worship Him together...if churches and congregations of Christ's people resorting together to God's service were once abolished and put away, we [would] have few good temples of God in men's souls, but all would within a while wear away...and clearly fall away."[12]

{Note: St. Thomas More wrote brilliantly on so many subjects having to do with the faith. His writing on virtue, however, may be some of the most common-sense advice for everyday people. Some examples are included below.}

"Even as the soul excels the body, so does the pure sweetness of spiritual pleasure surpass the joys of sense. In truth it is no joy, but a wretched counterfeit; and the reason why men run so madly after the false, is through ignorance of the value of the true...And trust me, that if men would accustom themselves to the task of spiritual pleasure, and of that sweet feeling that the virtuous have of the good hope of heaven, they would soon...despise the delights of sense."[13]

---

11 Bridgett (ed), *Wisdom and Wit,* 120.
12 Bridgett (ed), *Wisdom and Wit,* 129-130.
13 W. Jos. Walter, *Sir Thomas More; A Selection From His Works; As Well In Prose As In Verse* (Baltimore: Fielding Lucas, Jr. 1841), 282. In common domain but archaic language changed to more contemporary language)

"I will begin at the sin which is the very bed and root of all the vices, and that sin is pride, the mischievous mother of all kinds of vice. I have seen many…that…seemed far from pride, and yet… of that root they sprang. As for wrath and envy, they are the known offspring of pride; but what would seem farther from it than drunken gluttony? And yet you shall find more that drink themselves drunk from the pride of being called good-fellows, than for lust of the drink itself."[14]

"Envy is a very consumption and such a torment that all the tyrants in Sicily never devised a sorer…this vice is not only devilish, but foolish…It does all the hurt it can…It is the first-begotten daughter of Pride, and the devil is its father…The thought of death should be one of the best remedies against envy: for why envy your neighbor, when death may make you both [equals] the next night?… Since we are certain that death shall take away all that we envy any man for…we should never see cause to envy any man, but rather to pity him; and those most who have the most to be envied for, since they are those that have the most to lose.

"Wrath is another daughter of Pride. We see this in those who…cannot abide…to be contradicted and they fret and foam if their opinion is not accepted and their invention not magnified…are we not more angry for one breach of a commandment of our own, than for the breach of God's all ten; and with one…spiteful word spoken against ourselves than with many a blasphemy spoken of God…

---

14 Walter, *Sir Thomas More: A Selection From His Works*, 285.

St. Thomas More

"...Covetous men seem humble, and yet they are very proud; they seem wise, and yet they are very foolish. There is pride in the possession of their goods...They have enough for this day, for tomorrow, for this week, for the next, for a month, for years; they have lands, merchandise, offices, and other ways, and yet are they ever whining, mourning, for...fear of many years to come; as though God either would not, or was not able to keep his promise with us...

"Gluttony is the old evil that lost us paradise, and joined with pride of knowledge, drove our first parents, and us in them, from immortality to misery and death...If we see men die by famine...how great a matter we make of it; we march in processions, we pray for pity, and reckon the world at an end. But when people die of gluttony, we take no heed at all, but rather...blame the sickness rather than the gluttony [that causes the sickness].

"And if there be a man slain with a weapon, there is much speech made; the coroner is called, the inquest called, the verdict given...the felon arraigned, and he is sentenced to death. And yet if men were to study how many were slain with weapons, and how many eat and drink themselves to death, there would be found more dead of the cup and the kitchen than by the sword, and yet nothing is said of that at all."[15]

"When Judas betrays Him, Christ reviles the blasphemous hypocrisy of the traitor: 'With a kiss,' He says, 'do you betray the Son of Man?' Among all the circumstances surrounding an evil deed it is hard to find one more hateful to God than the perversion of the real

---

15 Walter, *Sir Thomas More: A Selection From His Works,* 287-296.

nature of good things to make them into instruments of our malice. Thus lying is hateful to God because words, which He appointed to express the mind's meaning, are twisted to deceptive purposes. Within this category of evil, it is a grave offense against God to misuse the law to inflict the very injuries it was intended to prevent."[16]

"It was for the sin of pride that God drove the angels from heaven. O let us resist its first beginnings, and tremble when we feel a high and proud thought entering our heart, and swelling it beyond measure. How foolish to pride ourselves on trifles that, properly are not ours…All that we have, from God have we received it; riches, power, beauty, strength, learning, wit, body, soul, all. And almost all these things are but lent us; we must resign them all, all except this soul of ours. And even that we must at last render into the hands of God; how careful, then, should we be to render it to Him worthy of his divine acceptance…It was pride of heart, the pride that disdained happy ignorance and would know more, that lost us paradise. The evil has been cancelled by the humiliation of the Son of God, who opened for us again the gates of heaven, that had been closed upon us by sin, and among sins by that greatest of all – pride. Let us then, beware that this sin close not to us the gate of the heavenly paradise…"[17]

---

16 Paul Thigpen, *Be Merry in God, 60 Reflections From the Writings of Saint Thomas More* (Ann Arbor: Servant Publications, 1999), 90.
17 Walter, *Sir Thomas More: A Selection From His Writings*, 297-298.

St. Thomas More

Prayers of St. Thomas More

"O blessed and glorious Trinity, whose justice has condemned to perpetual pain many proud and rebel angels, whom Your goodness had created to be partners of Your eternal glory; do You of Your tender mercy implant in my heart such meekness, that, by Your grace, I may so follow the motion of my good angel, and so Your bitter passion, I may become partner of Your bliss, with those blessed spirits that stood; and being confirmed now by Your grace, may stand for ever in Your glory. Amen."

"O my sweet Savior Christ, who, through Your gracious love to human-kind, kindly condescended to undergo the painful death of the Cross, suffer me not in return for all You have done for me, to be cold and lukewarm in my love to You; but after loving and serving You in this life, to come to the possession of You in the world that never ends. Amen."

"O Lord God, give us Your grace, not to read nor hear this Gospel of Your bitter passion, with our eyes and our ears, in the manner of a pastime, but that it may by meditation sink so deeply in our hearts, as to conduce to the everlasting profit of our souls. Amen."

"O Holy Trinity, Father, Son, and Holy Ghost, three equal and co-eternal Persons, and one Almighty God, have mercy on me, a vile subject, and sinful creature; meekly acknowledging before Your high Majesty my long-continued sinful life, even from my very childhood upwards. And now, O good and gracious Lord, as You gave me Your grace to acknowledge my sins, so also give me Your grace, not in word only, but in heart and spirit, with full and sorrowful contrition to repent them, and utterly forsake them. Forgive me those sins also, which, through my own defect, through evil affection or the force of custom, my reason is so blinded by sensuality, that I cannot discern as sins. O good Lord, illuminate my heart, and give me Your grace to know my sins, and to acknowledge them, to forgive me those that are forgotten through negligence, and bring them to my mind, with grace for me faithfully to confess them."[18]

DR. RONDA'S CONTEMPORARY APPLICATIONS AND PERSONAL REFLECTIONS

I first got to know St. Thomas More because of the famous film about his life: "A Man for All Seasons." This led me to read a long biography where I was amazed to find that he had to leave his beloved Carthusians because he was deemed too nervous for this kind of contemplative life. Since I am also a very nervous person who finds it hard to sit still in contemplative prayer unless I am given a special infused grace of prayer of quiet, I identified with Thomas More. I was also amazed to read that he married so soon after the death of his beloved wife, because some think that no widow or widower who was holy would re-marry and that is not the teaching of the Church.

I believe that the most significant part of the witness of St.

---

18 Walter, *Sir Thomas More: A Selection From His Writings,* 298-305.

St. Thomas More

Thomas More was his martyrdom over the disobedience to the Pope of his King. Some Catholics these days would never think that obedience to the Church in a divorce matter was important enough to die for. Such Catholics think that following your own conscience in what is called "the interior forum" is good enough. Such disobedience in marriage cases has led many into dissent about many other teachings of the Church. Those who want to avoid mortal sin and even more to wish for spiritual graces to become holy can never think that being married to a particular person against the directives of the Church is something so important that we can risk eternal happiness by choosing it. This comes down to idolatry of human love.

As well, unless we are invincibly ignorant we should not think that Churches founded by human beings are equal to that of the one founded by Our Lord, Jesus Christ – that is the one true Catholic Church. An example of invincible ignorance would be someone in a mission country who met Jesus only through a Protestant Church and never heard of the Catholic Church or only met witnesses who were counter witnesses to Her holiness.

I think that the writings of St. Thomas More about virtues and vices, because he was a layperson, have a style and pungency different for those of us who are lay people than those of consecrated religious. I laughed aloud reading the passage Kathleen Brouillette picked out on vanity concerning clothing and how the expensive cloth first belonged to the sheep. I have always been amazed at how we take such joy in being praised for our looks or our intelligence, gifts of God for which we have no merit whatsoever, more than for virtues that required our cooperation with God's grace to sustain!

On gluttony, the upper middle class in England, to which St. Thomas More belonged by birth, was famous for sumptuous eating and drinking. In our times obesity as contributing to death, as St. Thomas alludes to, is a huge health problem and alcoholism just as much, yet we rarely hear sermons about these vices. Anyone suffering from addiction, but hoping to become holy, needs to avail themselves of pastoral counseling, if that is available, or of those free self-help groups such as 12 Step or others that are Catholic oriented.

KATHLEEN'S CONTEMPORARY APPLICATIONS AND PERSONAL REFLECTIONS

I first became aware of St. Thomas More in my middle teens, when "A Man For All Seasons" won the Academy Award for Best Picture, and Paul Scofield won Best Actor for his portrayal of St. Thomas More. I was not yet a Catholic at the time, but the brilliant wit of St. Thomas, and his final words in particular, literally made my jaw drop in admiration. The film portrays St. Thomas as giving a coin to his executioner, telling him not to feel badly about what he was about to do, "You are sending me to God." I never forgot that line, or the man who reportedly said it. It was an extraordinary statement of faith that I heard at a time when I was seriously questioning the existence of God. But St. Thomas was so committed to Him, and to the truth of the Catholic Church, that he literally lost his head

St. Thomas More

defending it against King Henry VIII.

My second favorite quote from St. Thomas came to my attention some four years ago. He had written about the way Judas used a kiss as a twisted sign of affection in order to betray Jesus. The betrayal was bad enough, but the fact that he had misrepresented this sign of affection made it all the more abominable, according to our saint. He said, "Within this category of evil, it is a grave offense against God to misuse the law to inflict the very injuries it was intended to prevent."

How often in our society do we misrepresent and twist the meaning of things? Obviously the law has become a game whereby attorneys try to free people whom they know to be guilty. It's become a contest of wits to see who can outsmart whom. In like manner, perhaps, many of us misinterpret love of others to mean toleration of anything they do. People think nothing is "wrong" or "immoral" as long as no one is being hurt. Of course, we have little understanding of what it means to hurt someone, such as how premarital sex uses another and cheapens the spousal act. Nor do we look at how we are perverting God's plan by behaving not according to His perfect will, but for our temporal pleasure.

The deepest and most intimate gift of ourselves is given indiscriminately, and so rarely reflects a true gift or a deep love and sharing. We don't even call it making love anymore. It's "doing" someone, or "getting busy." Such perversion of God's intended meaning! And we are not the least bit concerned with offending Him.

St. Thomas points out that the things we think are doing us good are in reality doing us more harm than we can imagine – and it will likely be an eternal harm! His best advice is to always have before us our final end – death and facing God – and in that way we will never sin. But we have even twisted the notion of God's mercy to mean that everyone is forgiven everything (whether or not they repent) and everyone goes to heaven. So, the concept of sin that St. Thomas had in mind when he wrote his great advice is not on the minds of people anymore. I would hope to keep in my mind the image of Christ's suffering for me and remind myself to accept the crosses He allows in my life because He loves me and wills it for my good.

May St. Thomas More pray for us to our Lord, Who can neither deceive nor be deceived, that we may speak out for truth as Thomas More did, no matter what it may cost us, and may we ever progress in holiness until we reach heaven.

FOR PERSONAL REFLECTION AND GROUP SHARING

1. Does it make sense to you, as St. Thomas More asserts, that pride is the root of every vice?

2. Would you have the courage to defend the faith, even if it meant losing your head?

3. Do you find yourself falling for twisted ideas that make life easier? Does St. Thomas make you think more about looking out for deception?

4. Have you twisted the truth for your own ends at some time? Do you see that differently after reading the excerpts from St. Thomas?

5. Do you see suffering any differently after reading St. Thomas?

6. Are you more aware now of the need to think of God, of the saints in heaven as your aids, of the souls in purgatory in need of your prayers?

7. What, if anything, in the writings of St. Thomas More most applies to your own faith journey?

SAINT IGNATIUS (1491 – 1556)
THE SPIRITUAL EXERCISES

[Note to Reader: This chapter breaks with the usual format we have been using. First of all, we are substituting for the usual short biography, a longer one because it is so colorful and important for understanding the writings of our saint. Secondly, because the actual Spiritual Exercises are written for a spiritual director's use, not as a text to be read, we are substituting the way it is used by a contemporary Jesuit.]

Inigo de Loyola was born in 1491 in a Basque province of northern Spain.... At the age of sixteen years he was sent to serve as a page in the court of a nobleman of Castile. As a member of the household, he was frequently at court and developed a taste for all it presented, especially the ladies. He was much addicted to gambling, very contentious, and not above engaging in swordplay on occasion...

...(As an officer) during (a) battle a cannon ball struck Ignatius, wounding one leg and breaking the other. Because they admired his courage, the French soldiers carried him back to recuperate at his home, the castle of Loyola, rather than to prison.

His leg was set but did not heal, so it was necessary to break it again and reset it, all without anesthesia. Ignatius grew worse and was finally told by the doctors that he should prepare for death.

On the feast of Saints Peter and Paul (29 June) he took an unexpected turn for the better. The leg healed, but when it did the bone protruded below the knee and one leg was shorter than the other. This was unacceptable to Ignatius, who considered it a fate worse than death not to be able to wear the long, tight-fitting boots and hose of the courtier. Therefore he ordered the doctors to saw off the offending knob of bone and lengthen the leg by systematic stretching. Again, all of this was done without anesthesia. Unfortunately, this was not a successful procedure. All his life he walked with a limp because one leg was shorter than the other.

Conversion of St. Ignatius

During the long weeks of his recuperation, he was extremely bored and asked for some romance novels to pass the time. Luckily there were none in the castle of Loyola, but there was a copy of the life of Christ and a book on the saints. Desperate, Ignatius began to read them. The more he read, the more he considered the exploits of the saints worth imitating. However, at the same time he continued to have daydreams of fame and glory, along with fantasies of winning the love

of a certain noble lady of the court...He noticed, however, that after reading and thinking of the saints and Christ he was at peace and satisfied. Yet when he finished his long daydreams of his noble lady, he would feel restless and unsatisfied. Not only was this experience the beginning of his conversion, it was also the beginning of spiritual discernment, or discernment of spirits, which is associated with Ignatius and described in his *Spiritual Exercises*...

Eventually, completely converted from his old desires and plans of romance and worldly conquests, and recovered from his wounds enough to travel, he left the castle in 1522...

He proceeded to the Benedictine shrine of Our Lady of Montserrat, made a general confession, and knelt all night in vigil before Our Lady's altar... He left his sword and knife at the altar, went out and gave away all his fine clothes to a poor man, and dressed himself in rough clothes with sandals and a staff.

The Experience at Manresa

He continued towards Barcelona but stopped at a town called Manresa. He stayed in a cave outside the town, intending to linger only a few days, but he remained for ten months. He spent hours each day in prayer and also worked in a hospice. It was while here that the ideas for what are now known as the *Spiritual Exercises* began to take shape. It was also on the banks of this river that he had a vision which is regarded as the most significant in his life. The vision was more of an enlightenment, about which he later said that he learned more on that one occasion than he did in the rest of his life...

He finally arrived at Barcelona, took a boat to Italy, and ended up in Rome where he met Pope Adrian VI and requested permission to make a pilgrimage to the Holy Land....

The Company of Jesus

(Years later, after his theological schooling and ordination) Ignatius, along with two of his companions... decided to go to Rome and place themselves at the disposal of the Pope. It was a few miles outside of the city that Ignatius had the second most significant of his mystical experiences. At a chapel where they had stopped to pray, God the Father told Ignatius, "I will be favorable to you in Rome..." (He would go on to found the Society of Jesus, later called The Jesuits, that became most influential in the area of missionary work and education all over the world)....

... In 1556 he died. Ignatius was beatified on July 27, 1609 and canonized by Pope Gregory XV on March 12, 1622 together with St. Francis Xavier. Ignatius' feast day is celebrated by the universal Church and the Jesuits on July 31, the day he died.

Prayer of St. Ignatius

> Lord, Jesus Christ, take all my freedom, my memory, my understanding and my will.
> All that I have and cherish you have given me.
> I surrender it all to be guided by your will.
> Your grace and your love are wealth enough for me.
> Give me these, Lord Jesus, and I ask for nothing more.

Ignatius Loyola's *Spiritual Exercises* and its Influence on Education

by John J. Callahan, S.J. 1997 (used with permission)

Written originally as a four-part series, "Discovering A Sacred World" presents, in a very condensed form, the central themes and processes of the *Spiritual Exercises*...

I: Introduction and First Principle

... There have been hundreds of interpretations of the *Exercises* over the past 450 years. These chapters will attempt to explain some of the key elements of the method and vision of Ignatius' work. The hope is that the *Spiritual Exercises* may thereby become less a mystery and more an inspiration.

The Spiritual Exercises

The full title of Ignatius' book is: *Spiritual Exercises to Overcome Oneself and to Order One's Life...* The title could be paraphrased: "Spiritual exercises whose purpose is to lead a person to true spiritual freedom so that any choice or decision is made according to an ordered set of values rather than according to any disordered desire."

...*The Exercises* is about choice and decision-making. The thrust is toward action, not simply reflection...*The Exercises* aims to bring about an inner balance and steadiness within an individual so that, once fundamental values are determined, the person is not distracted or led astray by contrary passions or desires. This "balance" brings about an inner freedom to choose rightly.

What are "spiritual exercises?" According to Ignatius, just as running is an exercise which benefits the body, so spiritual exercises are activities which benefit the soul. Spiritual exercises encompass all the ways of making contact with God—"every method of examination of conscience, meditation, contemplation, vocal and mental prayer, and other spiritual activities." Ignatius was hardly a man of a single method.

The Exercises is divided into four parts called "weeks." The First Week is set in the context of God's love and its rejection through sin. The Second Week centers on the life of Jesus from its beginnings through his public ministry. The Third Week covers Jesus' passion and death. The Fourth Week looks upon the Risen Christ and the world renewed by the resurrection.

There are no fixed number of days within the "weeks." The number of days in each week depends on the progress of the person making the retreat. Normally, the exercises are finished after thirty days of silence and prayer. However, if a person cannot make the concentrated thirty-day retreat, Ignatius suggests that the exercises be made over the course of several months, with an hour each day reserved for prayer. This extended version of the exercises, sometimes called the "19th Annotation Retreat" or "Retreat in Everyday Life," is the most common way that busy people with many obligations make the exercises today.

Preparatory Exercise: The First Principle and Foundation

At the very beginning of *The Exercises*, Ignatius proposes a major "consideration." Called the "First Principle and Foundation," it sets forth the basic "ordered set of values" upon which the whole *Exercises* is based. It answers the question, "What should I most consider before making a decision?" or, put another way, "What should be the context of all the decisions I make?" Ignatius wastes no time; his first exercise presents a real challenge. He asks the person making the retreat (the "retreatant") to seriously consider that—

"Human beings are created to praise, reverence and serve God Our Lord and by this means to save their souls. The other things on the face of the earth are created for human beings to help them in working toward the goal for which they are created.

"Therefore, I am to make use of these other things insofar as they help me attain the goal and turn away from these other things insofar as they hinder me from attaining the goal. I must make myself indifferent to all created things, as far as I am allowed free choice and am not under any prohibition.

"Consequently, as far as I am concerned, I should not prefer health to sickness, riches to poverty, honor to dishonor, a long life to a short life. The same holds for all other things. My one desire and choice should be what is more conducive to reaching the goal for which I am created."

Though the First Principle and Foundation may appear, at first, like a catechism response of a young child, it is really quite profound. Four points:

1. The concept of "creation." Central to understanding the Principle and Foundation is seeing oneself as God's continuing creation. This creation is a dynamic, moment-by-moment activity shaped by a free, loving, self-giving God and by grateful, loving human beings who share the divine freedom. The "soul" is this free self, posited by God and engaged with God and things in continually creating something new. Evil arises from a human being's free decision to turn in on oneself and refuse God's loving desire.

2. The principle of tantum ... quantum ("as much ... so much"). The "other things on the face of the earth"—material things, genetic structure, physical and intellectual abilities, passions and feelings, hopes and desires, social status, friends, time, etc.—important as they are, do not compare in importance with that of cooperating with the creating God. A person either uses or does not use these created things depending only on whether or not they help or hinder this creative cooperation with God. "As much" as things help this cooperation, "so much" does one use them; insofar as things hinder this cooperation, they are avoided.

3. The principle of "indifference." Therefore, when making decisions, a person should be "indifferent" in regard to these "other things" until one is clear that God is directing the person in a certain way. The "other things" are not obstacles between God and the self. The question is how to use them properly.

Indifference is a distance from things that allows a person to freely choose "without prejudice." It is a distance from things that makes true vision possible. Ignatius is asking everyone to love themselves and all things as coming from God. Yet each is to "stand apart" from all created things in an inner freedom which awaits God's desire and invitation.

4. The principle of the magis ("more"). The "active indifference" of *The Exercises* is the exact opposite of unconcern, uniformity or mediocrity. Indifference does not exist for its own sake. Rather, it exists for an active choice, the free choice of "what is more conducive." Ignatius asks that a person not even consider choosing the second-rate. His challenge: freely choose the "more."

The First Principle and Education

>Love of God,
>love of self,
>love of all things as coming from God,
>recognition of one's place in creation,
>analysis and evaluation of what
>helps or hinders in achieving a life goal,
>inner freedom,
>self-discipline,
>choice,

the desire to be better and to do more —these make up the First Principle and Foundation both of the Ignatian vision and of Jesuit education.

Here is a way to try using Ignatian principles with regard to a choice in our own lives:

St. Ignatius Loyola

An Ignatian Framework for Making a Decision
by Jim Manney of Loyola Press from the web Ignatian Spirituality (used with permission)

11 Steps for Making a Decision Following the Ignatian Method

1. Identify the decision to be made or the issue to be resolved (Note from Dr. Ronda: this must be a choice between 2 good options, not between good vs. evil.)

The issue should be practical—about doing or not doing something.

It has to be real; that is, there really is a decision to be made—a question about whether you should or should not do something.

It must be an issue about which you have the right to make the decision.

You must have or be able to obtain the necessary information to decide intelligently.

If you have difficulty identifying the issue, follow this five-step procedure:

List the various issues you might be deciding about in the next few weeks or months, or in the next year's time.

List the actions you might take about these issues.

Make a list of pros and cons for each issue or possible action.

Rank the issues and possible actions in the order of preference as you currently experience them.

Use the issue or possible action ranked first as the focus of your discernment.

2. Formulate the issue in a proposal.

State it as a positive, concrete choice.

Make it as specific as possible (What you will do, where, and when).

State it in the way that God initially seems to be drawing you.

State it in the form of X vs. non-X or X vs. Y.

Example of an X vs. non-X proposal: "I will take enough courses next term so that I can graduate this coming May."

Example of an X vs. Y proposal: "I will stay in my current job with company A or I will accept a job offer from company B."

3. Pray for openness to God's will, and for freedom from pre-judgment and addictions.

Ask for that inner freedom and balance that allows you not to be inclined more toward one alternative or option than to the other. This means to ask to be free enough to be influenced only by this one value: which alternative will give most glory to God and be expressive of my own deepest self, my authentic self?

To arrive at this absolutely necessary inner freedom, you may wish to discuss the matter with a spiritually mature person who can help you. In particular, discuss what obstacles could be limiting your freedom by blocking you or inclining you to one alternative over the other.

Possible obstacles: projections, disordered attachments like inferiority complexes, superiority complexes, or glorified self-images; "shoulds" or "oughts" that tyrannize you; perfectionism, fears, materialistic greed, and possessiveness; past hurts and self-pity; competitiveness that leads to envy; impatience with yourself or others; lust, ingratitude, and irreverence; desire for control, power, status, prestige, exclusiveness, and so forth.

As preparation for your prayer, read over slowly, carefully, and attentively the following Scripture passages:

Luke 17:5-6	Mark 10:17-22	Luke 16:13
Luke 12:22-32	Matthew 5:13-16	Philippians 3:7-10
Matthew 13:44-46	Luke 14:33	Luke 11:5-13
Matthew 14:22-33	2 Timothy 1:7	Matthew 20:26-28
Luke 18:35-43	Matthew 7:24-25	

Note the passages that strike you most strongly. Make these passages the source from which you talk with God about the particular areas where you need freedom. Where do you need greater detachment about the alternatives or options in your proposal? Bring them to God in prayer. Ask above all for a deep love: love for God, for the people being affected by the decision, and for your own true self or authentic self. Pray that no self-centered attraction or aversion about a choice will sidetrack you from what the Holy Spirit is pointing you to. Ask for the guidance of the Holy Spirit in all this.

4. Gather all the necessary information.

Find out all the relevant specifics relating to the decision: Who? What? Where? When? How much? Why? Be satisfactorily informed.

Be sure to consult with everyone who will be intimately affected by the decision being made: spouse, children, other family, friends, colleagues. Get their input about it, including their feelings and desires.

Discuss this matter with someone sensitive to Christian spiritual values. This could be a friend, counselor, priest, or minister—someone who will be honest and objective with you. Discuss the matter in detail—its values and possibilities, your strengths and weaknesses.

5. Repeat the third step: Pray for openness to God's will.

Pray about the matter again in light of the data you have gathered and the counsel of others. Most likely new feelings and desires have been stirred up that need to be shared with God so that they might be purified of any prejudgment or disordered attachment. This is a "freedom check." Are you free enough to be influenced only by this one value: which alternative will give most glory to God and be expressive of your own deepest self, your authentic self?

6. State all the reasons for and all the reasons against each alternative in the proposal.

For a proposal of the X vs. non-X form, make two lists: "Advantages for me" and "Disadvantages for me." For a proposal of the X vs. Y form, make a table with four lists: "Advantages for Me" and "Disadvantages for me" for each alternative (See the table).

Stay with Company A		Take a New Job at Company B	
Advantages for Me	Disadvantages for Me	Advantages for Me	Disadvantages for Me
1.	1.	1.	1.
2.	2.	2.	2.
3.	3.	3.	3.

Begin with a short prayer asking God to be with you as you make your lists. Ask particularly for light to see clearly what God chooses for you and what will best honor and serve God, your neighbor, and your true self.

List all the reasons you can think of. Do not prejudge their merit. You will evaluate them in the next step.

7. Do a formal evaluation of all the advantages and disadvantages.

The point of this evaluation is to see which advantages and disadvantages seem to be coming from the influence of the Holy Spirit and which ones do not.

Attempt to get in contact with your motives and values. To do this well, you may have to spend considerable time on this step. It may take weeks if you are making a major life decision.

Repeat Step 3, praying for openness and freedom. Pray for light about factors that inhibit freedom and openness to God. Are there any? Beg God for the help to be detached from disordered attachments that might be influencing you. Pray for a deeper faith in God and love for God.

Evaluate the advantages and disadvantages by asking four questions:

Which reasons are the most important? Why?

What values are preserved or realized by each option? (Many advantages and disadvantages may be pointing to the same value.)

Which option more evidently leads to God's service and better serves the growth of your true self in the Holy Spirit?

Which option seems more consistent with your own faith journey and history with God?

8. Observe the direction of your will while reflecting on the advantages and disadvantages.

As you evaluate the choices, your desires will be influenced by the Holy Spirit; that is, your will becomes more inclined toward one option and less inclined toward the other. These inclinations may fluctuate between options. Pay attention to these inner movements. Pray for light from the Holy Spirit about them. Eventually, your will is likely to focus on one of the alternatives.

If your will does not settle on one choice but continues to fluctuate between the two, a disordered attachment may be influencing you. This is a signal to do some more prayer. Return to Step 3. Ask God to free you from any selfish inclinations and lead you to worthy motives. Pray that the Holy Spirit draws your will and its desires to God's will.

9. Ask God to give you feelings of consolation about the preferred option.

This is the third of three states of the discernment. First, you asked the Holy Spirit to transform your thoughts (listing advantages and disadvantages). Second, you asked the Holy Spirit to transform your desires (your will) while evaluating the lists of advantages and disadvantages. Now you ask the Holy Spirit to stir feelings of spiritual consolation. These are feelings of joy, enthusiasm, deeper faith, greater hope and trust, greater love, confidence, courage. These thoughts, desires, and feelings are all parts of your inner experience of the Holy Spirit guiding you to the truth.

These feelings of consolation accompany your desires when they are clearly pointed toward loving and serving God, others, and your true self. They are very different from the feelings that accompany your desires when they are influenced by disordered attachments aimed only at your selfish ways.

If your feelings fluctuate between consolation and desolation, you may be under the influence of mixed motives and disordered attachments. If so, return to Step 3: pray for freedom and openness to God.

10. Trust in God and make your decision, even if you are not certain about it.

11. Confirm the decision.

Live with the decision for a while to see whether your thoughts, desires, and feelings continue to support it. If not, new data is needed and the process must be redone.

DR. RONDA'S CONTEMPORARY APPLICATIONS AND PERSONAL REFLECTIONS

Many years ago I did the Spiritual Exercises in the long form that took about 3 months working on it a few hours every day under the direction of a Jesuit spiritual director. Recently, I was startled to hear that a parish in Southern California, St. Peter Chanel, under the auspices of the Oblates of the Virgin Mary, were offering the exercises to parishioners over a 2 year period, followed by a commitment to Daily Mass (possible because they have 5 Masses each weekday,

St. Ignatius Loyola

available at times any person could attend, before work, after work, mid-day, etc.) and to an hour of Adoration a day! Astounding! They also have confession before and during each Mass with even children standing on line voluntarily, not as part of a class or pushed to do so by their parents!

Assembling this chapter for the first class I gave in Spiritual Classics, I worked through my own example to make sure it was doable. I focused on a decision about visiting a new community of older women who wanted to be Sisters. It was easy to see the obstacles to making the trip. Luke 12:22-32 about not worrying about one's life on earth so much was apt. I remembered a word from the Lord to "stop scheming to avoid suffering." The scheming here would be fantasizing about perfect groups of widows and other women, all saints. In considering aversions to choices, I remembered how I usually feel very high on visits to places but then become highly critical after a short time. I decided to get more information about the future rule of this new community. Listing the pros and cons was very helpful. This gave me space to remember that spiritual directors in the past insisted I didn't belong in community at all, considering certain personality traits I had. By praying more to the Holy Spirit I was able to remember that the Vatican document on community religious life insists the community must come before any apostolate. But I feel clearly called to my teaching, writing, and speaking work and always want to put that first over community. This became the key point in deciding not to make the visit to this new group.

227

KATHLEEN'S CONTEMPORARY APPLICATIONS AND PERSONAL REFLECTIONS

I chose to read *The Exercises* and look at myself, rather than to use the decision method to make a choice. In the First Week the First Point is that of the sin of the angels: knowing God and seeing His majesty, having been created to serve and defend it, yet choosing in pride to rally against it and be tossed from heaven. The sin of Adam and Eve is the Second Point. In reference to it many, like my students, say, "If it wasn't for them, we'd still be in heaven." It seems easier for us to point fingers at others and see their sins rather than our own. In particular, it is hard to imagine how the angels and Adam and Eve could have seen God and known Him and yet disobeyed Him and sinned against Him.

For me, however, the Third Point is the one of most significance; bringing to mind the one sin that might be a mortal sin, condemning a person to hell for less than I have done. I can't do anything about the sin of the angels or of Adam and Eve. I can only look at myself and think how often I offend God with my mouth and my actions. I am not aware of having been in mortal sin, but I know I have more sins than I care to count. When I consider my unkindness, my opinionated, judgmental mind and heart, my anger, my unconstrained and imprudent passion, my PRIDE, and so very many other ways in which I sin against the goodness and love of my infinitely perfect God, I am near despair of ever being with Him in heaven. But for His infinite mercy and the most Precious Blood of Christ, there is no way for me to be pleasing in His sight. I often wonder how I can be so prideful when, in truth, even the good things I have done would not have been possible without the grace of God. I worry that the passion I feel for the faith is only pious platitudes and pretty words that mean nothing because I do not act on them.

In the Second Week, I also chose the Third Point in Part 2. Again, I say that I ask God to help me bear injury calmly and react kindly as He did, and that I want to choose Him over my own carnal pleasures. In truth, however, I still like my shoes and my shopping more than I probably should. I fast, but think too much, perhaps, about the days I can eat.

The Third Week contains two points that I find almost equally important. The Fifth Point is to consider how Divinity hides itself. It astounds me that Christ would choose to leave heaven, where angels and saints constantly sing praise to Him, in order to take on flesh and experience the hunger, weariness, thirst, betrayal, and temptation that we all experience. He chooses to die an ignominious death when He could have shown His power and might by annihilating His enemies. Surely, this is a point of great depth and much potential mediation.

But even more moving to me is the consideration of the Sixth Point: how He suffers all this for my sins, and what I ought to do and suffer for Him. Of course, Christ doesn't need my suffering, as I needed His. But I owe Him my suffering. I owe Him to endure the crosses that come into my life. I must trust that He allows them for my good, my purification. I must join my suffering to His suffering for the good of His Church and my fellow members of the Body of

Christ, whether on earth or in purgatory.

I tell my students that my job is to help them fall in love with God, because He is so deeply in love with them. Of course, they all look at each and roll their eyes as if I am some sort of nut case. Truth be told, the best way for me to teach them about loving God, is to first love Him myself. If I am in humble awe of what He has done, and respond to it by enduring and offering Him everything without reserve, they will see that. I must become like the great spiritual ones in this book, so that my extreme love of God will inspire in some small way a similar response in the ones I encounter. God help me.

FOR PERSONAL REFLECTION AND GROUP SHARING

Try this Ignatian method on a decision you are making now or might need to make in the near future. Share what you wish about this decision in writing or orally with the class. Or, if you prefer, as Kathleen did, go through *The Exercises* that can be found by googling a free online copy for each of the Four Weeks.

ST. TERESA OF AVILA (1515-1582) DOCTOR OF THE CHURCH, THE INTERIOR CASTLE

On March 28, 1515, Teresa de Ahumada y Cepeda was born in Avila, Castile, Spain. Her father was a devout Catholic, as was her mother, who was also of a Spanish noble family. Teresa, the fifth of twelve children, was only thirteen when her mother died.

Teresa spent a year and a half in an Augustinian convent before illness forced her to return home. She had learned much from the mother superior who, despite her strictness, impressed Teresa with her talk of God. Teresa decided at age twenty to become a Carmelite and entered the convent with the aid of her older brother, as her father was opposed.

At the time, the Carmelites were living a very relaxed life, social to the point of entertaining guests in their parlor. Teresa was still suffering from illness and emotional struggles. At one point, she was near death and was even paralyzed for several years until St. Joseph interceded for her.

When she was thirty years old, Teresa began to have mystical experiences and developed a great devotion to the wounded Christ that overtook her great fear of hell. At forty-five, she experienced levitation for the first time, as well as the famous transverberation of her heart.

Pope Pius IV was interested in reforming monastic orders. Teresa was at the forefront of reforming the Carmelites, opening new convents, and inspiring St. John of the Cross to assist her and to establish reformed monasteries for the male Carmelites.

Teresa died in 1582 amid the odor of sanctity. Her body was found to be incorrupt in 1583 and 1585. She was canonized in 1622 and named a Doctor of the Church by Pope Paul VI in 1970.

Excerpts from *The Interior Castle*[1]

First Mansions

While I was begging our Lord today to speak for me… I thought of the soul as resembling a castle, formed of a single diamond or a very transparent crystal, and containing many rooms, just as in heaven there are many mansions. (John 14:2)…

Would it not be gross ignorance, my daughters, if, when a man was questioned about his name, or country, or parents, he could not answer?... Stupid as this would be, it is unspeakably more foolish to care to learn nothing of our nature except that we possess bodies,

[1] St. Teresa of Avila, The Interior Castle, trans. The Benedictines of Stanbrook, (London: Thomas Baker, 1921) at Christian Classics Ethereal Library, http://www.ccel.org/ccel/teresa/castle2.pdf (In common domain but archaic language changed to more contemporary lanuage)

and only to realize vaguely that we have souls... Rarely do we reflect upon what gifts our souls may possess, Who dwells within them, or how extremely precious they are. Therefore we do little to preserve their beauty; all our care is concentrated on our bodies, which are but the coarse setting of the diamond, or the outer walls of the castle...

"I was recently told by a great theologian that souls without prayer are like bodies, palsied and lame, having hands and feet they cannot use. Just so, there are souls so infirm and accustomed to think of nothing but earthly matters, that there seems no cure for them. It appears impossible for them to retire into their own hearts...

"We will now think of the others who at last enter the precincts of the castle; they are still very worldly, yet have some desire to do right, and at times, though rarely, commend themselves to God's care. They think about their souls every now and then; although very busy, they pray a few times a month, with minds generally filled with a thousand other matters, for where their treasure is, there is their heart also. (Matt. 6:21)... At length they enter the first rooms in the basement of the castle, accompanied by numerous reptiles which disturb their peace, and prevent their seeing the beauty of the building; still, it is a great gain that these persons should have found their way in at all.

"I wish you to consider the state to which mortal sin brings this magnificent and beautiful castle... No night can be so dark... Suffice it to say that the sun in the center of the soul, which gave it such splendor and beauty, is totally eclipsed...

"...But fix your eyes on the keep, the court inhabited by the

King... this principal chamber is surrounded by many others. However large, magnificent, and spacious you imagine this castle to be, you cannot exaggerate it; the capacity of the soul is beyond all our understanding, and the Sun within this palace enlightens every part of it. A soul which gives itself to prayer, either much or little, should on no account be kept within narrow bounds. Since God has given it such great dignity, permit it to wander at will through the rooms of the castle, from the lowest to the highest...

"...The devil is so angry at this that he keeps legions of evil spirits hidden in each room to stop the progress of Christians, whom, being ignorant of this, he entraps in a thousand ways. He cannot so easily deceive souls which dwell nearer to the King as he can beginners still absorbed in the world, immersed in its pleasures, and eager for its honors and distinctions... such people are easily vanquished, although desirous not to offend God. Those conscious of being in this state must as often as possible have recourse to His Majesty, taking His Blessed Mother and the saints for their advocates to do battle for them...

"It is most important to withdraw from all unnecessary cares and business... in order to enter the second mansion... Do not trouble yourselves... with cares which do not concern you... (such as) to think every small fault she sees (is) a serious crime, and to watch constantly whether (others) do anything wrong... At the same time... never (noticing) her own shortcomings..."

Second Mansions

"These souls hear our Lord calling them... God here speaks to souls through words uttered by pious people, by sermons or good books... by means of sickness or troubles, or by some truth He teaches them during prayer, for tepid as they may be in seeking Him, yet God holds them very dear...for His Majesty is willing to wait for us many a day and even many a year, especially when He sees perseverance and good desires in our hearts...

"It is of the utmost importance for the beginner to associate with those who lead a spiritual life, and not only with those in the same mansion as herself, but with others who have travelled farther into the castle, who will aid her greatly and draw her to join them."

"If we start with the false principle of wishing God to follow our will and to lead us in the way we think best, upon what firm foundation can this spiritual edifice rest?... Therefore if you occasionally lapse into sin, do not lose heart and cease trying to advance, for God will draw good even out of our falls...it would be madness to think we could do so without sometimes retiring into our souls so as to know ourselves, or thinking of our failings and of what we owe to God, or frequently imploring His mercy.

Third Mansions

"Thanks to His mercy I believe there are many such people in the world: they are very desirous not to offend His Majesty even by venial sins, they love penance and spend hours in meditation, they employ their time well, exercise themselves in works of charity to their neighbors, are well-ordered in their conversation and dress, and those who own a household govern it well... but there is need of more than that for the Lord to possess entire dominion over the soul... Think of the saints, who have entered the Divine Presence, and you will see the difference between them and ourselves...

(Concerning aridity – dryness in prayer) "Where true humility exists, although God should never bestow consolations (note from Dr. Ronda: she means special graces such as locutions and visions), yet He gives a peace and resignation which make the soul happier than are others with sensible devotion. These consolations... are often given by the Divine Majesty to the weakest souls...God, wishing His elect to realize their own misery, often temporarily withdraws His favors: no more is needed to prove to us in a very short time what we really are...

"(A) person has more than sufficient means to live on, when an opportunity occurs for acquiring more property: if it is offered him, by all means let him accept it; but if he must go out of his way to obtain it and then continues working to gain more and more... he cannot possibly enter the mansions near the King...

"I wish it were—that they might not be content to creep on their way to God: a pace that will never bring them to their journey's end!... Let us exert ourselves, and leave our reason and our fears in His hands, paying no attention to the weaknesses of nature... (such as) regard for health... our bodies are not the chief factors in the work we have before us... the Lord never fails to repay our services... Who always bestows on us far more than we deserve, giving us greater happiness than could be obtained from any earthly pleasures and amusements."

"Let us look at our own faults, and not at other persons'. People who are extremely correct themselves are often shocked at everything they see...Our exterior comportment and manners may be better—this is well enough, but not of the first importance. We ought not to insist on every one following in our footsteps... Zeal for the good of souls, though given us by God, may often lead us astray..."

Fourth Mansions

"To reach the mansions we wish to enter, it is not so essential to think much as to love much... Love does not consist in great sweetness of devotion, but in a fervent determination to strive to please God in all things, in avoiding, as far as possible, all that would offend Him, and in praying for the increase of the glory and honor of His Son and for the growth of the Catholic Church...

(About distractions) "We cannot stop the revolution of the heavens as they rush with velocity upon their course, neither can we control our imagination... we think everything is lost, and that the time spent in God's presence is wasted. Meanwhile, the soul is perhaps entirely united to Him in the innermost mansions, while the imagination is in the precincts of the castle... Therefore we need not let ourselves be disturbed, nor give up prayer, as the devil is striving to persuade us... His Majesty wishes us to learn... to recognize the share taken in these troubles by our wandering imagination, our nature, and the devil's temptations, instead of laying all the blame on our souls.

Fifth Mansions

"Oh, my sisters, how shall I describe the riches, treasures, and joys contained in the fifth mansions! ...If you would purchase this treasure of which we are speaking, God would have you keep back nothing from Him, little or great. He will have it all; in proportion to what you know you have given will your reward be great or small... In the prayer of union the soul is asleep, fast asleep, as regards the world and itself: in fact, during the short time this state lasts it is deprived of all feeling whatever, being unable to think on any subject, even if it wished...it has died entirely to this world, to live more truly than ever in God. This is a delicious death, for the soul is deprived of the faculties it exercised while in the body: delicious because, (although not really the case), it seems to have left its mortal covering to abide more entirely in God. So completely does this take place, that I know not whether the body retains sufficient life to continue breathing...What will He not bestow, Who is so eager to give, and Who can give us all He desires!...

"Those who refuse to believe that God can do far more than this, and that He is pleased now, as in the past, to communicate Himself to His creatures, shut fast their hearts against receiving such favors themselves...

"Truly, the spirit does not recognize itself, being as different from what it was as is the white butterfly from the repulsive caterpillar. It does not know how it can have merited so great a good, or rather... it well knows it merits not. The soul desires to praise our Lord God and longs to sacrifice itself and die a thousand deaths for Him. It feels an unconquerable desire for... penances... for solitude and would have all men know God...

"Alas, what fresh trials begin to afflict the mind! Who would expect this after such a sublime grace? In fact in one way or another we must carry the cross all our lives... Who could ever have longed more eagerly to leave this life than did Christ? As He said at the Last Supper: 'With desire have I desired' this. (St. Luke 22:15) O Lord! Does not that bitter death You are to undergo present itself before Your eyes in all its pain and horror? 'No, for My ardent love and My desire to save souls are immeasurably stronger than the torments. This deeper sorrow I have suffered and still suffer while living here on earth, makes other pain seem as nothing in comparison.'"

Sixth Mansions

"Even when the mind is not recollected or even thinking of God, although no sound is heard, His Majesty arouses it suddenly as if by a swiftly flashing comet or by a clap of thunder. Yet the soul thus called by God hears Him well enough—so well, indeed, that sometimes, especially at first, it trembles and even cries out, although it feels no pain. It is conscious of having received a delicious wound... and hopes the hurt will never heal...The soul... know(s) that though He is present He will not manifest Himself so that it may enjoy Him. This causes a pain, keen although sweet and delicious...

"The devil cannot give such delicious pain: he may cause pleasure or delight which appears spiritual but is unable to add suffering, especially suffering of so keen a sort, united to peace and joy of soul. His power is limited to what is external; suffering produced by him is never accompanied with peace, but with anxieties and struggles… the great benefits left in the soul which, as a rule, is resolute to suffer for God and longs to bear many crosses. It is also far more determined than before to withdraw from worldly pleasures…

(Concerning locutions – words from God heard by the ears or in the depths of the heart) "I caution you on one point—although they may come from God, you must not esteem yourself more highly, for He often spoke to the Pharisees —all the good consists in profiting by His words. Take no more notice of any speeches you hear which disagree with the Holy Scriptures than if you heard them from Satan himself. Though they may only rise from your vivid imagination…

"These are the most certain signs of their being divine. The first and truest is the power and authority they carry with them… a soul is suffering all the sorrow and disquiet I have described: the mind is darkened and dry; but it is set at peace, freed from all trouble and filled with light merely by hearing the words: 'Be not troubled.'… Again, a person is troubled and greatly terrified at being told by her confessor and other people that her soul is under the influence of the evil one: she hears a single sentence which says, 'It is I, be not afraid,' and is at once freed from all fears and filled with consolation…

"The second sign is a great calm and a devout and peaceful

recollection which dwell in the soul together with a desire to praise God...

"The third proof is that these words do not pass from the memory but remain there for a very long time; sometimes they are never forgotten...

"...If the foregoing signs are present, we may feel fairly confident that these locutions are from God, though not so certain but that, if they refer to some weighty matter in which we are called upon to act or if they concern a third person, we should consult some confessor who is both learned and a servant of God...

"In one sort of rapture the soul... Such a one may piously believe her sins are now forgiven, supposing that she is in the disposition and has made use of the means required by the Church. The soul being thus purified, God unites it to Himself... our Lord favors it by discovering to it secrets such as heavenly mysteries... imprinted in the center of the soul and are never forgotten... all the earthly pleasures... (are) disappointing and base contrasted with the treasures which are to be enjoyed for ever—and yet even these are nothing compared with the possession for our own of the Lord of all treasures in heaven and earth... It is true that His Majesty grants such favors to whom He chooses; yet if we sought Him as He seeks us, He would give them to us all. He only longs for souls on whom He may bestow them...

"Our Lord sometimes causes in the soul a certain jubilation and a strange and mysterious kind of prayer. If He bestows this grace on you, praise Him fervently for it; I describe it so that you may know that it is something real... It often delights me, when in my sisters' company to see how the joy of their hearts is so great that they vie with one another in praising our Lord for placing them in this convent... I should like you to do this often, sisters, for when one begins she incites the rest to imitate her. How can your tongues be better employed when you are together than in praising God...?"

Seventh Mansions

"We now come to speak of divine and spiritual nuptials... The first time God bestows this grace, He, by an imaginary vision of His most sacred Humanity, reveals Himself to the soul so that it may understand and realize the sovereign gift it is receiving... (it) is like rain falling from heaven into a river or stream, becoming one and the same liquid, so that the river and rain water cannot be divided; or it resembles a streamlet flowing into the ocean, which cannot afterwards be disunited from it...

"...But in the other mansions there are still times of struggle, suffering, and fatigue... though tumults and wild beasts rage with great uproar in the other mansions, yet nothing of this enters the seventh mansions, nor drives the soul from it. Although the mind regrets these troubles, they do not disturb it nor rob it of its peace, for the passions are too subdued...

"(Those in this mansion) fear death no more than they would a delicious trance... Such a soul, thoroughly detached from all things, wishes to be either always alone or occupied on what benefits the souls of others: she feels neither aridity nor any interior troubles, but a constant tender recollection of our Lord Whom she wishes to praise unceasingly...

"Do not fancy that in spite of the strong desire and determination of these souls that they do not commit imperfections and even fall into many (venial) sins...

"...These graces are sent to strengthen our weakness so that we may imitate Him by suffering much... Fix your eyes on the Crucified One, and all will seem easy. If His Majesty proved His love for us by such stupendous labors and sufferings, how can you seek to please Him by words alone? Do you know what it is to be truly spiritual? It is for men to make themselves the slaves of God—branded with His mark, which is the cross. Since they have given Him their freedom, He can sell them as slaves to the whole world, as He was... unless you acquire the virtues and praise them, you will always be dwarfs... and please God no worse may befall you than making no progress, for you know that to stop is to go back if you love, you will never be content to come to a standstill."

St. Teresa's Bookmark

> Let nothing disturb you
> Nothing frighten you
> God never changes
> Patience endurance attains to all things
> Whom God possesses in nothing is wanting
> God alone is enough!

DR. RONDA'S CONTEMPORARY APPLICATIONS AND PERSONAL REFLECTIONS

I am so inspired by the writing of Thomas Dubay in *The Fire Within*. He offers much insight on St. Teresa of Avila and St. John of the Cross, so I will be summarizing his teachings about them in much of these applications and reflections.

St. Teresa of Avila was declared a Doctor of the Church because of such great spiritual books as *The Interior Castle*, her most famous. The Interior Castle shows us that we should not think vocal prayer is all God wants for us in this life. Consider that St. Mary Magdalene was praised for "choosing the better part." But many Catholics have no idea Jesus wants to bring us into close union with Him in prayer. Without a map, such as St. Teresa gives us in *The Interior Castle*, Dubay claims, we can become discouraged on such a journey. Reading St. Teresa is like seeing a photo of the top of a mountain before setting forth on the climb.

On the other hand, some of us think the highest degrees of prayer can be ours through methods such as centering prayer. Dubay warns that the key factor in being led closer to Christ is the willingness to follow the way of the Gospel. This way is full of the type of struggles St. Teresa tells us about in the first mansion. We need to become detached from many attachments (or what we would now call addictions, I would explain.) Reaching the inner rooms of the interior castle comes not from methods but from the desire to do God's will.

St. Teresa of Avila

A contemporary form of the contemplative prayer St. Teresa describes in the more interior mansions can be witnessed in Adoration of the Blessed Sacrament. I truly believe that thousands of Catholics who come to chapels around the world and sit still for an hour or more in front of the Eucharist in the monstrance are experiencing mystical prayer without having a name for it. How else explain how we can sit still so long and emerge peaceful instead of restless?

Reading St. Teresa's exciting spiritual books makes it possible to recognize that God could be inviting us into mansions we never imagined we could enter. As a philosophy professor and a married woman with children, I went to daily Mass, prayed the rosary, and morning, evening and night prayer. I also belonged to a charismatic prayer group. A parish woman asked me if I would like to have the Pilgrim Virgin of Our Lady of Fatima come to our house for a week. As explained in other writings of mine, this ushered me into some of the graces described for St. Teresa in those famous mansions of hers.

Today, many decades later, I have had the joy of watching the long film on the life of St. Teresa of Avila made by Spanish professionals and so I can picture her even better than from readings. You can find it by googling it on EWTN. My favorite spiritual maxim is St. Teresa's "God alone is enough." When forced to let go of people I love, dreams of earthly security, or other wants, I think of St. Teresa's spiritual wisdom and surrender.

KATHLEEN'S CONTEMPORARY APPLICATIONS AND PERSONAL REFLECTIONS

The First Mansion is a critical place for me. I struggle with self-knowledge and with humility. Often, I fall subject to scruples and it's hard for me to know when I am seeing rightly. A former spiritual director once told me I had a "terminal case of scrupulosity." I wish he might have prescribed a cure but we never got that far.

Still, it's crucial for us to know who we are in relation to God. This generation of entitlement is much more fixed on "what's in it for me" and what they refer to as "feeding my spirit" than on serving God and seeking His will. Unless we can see our complete dependence upon Him, and His great mercy and love in bestowing upon us the unmerited graces and blessings He does, how can we feel appreciation? How can we truly seek Him when we are really seeking our own will and desire, looking at Him as a genie in heaven granting our wishes, if indeed we look at Him at all? If we don't look at His perfect virtue, how can we aspire to it? Truly, as St. Teresa says, there are many serpents in this mansion and we are in danger of being so deceived by them that we never find our way beyond this dwelling, if ever we even enter it.

If we progress to the Second Mansion, as I hope I have done, we still fall backward sometimes. But in this place, we seek and sometimes hear the voice of God. Yet if we are scrupulous, we can become discouraged at our imperfection and inability to be what God wants us to be, and what we want to be for His glory. But we cannot give up, or be content to remain here. For truly, we never remain stable. We are either pressing onward, or we are going backward. Perseverance is so crucial. And yet we cannot persevere without God's grace. Here we are given friends along the way to encourage us and even to speak God's will to us. Our intellect and will begin to urge us to choose God over those visible things that may be more intriguing and give us more instant, if temporary, gratification. But that is not the foundation on which to build our spiritual castle! We must endure the struggle and bear the cross and allow God to help us go on when we stumble under its weight. All the while, the key is prayer.

The Third Mansion is entered through awe of God. It is by perseverance and grace that we have come this far. God help me not to look at what I think You owe me for my service to You. Truly, no service will ever repay You for what You have done for me. I can never do enough or be enough and our being, St. Teresa says, is the only thing God wants of us—the clear intent of our will aligned with His. Would that all mankind could see how blessed we are and how much we owe to God's great mercy. Our perspective would change so much. The challenge in this Mansion is to grow in knowledge of God while not becoming so familiar with Him that we lose our sense of awe. No matter how much we serve or suffer, we will never serve or suffer as much as Jesus did. We must always remember humility and abandonment to God's will in order to reach perfection, which is, Teresa says, about loving and not our own consolation.

The Fourth Mansion, coming closer to God, is more beautiful than previous ones and begins our entry into the supernatural. Here some temptation can be beneficial in order for the soul to gain merit. St. Teresa describes the difference between consolation and divine sweetness, the one coming from our own efforts and worldly achievements, the other coming from God and making us delight in it more than in worldly joys. We must remember that this divine sweetness is not anything we have merited; it comes only from God's great goodness.

In this Mansion is the description of my own struggle. Here, St. Teresa insists, if we want to make progress it is important not that we think much, but that we love much. Here, then, is where I need to get my faith out of my head and into my heart. I take courage, however, from her assertion that we can be fully present to God in soul even while battling distractions of the mind and may even gain merit from battling these creatures of temptation. She holds that we cannot give up eating or drinking and should not expect to give up thinking. We need to just accept our imperfections and entrust them to God. We will have so much more peace when we do so, and be able to focus on God rather than on the temptation.

The greatest peace and blessings come not from our own effort in prayer, but from God's goodness, usually when we least expect it. Yet we can never stop trying to overcome distraction or to come to know God or come to know ourselves. All of these steps prepare and expand our souls to receive the blessings He sends, especially when He draws us into a prayer of recollection. It is only with His help and His grace that we can concentrate on Him and forget ourselves.

A confessor of mine once told me that we do not need to think less of ourselves, but to think of ourselves less. St. Teresa advises that we not try to deceive our faculties but instead let them do their job until God assigns them a higher one. The intellect does not discover the condition of the soul, rather it is the will that does so. When the will is guiding the soul to rest in God, He will do all else according to His mercy. This is a very consoling and encouraging thought to someone like me, who struggles to give up control. I do now find myself, little by little (if not yet enough) drawing away from worldly pleasures. I believe and hope it is because of my love for God. More likely, it is because of His love for me.

In the Fifth Mansion, St. Teresa discusses the Prayer of Union. We must wait for God to help us. He gives to us in proportion as we have given to Him. We must be careful of doing only the externals and concentrate instead on the internal as we desire and approach righteousness. There is no technique for suspending consciousness. If we pay no attention to the little distractions to which she refers then they can do no harm. Eventually, God will take us to a union with Him that the enemy cannot penetrate. We can't get in on our own. What a reassuring thought! It really does take the pressure off. Just love God, be aware of Him, give Him everything and let Him do the rest.

In the Sixth Mansion, the soul desires only union with God. She is wounded again and again. The waiting for this union is so painful. There are trials and tribulations to be endured. The difference between the trials of these souls and the trials of the rest of us is that the soul in the Sixth Mansion understands that it is God who begets in her any measure of good. She praises Him instead of moaning and whining like I do, for example. This soul embraces the cross and knows God sends it for her good. These souls flourish in virtue as a result of the trials endured in the Sixth Mansion, whereas I would be discouraged by them, and possibly give up spiritual pursuits. The soul in union with God knows He sends these for good. The pain is an offering to God and it is suffered willingly because of the great love the soul feels for Him. So few of us are there, or ever will be there.

The Seventh Mansion is the complete spiritual marriage between the soul and God. The dwelling for God within us is another heaven. In the very center of the soul is God's own dwelling. The soul that might not have been called there before is called now. There is a vision of the Holy Trinity, understanding of things never before understood, grasping of oneness. The Three-in-One never leaves the soul again. Still, there is greater care than ever not to offend Him. The love is greater than ever. Will I ever be selfless enough to allow God to accomplish that in me?

FOR PERSONAL REFLECTION AND GROUP SHARING

Write a response to the theme of each mansion, as Kathleen did, OR answer all of these questions:

First Mansion: If you think you are not worldly ask yourself, what is a good day for me? Lots of pleasures? Few pains? People admired me? vs. I went to Mass, prayed well, and served others? What optional pleasurable activities might you omit to have more time for the things of the soul?

Second Mansion: Do I listen to the voice of God in my heart drawing me to virtue and away from self-deceit about my known faults, such as gluttony, shopaholism, gossip or worse?

Third Mansion: Do you agree with St. Teresa that often special graces are given more to the weak to encourage them than to the strong in faith? Even if I am always right, do I love to feel superior by criticizing others and by blaming them?

Fourth Mansion: Do I seek time to be alone with God outwardly or inwardly during Mass, Adoration, a personal prayer time?

Fifth Mansion: Do I beg to surrender to God, to be totally His so that He can live in me?

Sixth Mansion: If I have received any special mystical graces, have I checked them out with a spiritual director? If they have been deemed to come probably from God, do I thank God often for them? If I have not received many such graces, do I pray for whatever graces I need to become closer to God?

Seventh Mansion: Do I want to be closer and closer to the transforming union with God no matter what the sufferings entailed or do I really mostly want God to help me to do my will?

ST. JOHN OF THE CROSS (1542-1591) DOCTOR OF THE CHURCH
ASCENT OF MT. CARMEL, AND SHORT EXCERPTS FROM OTHER BOOKS

The man who would be known to the world as John of the Cross was born in Spain in 1542. His father, of the working class, died soon after his birth. His struggling mother put John for a while in an orphanage in Medina del Campo. As a teen he worked as a nurse but also attended a Jesuit college. At 21 he became a Carmelite, studied at the famous University of Salamanca, and for the priesthood. He was thinking that his order was too lax when he met Teresa of Avila. She convinced him to help start a men's branch of the reformed movement.

In 1577, friars who opposed the reform kidnapped him and kept him in a prison in Toledo. He was confined to a dark cell and brutalized. After a time, Our Lady instructed him on how to escape in the night from his prison cell. The image of escaping on a dark night became the metaphor for many of his writings. While in prison he wrote the poetry which, later, after his escape, became the basis for the famous commentaries that are among the most influential and beautiful of all spiritual classics: *The Ascent of Mount Carmel, The*

Dark Night of the Soul, The Spiritual Canticle and *The Living Flame of Love* are the longest.

Whereas John's first persecutors hated him for being stricter than they, within the new reformed order he was persecuted for being a moderate. St. John of the Cross died in 1591 at 49 years of age.

The Ascent of Mount Carmel

To reach satisfaction in all[1]

desire its possession in nothing.

To come to possession in all

desire the possession of nothing.

To arrive at being all

desire to be nothing.

To come to the knowledge of all

desire the knowledge of nothing.

To come to the pleasure you have not

you must go by the way in which you enjoy not.

To come to the knowledge you have not

you must go by the way in which you know not.

To come to the possession you have not

you must go by the way in which you possess not.

---

1 John of the Cross: *Selected Writings* - translated & introduced by Kieran Kavanaugh OCD. Preface by Ernest Larkin, O. Carm. Paulist Press ISBN 0-8091-2839-X

St. John of the Cross

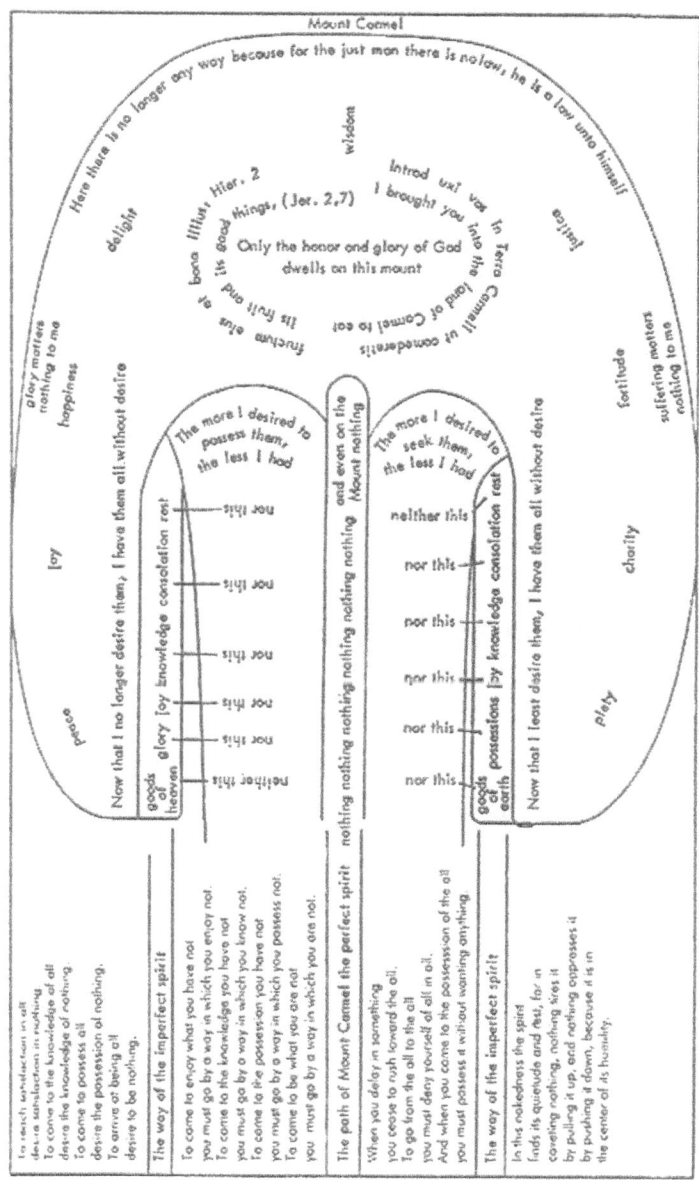

ENGLISH TRANSLATION OF TERMS USED IN ST. JOHN'S ORIGINAL DRAWING.

To come by the what you are not
you must go by a way in which you are not.
When you turn toward something
you cease to cast yourself upon the all.
For to go from all to the all
you must deny yourself of all in all.
And when you come to the possession of the all
you must possess it without wanting anything.
Because if you desire to have something in all
your treasure in God is not purely your all.

Following is the poem which is the basis of the commentary of St. John in the body of the *Ascent of Mt. Carmel*[2]:

On a dark night, Kindled in love with yearnings
—oh, happy chance!—
I went forth without being observed,
My house being now at rest.
In darkness and secure,
By the secret ladder, disguised
—oh, happy chance!—
In darkness and in concealment,
My house being now at rest.

---

[2] Saint John of the Cross, *Ascent of Mount Carmel*, Trans. Peers, Allison, E., At Christian Classics Ethereal Library (CCEL): http://www.ccel.org/ccel/john_cross/ascent.i.html In common domain (Slight modernization of language by editors).

St. John of the Cross

In the happy night,

In secret, when none saw me,

Nor I beheld aught,

Without light or guide, save that which burned in my heart.

This light guided me

More surely than the light of noonday,

To the place where he (well I knew who!) was awaiting me

—A place where none appeared.

Oh, night that guided me,

Oh, night more lovely than the dawn,

Oh, night that joined Beloved with lover,

Lover transformed in the Beloved!

Upon my flowery breast,

Kept wholly for himself alone,

There he stayed sleeping, and I caressed him,

And the fanning of the cedars made a breeze.

The breeze blew from the turret

As I parted his locks;

With his gentle hand he wounded my neck

And caused all my senses to be suspended.

I remained, lost in oblivion;

My face I reclined on the Beloved.

All ceased and I abandoned myself,

Leaving my cares forgotten among the lilies.

Here, now, is an example of the prose writing of St. John of the

Cross from his commentary on the above mystical poem:

Some remarks about the two different nights through which spiritual persons pass in both the lower and higher parts of their nature. A commentary on the first stanza.

[First Stanza]
One dark night,
fired with love's urgent longings
—ah, the sheer grace!—
I went out unseen,
my house being now all stilled.

In this first stanza the soul sings of the happy fortune and chance which it experienced in going forth from all things that are without, and from the desires and imperfections that are in the sensual part of man because of the disordered state of his reason. For the understanding of this it must be known that, for a soul to attain to the state of perfection, it has ordinarily first to pass through two principal kinds of night, which spiritual persons call purgations or purifications of the soul; and here we call them nights, for in both of them the soul journeys, as it were, by night, in darkness.

2. The first night or purgation is of the sensual part of the soul, which is treated in the present stanza, and will be treated in the first part of this book. And the second is of the spiritual part; of this speaks the second stanza…

3. And this first night pertains to beginners, occurring at the time when God begins to bring them into the state of contemplation; in this night the spirit likewise has a part, as we shall say in due course. And the second night, or purification, pertains to those who are already proficient, occurring at the time when God desires to bring them to the state of union with God. And this latter night is a more obscure and dark and terrible purgation, as we shall say afterwards.

4. Briefly, then, the soul means by this stanza that it went forth (being led by God) for love of Him alone, enkindled in love of Him, upon a dark night, which is the privation and purgation of all its sensual desires, with respect to all outward things of the world and to those which were delectable to its flesh, and likewise with respect to the desires of its will. This all comes to pass in this purgation of sense; for which cause the soul says that it went forth while its house was still at rest; which house is its sensual part, the desires being at rest and asleep in it, as it is to them. For there is no going forth from the pains and afflictions of the secret places of the desires until these be mortified and put to sleep. And this, the soul says, was a happy chance for it — namely, it is going forth without being observed: that is, without any desire of its flesh or any other thing being able to hinder it. And likewise, because it went out by night — which signifies the privation of all these things wrought in it by God, which privation was night for it.

5. And it was a happy chance that God should lead it into this night, from which there came to it so much good; for, of itself, the

soul would not have succeeded in entering therein, because no man of himself can succeed in voiding himself of all his desires in order to come to God.

6. This is, in brief, the exposition of the stanza; and we shall now have to go through it, line by line, setting down one line after another, and expounding that which pertains to our purpose. And the same method is followed in the other stanzas, as I said in the Prologue — namely, that each stanza will be set down and expounded, and afterwards each line.

[Note from Dr. Ronda: *The Ascent of Mt. Carmel* is, perhaps, the most thorough spiritual writing ever composed about the purgative way or ascetical path. It describes in detail the way in which attachment to created things and people is an obstacle to growing in the perfect love of God and neighbor that comes with ascent to the peak of 'Mt. Carmel.'

By contrast, St. John of the Cross' other famous treatises, *The Dark Night of the Soul*, *The Spiritual Canticle*, and *The Living Flame of Love*, although also containing much advice about detachment, also display the incredible mystical rewards of the strife of the purgative way to be found in the illuminate way and the unitive way.

We offer *The Spiritual Canticle* to wet your appetite for reading more of the writings of this giant of the Catholic faith. Based on the Song of Songs of the Old Testament, you need to remember that the soul can be drawn by the Holy Spirit to know itself to be the beloved bride of God.

St. John of the Cross

The Spiritual Canticle[3]

I

THE BRIDE

Where have You hidden Yourself,
And abandoned me in my groaning, O my Beloved?
You have fled like the hart,
Having wounded me.
I ran after You, crying; but You were gone.

II

O shepherds, you who go
Through the sheepcots up the hill,
If you shall see Him
Whom I love the most,
Tell Him I languish, suffer, and die.

III

In search of my Love
I will go over mountains and strands;
I will gather no flowers,

---

[3] St. John of the Cross, Trans. Lewis, David. CCEL: http://www.ccel.org/ccel/john_cross/canticle.i.html

I will fear no wild beasts;
And pass by the mighty and the frontiers.

IV

O groves and thickets
Planted by the hand of the Beloved;
O verdant meads
Enameled with flowers,
Tell me, has He passed by you?

V

ANSWER OF THE CREATURES

A thousand graces diffusing
He passed through the groves in haste,
And merely regarding them
As He passed
Clothed them with His beauty.

VI

THE BRIDE

Oh! who can heal me?

St. John of the Cross

Give me at once Yourself,
Send me no more
A messenger
Who cannot tell me what I wish.

VII

All they who serve are telling me
Of Your unnumbered graces;
And all wound me more and more,
And something leaves me dying,
I know not what, of which they are darkly speaking.

VIII

But how you persevere, O life,
Not living where you live;
The arrows bring death
Which you receive
From your conceptions of the Beloved.

IX

Why, after wounding
This heart, have You not healed it?
And why, after stealing it,

Have You thus abandoned it,
And not carried away the stolen prey?

X

Quench my troubles,
For no one else can soothe them;
And let my eyes behold You,
For You are their light,
And I will keep them for You alone.

XI

Reveal Your presence,
And let the vision and Your beauty kill me,
Behold the malady
Of love is incurable
Except in Your presence and before Your face.

XII

O crystal well!
Oh that on Your silvered surface
You would mirror forth at once
Those eyes desired
Which are outlined in my heart!

XIII

Turn them away, O my Beloved!
I am on the wing:

THE BRIDEGROOM

Return, My Dove!
The wounded hart
Looms on the hill
In the air of your flight and is refreshed.

XIV

My Beloved is the mountains,
The solitary wooded valleys,
The strange islands,
The roaring torrents,
The whisper of the amorous gales;

XV

The tranquil night
At the approaches of the dawn,
The silent music,
The murmuring solitude,

The supper which revives, and enkindles love.

XVI

Catch us the foxes,
For our vineyard has flourished;
While of roses
We make a nosegay,
And let no one appear on the hill.

XVII

O killing north wind, cease!
Come, south wind, that awakens love!
Blow through my garden,
And let its odors flow,
And the Beloved shall feed among the flowers.

XVIII

O nymphs of Judea!
While amid the flowers and the rose-trees
The amber sends forth its perfume,
Tarry in the suburbs,
And touch not our thresholds.

XIX

Hide yourself, O my Beloved!
Turn Your face to the mountains,
Do not speak,
But regard the companions
Of her who is traveling amidst strange islands.

XX

THE BRIDEGROOM

Light-winged birds,
Lions, fawns, bounding does,
Mountains, valleys, strands,
Waters, winds, heat,
And the terrors that keep watch by night;

XXI

By the soft lyres
And the siren strains, I adjure you,
Let your fury cease,
And touch not the wall,
That the bride may sleep in greater security.

XXII

The bride has entered
The pleasant and desirable garden,
And there reposes to her heart's content;
Her neck reclining
On the sweet arms of the Beloved.

XXIII

Beneath the apple-tree
There were you betrothed;
There I gave you My hand,
And you were redeemed
Where your mother was corrupted.

XXIV

THE BRIDE

Our bed is of flowers
By dens of lions encompassed,
Hung with purple,
Made in peace,
And crowned with a thousand shields of gold.

XXV

In Your footsteps
The young ones run Your way;
At the touch of the fire
And by the spiced wine,
The divine balsam flows.

XXVI

In the inner cellar
Of my Beloved have I drunk; and when I went forth
Over all the plain
I knew nothing,
And lost the flock I followed before.

XXVII

There He gave me His breasts,
There He taught me the science full of sweetness.
And there I gave to Him
Myself without reserve;
There I promised to be His bride.

XXVIII

My soul is occupied,
And all my substance in His service;
Now I guard no flock,
Nor have I any other employment:
My sole occupation is love.

XXIX

If, then, on the common land
I am no longer seen or found,
You will say that I am lost;
That, being enamored,
I lost myself; and yet was found.

XXX

Of emeralds, and of flowers
In the early morning gathered,
We will make the garlands,
Flowering in Your love,
And bound together with one hair of my head.

St. John of the Cross

XXXI

By that one hair
You have observed fluttering on my neck,
And on my neck regarded,
You were captivated;
And wounded by one of my eyes.

XXXII

When You regarded me,
Your eyes imprinted in me Your grace:
For this You loved me again,
And thereby my eyes merited
To adore what in You they saw

XXXIII

Despise me not,
For if I was swarthy once
You can regard me now;
Since You have regarded me,
Grace and beauty have You given me.

XXXIV

THE BRIDEGROOM

The little white dove
Has returned to the ark with the bough;
And now the turtle-dove
Its desired mate
On the green banks has found.

XXXV

In solitude she lived,
And in solitude built her nest;
And in solitude, alone
Has the Beloved guided her,
In solitude also wounded with love.

XXXVI

THE BRIDE

Let us rejoice, O my Beloved!
Let us go forth to see ourselves in Your beauty,
To the mountain and the hill,
Where the pure water flows:

Let us enter into the heart of the thicket.

XXXVII

We shall go at once
To the deep caverns of the rock
Which are all secret,
There we shall enter in
And taste of the new wine of the pomegranate.

XXXVIII

There you will show me
That which my soul desired;
And there You will give at once,
O You, my life!
That which You gave me the other day.

XXXIX

The breathing of the air,
The song of the sweet nightingale,
The grove and its beauty
In the serene night,
With the flame that consumes, and gives no pains.

XL

None saw it;
Neither did Aminadab appear
The siege was intermitted,
And the cavalry dismounted
At the sight of the waters.

DR. RONDA'S CONTEMPORARY APPLICATIONS AND PERSONAL REFLECTIONS

A book I find the most helpful in considering St. John of the Cross is *The Fire Within* by Fr. Thomas Dubay (San Francisco: Ignatius Press, 1989).

Basically, Dubay proves that the spiritual doctrine of St. John of the Cross, far from being only for enclosed Carmelite contemplatives, has nothing in it that cannot be found in Holy Scripture. The goal of holiness is something the Holy Spirit taught in the Old and New Testaments. In line with the title of Dubay's book we have Jesus proclaiming that "I have come to cast fire on the earth and how I wish it were already blazing." (Luke 12:49) How could St. Paul claim that "having nothing I possess all things" (2 Corinthians 6: 10) unless he was a mystic as well as an apostle?

Spiritual stages such as purgation in St. John of the Cross' *Ascent of Mt. Carmel* were experienced by all the prophets of the Old

Testament and can be found continually in the Psalms. The rapturous experience of God described in poetic language by St. John of the Cross is expressed in Scripture in such lines as "taste and see how good is the Lord." (Psalm 34:5) We can experience, even in this valley of tears, remarkable spiritual delights amidst the purifying sufferings of life.

Passages about longing to see "the face" of God signify that none of us is to be content with blind faith as if mystical glimpses or touches of grace in the heart were only for eccentric wild visionaries. Dubay teaches that we should avoid the extreme of thinking that everything in spiritual experience is from God or that it is all nonsense. For when we read St. John, do not our hearts long for such union with God?

At a point in my life where I was deeply disappointed in human love, I asked a holy contemplative Jewish convert to the Catholic faith, Charles Rich, what I should read. For more about this extraordinary spiritual mentor, see www.rondachervin.com link to Friends of Charles Rich. He suggested St. John of the Cross. He added, however, that many spiritual directors of lay people tell them not to read John of the Cross because he could be easily misunderstood.

I loved reading St. John of the Cross because of the sublimity of his poetry and the philosophical analysis of each verse that brought me back down to the struggle part of spirituality. What is there in John's image of spiritual union that is so poignant and thrilling? Is it not that underneath all the layers of disillusioned cynicism, each of us still longs for absolute fulfillment – to give and receive perfect love? We know that human beings can give such love only fleetingly. The kind that lasts is warm and tender, but rarely intense and exalting. It is incredible to think that God could love us in this way. Yet secretly, we do believe it is possible... from time to time we recognize that there is a stream of pure, beautiful love inside us, waiting for its opportunity to flow. To come into such a mystery we have to be alone not only physically but interiorly. We see that the great mystics lived so securely centered in God that they brought Him with them everywhere, even into ordinary life.

KATHLEEN'S CONTEMPORARY APPLICATIONS AND PERSONAL REFLECTIONS

I notice that in presentations on the faith I often use the expression, "it's that simple." That phrase is on the tips of my fingers again as I begin writing on St. John of the Cross. In considering *The Ascent of Mt. Carmel*, I see that St. John makes the acquisition of holiness and perfect union with God seem amazingly simple: get rid of everything that is not what you seek. If we seek to be or know or possess our goal, we get there by denying ourselves anything that is not the goal.

St. John describes the ascent with an "all or nothing" comparison. We cannot have the "all" unless or until we are content to have nothing else. We must "keep our eyes on the prize" so to speak. If the prize is God (and He is the prize for every soul whether we realize that or not), then absolutely nothing else can interfere or take our attention from Him. Most touching to me in this writing by St. John is, "when you turn toward something you cease to cast yourself upon the all." When you take your eyes off the prize, you lose focus. Then the energy that should be spent in pursuit of it is wasted on the extraneous. If you want God, focus on nothing else. It's that simple.

In *The Spiritual Canticle* St. John describes the seeking. A soul that has experienced something of the love of God wants nothing else and is focused on it. While God hides Himself at times, the soul seeks Him more and more. The time spent without the experience is heartbreaking and frustrating, with the soul pleading with God not to abandon this heart He has stolen.

Strangely, when the circumstances of our lives change, our perspective and focus change as well. In the aftermath of Hurricane Sandy (the "superstorm" which hit New York, New Jersey, and parts of Connecticut), what touches me about *The Spiritual Canticle* is perhaps different than what might have touched me before. I look at Stanza X, "Quench my troubles, for no one else can soothe them." With the storm approaching, the real possibility of losing everything we own was a frightening one. When we drove away from our home on Monday morning, with the winds picking up and the waters becoming angry, I prayed a prayer that I pray every morning. This time, however, it meant something so much different: "O Jesus, our Lord and our brother. We recommend our family and all that is ours to your protection. We confide all to your most holy love." I was doing, literally, just that on this day. What would happen to our home and possessions, pictures and memories was completely out of my control.

The next sentence in Stanza X takes up the theme of keeping focused on God, as we saw it in *The Ascent of Mt. Carmel*, "and let my eyes behold you, for you are their light, and I will keep them for You alone." Here, the soul is asking to see God; the goal and prize. But it also is reminded that the focus can be nowhere else. For me, on this day, however, I did behold God. We came home to a place completely intact! With devastation all around us, homes floating in Long Island Sound, boats on land, power out everywhere – we had a safe home, no water, no damage, and no loss of power. During Hurricane Irene, we lost power for a week, but still recognized how unbelievably lucky we were. During storm-of-the-century Sandy, we had not even that inconvenience. Surely, after the prayers of so many wonderful people, what we saw on our arrival at our home was God! Nothing else can explain the miraculous mercy that was ours. It's that simple.

The Living Flame of Love Stanza 2 talks of God's gentle touch, eternal life and the paying of our debt. It closes with, "In killing you changed death to life." God seems so often to work in ways that make no sense, seem contradictory or are unexplainable. How does killing change death to life except in the Crucifixion of Christ? For me, following Hurricane Sandy, how did devastation show mercy and the kindness of God except that in the face of the greatest natural challenge of my lifetime I saw the miracle of a home and a life unscathed in the midst of the destruction all around me.

With all the tragic stories being told in the aftermath of Sandy, I understand the feelings of survivors of disasters who say, "Why me?" I understand the guilt of those who are not lost in wartime when their buddies are dying all around them. "Why me?" I am so humbly grateful for the miracle we experienced and the mercy we did not deserve (that's why they call it mercy!).

Even though St. John talks, in *The Dark Night of the Soul*, about the end of the sweet caresses of God as He makes us learn to stand on our own two feet, to grow and mature in our faith, we know that God also gives us something of His loving consolation when we need the courage to go on. We are tested sometimes. I have often been tested in ways that made me say, "You know, God, what you think I can handle and what I think I can handle are two completely different things!" But in the darkness of that week, when I was forced to put all my trust in God, to keep my eyes on the prize of His mercy and love, to surrender absolutely everything to Him, He allowed me to find Him whom I sought. Keeping my eyes on God and His mercy, and on nothing else, He allowed me to find Him for a brief moment as I experienced what could only have been His loving touch and protection. It's that simple.

FOR PERSONAL REFLECTION AND GROUP SHARING

Because we believe that the Holy Spirit works in a personal way in the soul of the reader of mystical writings, instead of asking specific questions we are asking you to share what your own experience is as you meditate on these radiant but sometimes overwhelming excerpts from these books by St. John of the Cross. What do they make you see, or feel, or wonder? Does he give you a new perspective at all?

ST. FRANCIS DE SALES, BISHOP (1567-1622)
INTRODUCTION TO THE DEVOUT LIFE

Born in Savoy to an aristocratic family, St. Francis' father wanted him to become a magistrate.[1] After a terrible and prolonged bout with despair, he was suddenly freed as he knelt before a miraculous image of Our Lady; he made a vow of chastity and consecrated himself to the Blessed Virgin Mary. After his studies he was about to become a senator. His father had selected an heiress of a noble family in Savoy as a wife for him, but Francis declared his intention of embracing the ecclesiastical life. A sharp struggle ensued, but Francis received Holy Orders (1593).

Francis devoted himself to preaching, hearing confessions, and the other work of his ministry. Risking his life, he journeyed through the entire district of Le Chablais, preaching constantly. He confuted the Calvinist preachers sent by Geneva to oppose him and converted some prominent Calvinists. A large part of the inhabitants of Le Chablais returned to the true fold.

---

1 *The Catholic Encyclopedia*, vol. VI, ed. Charles G. Herbermann et al. (New York: The Encyclopedia Press, 1913), 220-221.

The king made him preach the Lent at Court, and wished to keep him in France. He urged him to continue, by his sermons and writings, to teach those souls that had to live in the world how to have confidence in God, and how to be genuinely and truly pious—graces of which he saw the great necessity.

Francis was consecrated Bishop of Geneva in 1602. His first step was to institute catechetical instructions for the faithful, both young and old. He carefully visited the parishes scattered through the rugged mountains of his diocese. He reformed the religious communities. His goodness, patience and mildness became proverbial. He had an intense love for the poor. His food was plain, his dress and his household simple. He completely dispensed with superfluities and lived with the greatest economy, in order to be able to provide more abundantly for the wants of the needy. He heard confessions, gave advice, and preached incessantly. He wrote innumerable letters and books. His most famous work is *Introduction to the Devout Life*, a work intended to lead the soul living in the world into the paths of devotion. *The Introduction*, which is a masterpiece of psychology, practical morality, and common sense, was translated into nearly every language even in the lifetime of the author.

Together with St. Jane Frances de Chantal, he founded (1607) the Institute of the Visitation of the Blessed Virgin, for young girls and widows. During his last stay in Paris, he had to go into the pulpit each day to satisfy the pious wishes of those who thronged to hear him. "Never," said they, "have such holy, such apostolic sermons been preached."

St. Francis de Sales

Excerpts from Introduction to the Devout Life[2]

It is too true that I who write about the devout life am not myself devout, but most certainly I am not without the wish to become so, and it is this wish which encourages me to teach you. A notable literary man has said that a good way to learn is to study, a better to listen, and the best to teach. And ST. Augustine, writing to the devout Flora, says: giving is a claim to receive, and teaching a way to learn...

And so, friendly reader, it seems to me that as a Bishop, God wills me to frame in the hearts of His children not merely ordinary goodness, but yet more His own most precious devotion; and on my part I undertake willingly to do so, as much out of obedience to the call of duty as in the hope that, while fixing the image in others' hearts, my own may haply conceive a holy love; and that if His Divine Majesty sees me deeply in love, He may give her to me in an eternal marriage. The beautiful and chaste Rebecca, as she watered Isaac's camels, was destined to be his bride, and received his golden earrings and bracelets, and so I rely on the boundless goodness of my God, that while I lead His beloved lambs to the wholesome fountain of devotion, He will take my soul to be His bride, giving me earrings of the golden words of love, and strengthening my arms to carry out its works, wherein lies the essence of all true devotion, for which I pray His Heavenly Majesty to grant to me and to all the children of

---

2 Francis de Sales, *Introduction to the Devout Life* at www.ccel.org. In common domain but archaic language changed to more contemporary language by the editors.

His Church—that Church to which I would ever submit all my writings, actions, words, will and thoughts.

You aim at a devout life... because as a Christian you know that such devotion is most acceptable to God's Divine Majesty. But seeing that the small errors people are wont to commit in the beginning of any under taking are apt to wax greater as they advance, and to become irreparable at last, it is most important that you should thoroughly understand wherein lies the grace of true devotion—and that because while there undoubtedly is such a true devotion, there are also many spurious and idle semblances thereof; and unless you know which is real, you may mistake, and waste your energy in pursuing an empty, profitless shadow.

One man sets great value on fasting, and believes himself to be leading a very devout life... although... his heart is full of bitterness—and while he will not moisten his lips with wine, perhaps not even with water, in his great abstinence, he does not scruple to steep them in his neighbor's blood, through slander and detraction. Another man reckons himself as devout because he repeats many prayers daily, although at the same time he does not refrain from all manner of angry, irritating, conceited or insulting speeches among his family and neighbors. This man freely opens his purse in almsgiving, but closes his heart to all gentle and forgiving feelings towards those who are opposed to him; while that one is ready enough to forgive his enemies, but will never pay his rightful debts save under pressure. Meanwhile all these people are conventionally called religious, but nevertheless they are in no true sense really devout.

... All true and living devotion presupposes the love of God—and indeed it is neither more nor less than a very real love of God, though not always of the same kind; for that Love one while shining on the soul we call grace, which makes us acceptable to His Divine Majesty—when it strengthens us to do well, it is called charity—but when it attains its fullest perfection, in which it not only leads us to do well, but to act carefully, diligently, and promptly, then it is called devotion.

...The world runs down true devotion, painting devout people with gloomy, melancholy aspect, and affirming that religion makes them dismal and unpleasant... The world, looking on, sees that devout persons fast, watch and pray, endure injury patiently, minister to the sick and poor, restrain their temper, check and subdue their passions, deny themselves in all sensual indulgence, and do many other things which in themselves are hard and difficult. But the world sees nothing of that inward, heartfelt devotion which makes all these actions pleasant and easy... the devout soul finds bitter herbs along its path of devotion, they are all turned to sweetness and pleasantness as it treads.... And if devotion can sweeten such cruel torments, and even death itself, how much more will it give a charm to ordinary good deeds?

Ponder Jacob's ladder—it is a true picture of the devout life; the two poles which support the steps are types of prayer which seek the love of God, and the Sacraments which confer that love; while the steps themselves are simply the degrees of love by which we go on from virtue to virtue...

God... commanded... Christians... to bring forth fruits of devotion, each one according to his kind and vocation. A different exercise of devotion is required of each—the noble, the artisan, the servant, the prince, the maiden and the wife; and furthermore such practice must be modified according to the strength, the calling, and the duties of each individual.

It is an error, nay more, a very heresy, to seek to banish the devout life from the soldier's guardroom, the mechanic's workshop, the prince's court, or the domestic hearth. Of course a purely contemplative devotion, such as is specially proper to the religious and monastic life, cannot be practiced in these outer vocations, but there are various other kinds of devotion well-suited to lead those whose calling is secular...

...The soul which aims at the dignity of becoming the spouse of Christ, must put off the old man, and put on the new man, forsaking sin: moreover, it must pare and shave away every impediment which can hinder the love of God... The ordinary purification, whether of body or soul, is only accomplished by slow degrees, step by step, gradually and painfully.

God did not bring you into the world because He had any need of you, useless as you are; but solely that He might show forth His Goodness in you, giving you His grace and glory. And to this end He gave you understanding that you might know Him, memory that you might think of Him, a will that you might love Him, imagination that you might realize His mercies, sight that you might behold the marvels of His works, speech that you might praise Him...

...We have certain natural inclinations, which are not strictly speaking either mortal or venial sins, but rather imperfections; and the acts in which they take shape, failings and deficiencies... Some people are naturally easy, some oppositions; some are indisposed to accept other men's opinions, some naturally disposed to be cross, some to be affectionate—in short, there is hardly anyone in whom some such imperfections do not exist. Now, although they are natural and instinctive in each person, they may be remedied and corrected...

But especially I commend earnest mental prayer to you, more particularly such as bears upon the life and passion of our Lord. If you contemplate Him frequently in meditation, your whole soul will be filled with Him, you will grow in His likeness, and your actions will be molded on His. He is the Light of the world; therefore in Him, by Him, and for Him we shall be enlightened and illuminated... (if) we cleave to the Savior in meditation, listening to His words, watching His actions and intentions, we shall learn in time, through His Grace, to speak, act and will like Himself.

Above all things... strive when your meditation is ended to retain the thoughts and resolutions you have made as your earnest practice throughout the day.

...Aspire continually to God, by brief, ardent uplifting of heart; praise His excellence, invoke His aid, cast yourself in spirit at the foot of His cross, adore His goodness, offer your whole soul a thousand times a day to Him, fix your inward gaze upon Him, stretch out your hands to be led by Him, as a little child to its father, clasp Him to your breast as a fragrant nosegay, upraise Him in your soul as a standard. In short, kindle by every possible act your love for God, your tender, passionate desire for the Heavenly Bridegroom of souls.

In order to join in (Mass) rightly...you must...: (1) In the beginning, and before the priest goes up to the altar, make your preparation with his—placing yourself in God's presence, confessing your unworthiness, and asking forgiveness. (2) Until the Gospel, dwell simply and generally upon the coming and the life of our Lord in this world. (3) From the Gospel to the end of the creed, dwell upon our dear Lord's teaching, and renew your resolution to live and die in the faith of the Holy Catholic Church. (4) From thence, fix your heart on the mysteries of the Word, and unite yourself to the death and passion of our Redeemer, now actually and essentially set forth in this holy sacrifice, which, together with the priest and all the congregation, you offer to God the Father, to His glory and your own salvation. (5) Up to the moment of communicating, offer all the longings and desires of your heart, above all desiring most earnestly to be united forever to our Savior by His eternal love. (6) From the time of Communion to the end, thank His gracious majesty for His incarnation, His life, death, passion, and the love which He sets forth in this holy sacrifice, entreating through it His favor for yourself, your relations and friends, and the whole Church; and humbling yourself sincerely, devoutly receive the blessing which our dear Lord gives you through the channel of His minister.

Our Savior has bequeathed the sacrament of penitence and confession to His Church, in order that therein we may be cleansed from all our sins, however and whenever we may have been soiled thereby. Therefore… never allow your heart to abide heavy with sin, seeing that there is so sure and safe a remedy at hand. Make your confession humbly and devoutly every week… although your conscience is not burdened with mortal sin; for in confession you do not only receive absolution for your venial sins, but you also receive great strength to help you in avoiding them henceforth, clearer light to discover your failings, and abundant grace to make up whatever loss you have incurred through those faults. You exercise the graces of humility, obedience, simplicity and love, and by this one act of confession you practice more virtue than in any other.

In practicing any virtue, it is well to choose that which is most according to our duty, rather than most according to our taste… the Apostles, whose mission it was to preach the Gospel, and feed souls with the bread of life, judged well that it was not right for them to hinder this holy work in order to minister to the material wants of the poor, weighty as that work was also. Every calling stands in special need of some special virtue… but each should cultivate chiefly those which are important to the manner of life to which he is called… It is well for everybody to select some special virtue at which to aim, not as neglecting any others, but as an object and pursuit to the mind.

Call often to mind that our Savior redeemed us by bearing and suffering, and in like manner we must seek our own salvation amid sufferings and afflictions; bearing insults, contradictions and troubles with all the gentleness we can possibly command. Do not limit your patience to this or that kind of trial, but extend it universally to whatever God may send, or allow to befall you… to bear such injustice at the hands of good men, of friends and relations, is a great test of patience… Be patient, not only with respect to the main trials which beset you, but also under the accidental and accessory annoyances which arise out of them… Complain as little as possible of your wrongs… When you are sick, offer all your pains and weakness to our Dear Lord, and ask Him to unite them to the sufferings which He bore for you… Gaze often inwardly upon Jesus Christ crucified, naked, blasphemed, falsely accused, forsaken, overwhelmed with every possible grief and sorrow, and remember that none of your sufferings can ever be compared to His, either in kind or degree, and that you can never suffer anything for Him worthy to be weighed against what He has borne for you.

…Be careful and diligent in all your affairs; God, Who commits them to you, wills you to give them your best attention; but strive not to be anxious and solicitous, that is to say, do not set about your work with restlessness and excitement, and do not give way to bustle and eagerness in what you do—every form of excitement affects both judgment and reason, and hinders a right performance of the very thing which excites us… Accept the duties which come upon you quietly, and try to fulfill them methodically, one after another. If you attempt to do everything at once, or with confusion, you will only encumber yourself with your own exertions, and by dint of perplexing your mind you will probably be overwhelmed and accomplish nothing… In all your affairs lean solely on God's providence, by means of which alone your plans can succeed. Meanwhile, on your part work on in quiet cooperation with Him, and then rest satisfied that if you have trusted entirely to Him you will always obtain such a measure of success as is most profitable for you, whether it seems so or not to your own individual judgment.

Anxiety of mind is not so much an abstract temptation, as the source whence various temptations arise. Sadness, when defined, is the mental grief we feel because of our involuntary ailments—whether the evil is exterior, such as poverty, sickness or contempt; or interior, such as ignorance, dryness, depression or temptation... If anyone strives to be delivered from his troubles out of love of God, he will strive patiently, gently, humbly and calmly, looking for deliverance rather to God's Goodness and Providence than to his own industry or efforts; but if self-love is the prevailing object he will grow hot and eager in seeking relief, as though all depended more upon himself than upon God. I do not say that the person thinks so, but he acts eagerly as though he did think it... This restless anxiety is the greatest evil which can happen to the soul, sin only excepted... so if our heart be disturbed and anxious, it loses power to retain such graces as it has, as well as strength to resist the temptations of the Evil One...

Anxiety arises from an unregulated desire to be delivered from any pressing evil, or to obtain some hoped-for good. Nevertheless nothing tends so greatly to enhance the one or retard the other as over-eagerness and anxiety... When you are conscious that you are growing anxious, commend yourself to God... If you can lay your anxiety before your spiritual guide, or at least before some trusty and devout friend, you may be sure that you will find great solace.

DR. RONDA'S CONTEMPORARY APPLICATIONS AND PERSONAL REFLECTIONS

Whenever I reread the *Introduction to the Devout Life*, I always think that I am going to find it too elementary and then have to hang my head that I have not mastered all that he advises in spite of thinking myself to be "advanced." On needing a mentor in the challenges of trying to be a good Christian, I have been so blessed with wonderful spiritual directors in the many places I have taught. Recently I read a book about spiritual direction by Thomas Dubay, the same theologian I cited concerning St. John of the Cross. He insists that even if it is hard to find a priest spiritual director we should pray for some kind of mentor even if "only" a good friend. I absolutely agree with De Sales that we need to bring our troubles to someone who is going to help us rather than add complaints about life to our own and help us to despise our enemies! I thank God for so many such friends sent me throughout the many phases of my life.

I find very helpful the way St. Francis de Sales gets into the nitty-gritty on virtues such as patience and impatience. For more contemporary examples you might see my booklet "The Way of Love: Overcoming Obstacles to Love" (part of a large book called *Way of Love* you can find on Amazon if you add my name to the title.) Or, consider how the passage about preserving chastity related to such widespread contemporary vices as porn.

Some Catholics use the concepts of St. Francis de Sales about different vocations to justify luxurious living for lay people. From reading biographies of holy people of the times of St. Francis and his followers, I think he means that they couldn't live like monks, not that they could eat, dress, and furnish their homes with luxuries. To make it contemporary, a business man/woman has to wear suits, not tattered Franciscan robes. It is necessary to wine and dine others as part of a life in management of companies. A pianist has to have a piano and nice clothing for performances. How different this is, however, from having closets stuffed with garments hardly ever worn or a large screen TV in every room of a large house.

KATHLEEN'S CONTEMPORARY APPLICATIONs AND PERSONAL REFLECTIONS

In the very first paragraph of St. Francis de Sales' *Introduction to the Devout Life*, I am struck by something he writes that was also said to me this very week in confession. We can think we are being devout through our pious practices when, in reality, our hearts are full of anger and pettiness toward our brothers and sisters in Christ. In fact, the idea of fasting is what was addressed specifically in confession. St. Francis says in fasting from food I may be full of bitterness in my heart, in keeping wine and even water from my lips, I may "steep them in (my) neighbor's blood, through slander and detraction." I am reminded that the Scripture tells us, "it is mercy I desire and not sacrifice." What good is it for me to rattle off prayers with my mouth, or keep food and drink from it, if I am using it to complain about and criticize my fellows? What does it matter to keep things out of my body if my heart is full of contempt and devoid of love? Or how can I love God if I am thinking only of tomorrow when I can eat again? I can only believe this is a message meant for me from our Lord since it came to me twice in one week through His loved ones. I believe He wants me to look at what I am doing and what is in my heart.

All of the previous writers we have studied have encouraged a true desire for God. St. Francis de Sales describes devotion as a deep and great love for God that enables us to endure with joy and ease all the slow, painful steps toward holiness. I am still in the struggling stage. It seems that all of my spiritual life is about fasting these days: from food, yes, but also from anger and pettiness, from desire to retaliate when I have been wronged, from the urge to offer my opinion. For me now, all this fasting is about me decreasing while the Lord increases, to paraphrase St. Paul. I seek to deny myself, pick up my cross, and follow Him.

We read in Thomas a Kempis, "Who hath a harder battle to fight than he who striveth for self-mastery?" It seems to me that fasting from whatever ties us to earthly things is the way to self-mastery. St. Francis de Sales offers a way to achieve this through a great love of God. The way to love God, no matter our station in life, is to get beyond these things that distract us from Him. Paradoxically, we can easily get beyond them through the motivation to love Him.

Again, as with other writers we have considered in this course, St. Francis de Sales encourages us to keep our eyes on the prize and not to become discouraged by our imperfections. We cannot, he says, end our struggle for self-mastery except with death. But we take courage in the knowledge that we are not left alone in our attempts for, as we know, God gives us His very own life and love to aide us through the gift of grace in the Sacraments.

If we are mindful of God's goodness and mercy in drawing us away from sin and providing us strength in the Sacraments, we cannot fail to be in awe of His almighty power. With proper perspective, we are in awe of His love and grateful for it. We will strive not to fall again into sin, and to achieve self-mastery for love of Him.

FOR PERSONAL REFLECTION AND GROUP SHARING

1. Did you ever think spirituality was only for the consecrated, not for lay people?

2. Have you ever known others whose spirituality seemed to you to be unsuited to the nature of their vocations in the world? For example, those who pray long hours at Adoration but neglect the family? Have you, yourself, ever fallen into a partly false spirituality on this account?

3. Have you had spiritual mentoring? Do you pray for such help?

4. What stood out for you in St. Francis de Sales' treatment of patience? Can you give personal examples about patience or impatience?

5. In relation to St. Francis de Sales' admonitions concerning worry about our endeavors, think about how much you worry about success in school, the workplace, Church work. What part of De Sales' advice could you use to become more tranquil about such matters?

Give your own example of some source of chronic anxiety in your life and how the wisdom of De Sales could be applied.

BROTHER LAWRENCE (C. 1605-1691)
THE PRACTICE OF THE PRESENCE OF GOD

Brother Lawrence was born Nicholas Herman in Loraine in France, and became a soldier in his youth. Lacking education, he later became a lay brother in the Discalced Carmelites in Paris, and was known as Brother Lawrence of the Resurrection. He was assigned the task of cook at the monastery and didn't like the work. But he did it for the glory of God and offered everything to Him.

Brother Lawrence shared his secret of holiness and peace with anyone who asked: practice being in the presence of God and talking with him all the time.

Excerpts from *The Practice of the Presence of God*[1]
(as compiled by Fr. de Beaufort)

First Conversation

The first time I saw Brother Lawrence was on the 3rd of August, 1666. He told me that God had done him a singular favor, in his conversion at the age of eighteen. That in the winter, seeing a tree stripped of its leaves, and considering that within a little time, the leaves would be renewed, and after that the flowers and fruit appear, he received a high view of the providence and power of God, which has never since been effaced from his soul. That this view had perfectly set him loose from the world, and kindled in him such a love for God, that he could not tell whether it had increased in above forty years that he had lived since…

…He had desired to be received into a monastery, thinking that he would there be made to smart for his awkwardness and the faults he should commit, and so he should sacrifice to God his life, with its pleasures: but …God had disappointed him, he having met with nothing but satisfaction in that state.

…We should establish ourselves in a sense of God's presence, by continually conversing with Him…it was a shameful thing to quit His conversation, to think of trifles and fooleries.

…We should feed and nourish our souls with high notions of

---

[1] Brother Lawrence, *The Practice of the Presence of God* (London: The Epworth Press) at www.ccel.org. In common domain but archaic language changed to more contemporary langauge by the editors.

God; which would yield us great joy in being devoted to Him.

...The way of faith was the spirit of the Church, and...it was sufficient to bring us to a high degree of perfection.

...We ought to give ourselves up to God, with regard to things both temporal and spiritual, and seek our satisfaction only in the fulfilling of His will, whether He lead us by suffering or by consolation, for all would be equal to a soul truly resigned.

Second Conversation

(Brother Lawrence told me) that he had always been governed by love, without selfish views; and that having resolved to make the love of God the end of all his actions, he had found reasons to be well satisfied with his method. That he was pleased when he could take up a straw from the ground for the love of GOD, seeking Him only, and nothing else, not even His gifts...

That in order to form a habit of conversing with God continually, and referring all we do to Him; we must at first apply to Him with some diligence: that after a little care we should find His love inwardly excite us to it without any difficulty.

That he expected after the pleasant days God had given him, he should have his turn of pain and suffering; but that he was not uneasy about it, knowing very well, that as he could do nothing of himself, God would not fail to give him the strength to bear them.

That when an occasion of practicing some virtue offered, he addressed himself to God, saying, Lord, I cannot do this unless You enable me; and that then he received strength more than sufficient.

That when he had failed in his duty, he only confessed his fault, saying to God, I shall never do otherwise, if You leave me to myself; It is You who must hinder my falling, and mend what is amiss. That after this, he gave himself no further uneasiness about it.

That we ought to act with God in the greatest simplicity, speaking to Him frankly and plainly, and imploring His assistance in our affairs, just as they happen. That God never failed to grant it, as he had often experienced.

…In his business in the kitchen (to which he had naturally a great aversion), having accustomed himself to do everything there for the love of God, and with prayer, upon all occasions, for His grace to do his work well, he had found everything easy, during the fifteen years that he had been employed there.

…Useless thoughts spoil all: …the mischief began there; but that we ought to reject them as soon as we perceived their impertinence to the matter in hand, or our salvation; and return to our communion with God.

…(He told me) that our only business was to love and delight ourselves in God.

That all possible kinds of penances, if they were void of the love of God, could not efface a single sin. That we ought, without anxiety, to expect the pardon of our sins from the Blood of Jesus Christ, only endeavoring to love Him with all our hearts. That God seemed to have granted the greatest favors to the greatest sinners, as more signal monuments of His mercy.

Third Conversation

He told me, that the foundation of the spiritual life in him had been a high notion, and esteem of God in faith; which when he had once well-conceived, he had no other care at first, but faithfully to reject every other thought, that he might perform all his actions for the love of God. That when sometimes he had not thought of God for a good while, he did not disquiet himself for it; but after having acknowledged his wretchedness to God, he returned to Him with so much the greater trust in Him, by how much he found himself more wretched to have forgot Him.

That the trust we put in God honors Him much, and draws down great graces.

…When outward business diverted him a little from the thought of God, a fresh remembrance coming from God invested his soul, and so inflamed and transported him that it was difficult for him to contain himself…

That he expected hereafter some great pain of body or mind; that the worst that could happen to him was, to lose that sense of God, which he had enjoyed so long but that the goodness of God assured him He would not forsake him utterly, and that He would give him strength to bear whatever evil He permitted to happen to him; and therefore that he feared nothing, and had no occasion to consult with anybody about his state. That when he attempted to do it, he had always come away more perplexed; and that as he was conscious of his readiness to lay down his life for the love of God, he had no apprehension of danger. That perfect resignation to God was a sure way to heaven, a way in which we had always sufficient light for our conduct.

That in the beginning of the spiritual life, we ought to be faithful in doing our duty and denying ourselves; but after that unspeakable pleasure followed: that in difficulties we need only have recourse to Jesus Christ, and beg His grace, with which everything became easy.

That many do not advance in Christian progress, because they stick in penances, and particular exercises, while they neglect the love of God, which is the end. That this appeared plainly by their works, and was the reason why we see so little virtue.

That there is neither art nor science for going to God, but only a heart resolutely determined to apply itself to nothing but Him, or for His sake, and to love Him only.

Fourth Conversation

He discoursed with me very frequently, and with great openness of heart, concerning his manner of going to God, of which some part is related already.

He told me, that all consists in one hearty renunciation of everything which we are sensible does not lead to God that we might accustom ourselves to continual conversation with Him, with freedom and in simplicity. That we need only to recognize God intimately present with us, to address ourselves to Him every moment, that we may beg His assistance for knowing His will in things doubtful, and for rightly performing those which we plainly see He requires of us, offering them to Him before we do them and giving Him thanks when we have done.

That in this conversation with God, we are also employed in praising, adoring, and loving Him incessantly, for His infinite goodness and perfection…

That God always gave us light in our doubts, when we had no other design but to please Him.

That our sanctification did not depend upon changing our works, but in doing that for God's sake, which we commonly do for our own. That it was lamentable to see how many people mistook the means for the end, addicting themselves to certain works, which they performed very imperfectly, by reason of their human or selfish regards…

That his prayer was nothing else but a sense of the presence of God, his soul being at that time insensible to everything but Divine love; and that when the appointed times of prayer were past, he found no difference because he still continued with God, praising and blessing Him with all his might, so that he passed his life in continual joy; yet hoped that God would give him somewhat to suffer, when he should grow stronger.

That we ought, once and for all, heartily to put our whole trust in God, and make a total surrender of ourselves to Him, secure that He would not deceive us.

That we ought not to be weary of doing little things for the love of God, who regards not the greatness of the work, but the love with which it is performed. That we should not wonder if, in the beginning, we often failed in our endeavors, but that at last we should gain a habit, which will naturally produce its acts in us, without our care, and to our exceeding great delight…

That all things are possible to him who believes, that they are less difficult to him who hopes, they are more easy to him who loves, and still more easy to him who perseveres in the practice of these three virtues.

That the end we ought to propose to ourselves is to become, in this life, the most perfect worshippers of God we can possibly be, as we hope to be through all eternity…

…In the beginning of his novitiate he spent the hours appointed for private prayer thinking of God, so as to convince his mind of, and to impress deeply upon his heart, the Divine existence rather by devout sentiments, and submission to the lights of faith, than by studied reasonings and elaborate meditations. That by this short and sure method, he exercised himself in the knowledge and love of God, resolving to use his utmost to endeavor to live in a continual sense of His Presence, and, if possible, never to forget Him more.

…When he began his business, he said to God, with a filial trust in Him, "Oh my God, since You are with me, and I must now, in obedience to Your commands, apply my mind to these outward things, I beseech You to grant me the grace to continue in Your Presence; and to this end grant me Your assistance, receive all my works, and possess all my affections."

As he proceeded in his work, he continued his familiar conversation with his Maker, imploring His grace, and offering to Him all his actions.

When he had finished, he examined how he had discharged his duty; if he found well, he returned thanks to God; if otherwise, he asked pardon; and without being discouraged, he set his mind right again, and continued his exercise of the presence of God, as if he had never deviated from it. "Thus," said he, "by rising after my falls, and by frequently renewed acts of faith and love, I am come to a state, wherein it would be as difficult for me not to think of God, as it was at first to accustom myself to it."

Letters

First Letter

...After having given myself wholly to God, to make all the satisfaction I could for my sins, I renounced, for the love of Him, everything that was not He; and I began to live as if there was none but He and I in the world. Sometimes I considered myself before Him as a poor criminal at the feet of his judge; at other times I beheld Him in my heart as my Father, as my God: I worshipped Him the oftenest that I could, keeping my mind in His holy Presence, and recalling it as often as I found it wandered from Him. I found no small pain in this exercise, and yet I continued it, notwithstanding all the difficulties that occurred, without troubling or disquieting myself when my mind had wandered involuntarily...for at all times, every hour, every minute, even in the height of my business, I drove away from my mind everything that was capable of interrupting my thought of God.

…But when we are faithful to keep ourselves in His holy Presence, and set Him always before us, this not only hinders our offending Him, and doing anything that may displease Him, at least willfully, but it also begets in us a holy freedom, and if I may so speak, a familiarity with God…In fine, by often repeating these acts, they become habitual, and the presence of God is rendered as it were natural to us. Give Him thanks, if you please, with me, for His great goodness towards me, which I can never sufficiently admire, for the many favors He has done to so miserable a sinner as I am. May all things praise Him. Amen.

Second Letter

…Sometimes I consider myself…as a stone before a carver, whereof he is to make a statue: presenting myself thus before God, I desire Him to make His perfect image in my soul, and render me entirely like Himself.

At other times, when I apply myself to prayer, I feel all my spirit and all my soul lift itself up without any care or effort of mine; and it continues as it were suspended and firmly fixed in God, as in its center and place of rest…

Fifth Letter

I will send you one of those books which treat of the presence of God; a subject which, in my opinion, contains the whole spiritual life; and it seems to me that whoever duly practices it will soon become spiritual.

I know that for the right practice of it, the heart must be empty of all other things; because God will possess the heart alone; and as He cannot possess it alone, without emptying it of all besides, so neither can He act there, and do in it whatever He pleases, unless it is left vacant to Him.

There is not in the world a kind of life more sweet and delightful, than that of a continual conversation with God: those only can comprehend it who practice and experience it; yet I do not advise you to do it from that motive; it is not pleasure which we ought to seek in this exercise; but let us do it from a principle of love, and because God would have us.

Were I a preacher, I should above all other things preach the practice of the presence of God; and were I director, I should advise all the world to do it: so necessary do I think it, and so easy too...

Seventh Letter

...It will be of great importance if you can leave the care of your affairs to, and spend the remainder of your life only in worshiping God. He requires no great matter of us; a little remembrance of Him from time to time, a little adoration: sometimes to pray for His grace, sometimes to offer Him your sufferings, and sometimes to return Him thanks for the favors He has given you, and still gives you, in the midst of your troubles, and to console yourself with Him as often as you can. Lift up your heart to Him sometimes even at your meals, and when you are in company: the least little remembrance will always be acceptable to Him. You need not cry very loud; He is nearer to us than we are aware of.

It is not necessary for being with God to be always at church; we may make an oratory of our heart, wherein to retire from time to time, to converse with Him in meekness, humility, and love. Everyone is capable of such familiar conversation with God, some more, some less: He knows what we can do. Let us begin then; perhaps He expects but one generous resolution on our part. Have courage…

Ninth Letter

…We cannot escape the dangers which abound in life, without the actual and continual help of God; let us then pray to Him for it continually. How can we pray to Him without being with Him? How can we be with Him but in thinking of Him often? And how can we often think of Him, but by a holy habit which we should form of it? You tell me that I am always saying the same thing: it is true, for this is the best and easiest method I know; and as I use no other, I advise all the world to it. We must know before we can love. In order to know God, we must often think of Him; and when we come to love Him, we shall then also think of Him often, for our heart will be with our treasure…

Eleventh Letter

I do not pray that you may be delivered from your pains; but I pray God earnestly that He would give you strength and patience to bear them as long as He pleases. Comfort yourself with Him who holds you fastened to the cross: He will loose you when He thinks fit. Happy those who suffer with Him: accustom yourself to suffer in that manner, and seek from Him the strength to endure as much, and as long, as He shall judge to be necessary for you...

Twelfth Letter

If we were well accustomed to the exercise of the presence of God, all bodily diseases would be much alleviated thereby. God often permits that we should suffer a little, to purify our souls, and oblige us to continue with Him.

Take courage, offer Him your pains incessantly, pray to Him for strength to endure them...

God has many ways of drawing us to Himself. He sometimes hides Himself from us: but faith alone, which will not fail us in time of need, ought to be our support, and the foundation of our confidence, which must be all in God.

Fifteenth Letter

God knows best what is needful for us, and all that He does is for our good. If we knew how much He loves us, we should be always ready to received equally and with indifference from His hand the sweet and the bitter; all would please that came from Him....

DR. RONDA'S CONTEMPORARY APPLICATIONS AND PERSONAL REFLECTIONS

I have always found it noteworthy that Christians who would never want to read such giants as St. Teresa of Avila or St. John of the Cross, will often delight in reading smaller masterpieces such as *The Practice of the Presence of God* by un-canonized "littler" holy writers.

In the 20th century, a book in some ways similar to that of Brother Lawrence was *The Way of the Pilgrim*. It describes the adventures and graces of an uneducated Russian peasant who endeavored to repeat this prayer incessantly at all times: "Lord Jesus, Son of David, have mercy on me a poor sinner." Because I sometimes do pray this way myself "between things" I always think that I am also a disciple of Brother Lawrence. However, when I re-read Brother Lawrence from time to time I realize this is not true. I certainly often turn to God the Father, God the Holy Spirit, Our Lord Jesus Christ, Mary, Joseph and many saints each day, and beg them to help me. That is not quite the same as confiding in them all my thoughts, leaving room for a word from them in my heart or just a sense of some truth I have been ignoring as my brain frantically works on ways to cope with the obstacles of life.

This reading, working on the excerpts, I did increase my time in conversation with the Holy ones with great profit of insight and comfort.

KATHLEEN'S CONTEMPORARY APPLICATIONS AND PERSONAL REFLECTIONS

Especially in light of the over-scheduled, noise-polluted society in which we live, I found Brother Lawrence's *Practice of the Presence of God* to be another of those "it's that simple" subjects. Brother Lawrence simply did everything in God's presence. He offered every thought, every action, every word to God. If he found his mind wandering, he immediately brought it back. If he busied himself with anything that was not of God, upon realizing it, he would immediately turn back to God. I am trying each day to remind myself to be in God's presence. I am remembering more each day to look inside myself, rather than "out there somewhere" to find Him. I try to accept whatever comes by reminding myself that I am having the day God wants me to have – and that everything has a reason, coming from His great love for me and desire for my good.

Brother Lawrence found that he could speak to God about everything – plainly, simply, and as it happened. He found that he never sought help without receiving it. God is present everywhere and in everything. It is incumbent upon us to be conscious of that and to call upon Him in every circumstance. We say that God wants us to come to Him with everything, but how often do we do it?

I often tell my students that they may see me driving around town with my lips moving. I am talking aloud to God. I do it every day. Sadly, I am most often asking Him for favors or complaining about my struggles and begging for mercy. But I am striving to come to Him about everything. I invite Him into every situation. I ask His guidance and blessing. I seek His forgiveness. One day, I hope my will may be aligned with His. My mantra is, "Give Him glory and attain salvation."

In Brother Lawrence we find a common sense approach to union with God. He is a great reminder that we cannot find our way to God without His help and His grace. We all are called to God, but we will not all reach Him in the same way. What is beneficial to one may not be so to another. Brother Lawrence found the paths marked out by others to be discouraging to him. He sought simply to love God above everything else and to turn toward God in all times and circumstances. He offered himself to God and found God ready and waiting to accept that gift. If our perspective and priorities are correct, if we are in awe of Him, we will seek to please Him and never to offend Him. If we practice being with Him, over and over, until we achieve it, we will come to know Him. If we truly know Him, we will love Him. Brother Lawrence seems to have shown us – before Winston Churchill ever said it – "Never give up, never give up, never, never, never, never, never give up!"

FOR PERSONAL REFLECTION AND GROUP SHARING

Try to go through an entire day practicing the Presence of God. Share your experience.

ST. LOUIS MARIE DE MONTFORT (1673 – 1716)
TRUE DEVOTION TO MARY

St. Louis de Montfort was born January 31, 1673. As a child, he prayed before Jesus in the Blessed Sacrament, gave alms to the poor, and made visitations to the Church before and after school. He studied theology in Paris at age nineteen and was ordained at age twenty-seven. Louis was an extremely gifted speaker and was able to move even hardened soldiers to confess their sins and ask the Lord's forgiveness.

His great love and reverence for Our Lady moved him to write *True Devotion to Mary* and *The Secret of the Rosary*, two of the most widely read and popular books ever written on devotion to the Blessed Mother. St. Louis de Monfort died April 28, 1716, was beatified by Pope Leo XIII in 1888, and canonized by Pope Pius XII in 1947.

Excerpts from True Devotion to Mary[1]

Treatise on True Devotion to the Blessed Virgin

Part I: True Devotion to our Lady in General

Ch. 2: In what Devotion to Mary Consists

Principal practices of devotion to Mary

115. There are several interior practices of true devotion to the Blessed Virgin. Here briefly are the main ones:

1. Honoring her, as the worthy Mother of God, by the cult of hyperdulia (this means veneration above that of other saints but never considering her a sort of goddess), that is, esteeming and honoring her more than all the other saints as the masterpiece of grace and the foremost in holiness after Jesus Christ, true God and true man.
2. Meditating on her virtues, her privileges and her actions.
3. Contemplating her sublime dignity.
4. Offering to her acts of love, praise and gratitude.
5. Invoking her with a joyful heart.
6. Offering ourselves to her and uniting ourselves to her.
7. Doing everything to please her.
8. Beginning, carrying out and completing our actions through her, in her, with her, and for her in order to do them through Jesus, in Jesus, with Jesus, and for Jesus, our last end. We shall

---

[1] St. Louis de Montfort, *Treatise on True Devotion to the Blessed Virgin*, http://www.ewtn.com/library/Montfort/TRUEDEVO.HTM.

explain this last practice later.

116. True devotion to our Lady has also several exterior practices. Here are the principal ones:
1. Enrolling in her confraternities and joining her sodalities.
2. Joining religious orders dedicated to her.
3. Making her privileges known and appreciated.
4. Giving alms, fasting, performing interior and exterior acts of self-denial in her honor.
5. Carrying such signs of devotion to her as the rosary, the scapular, or a little chain.
6. Reciting with attention, devotion and reverence the fifteen decades of the Rosary in honor of the fifteen principal mysteries of our Lord, or at least five decades in honor of:

> the Joyful mysteries - the Annunciation, the Visitation, the Birth of our Lord, the Purification, the Finding of the Child Jesus in the temple;
>
> or the Sorrowful mysteries: the Agony in the Garden, the Scourging, the Crowning with thorns, the Carrying of the Cross, and the Crucifixion;
>
> or the Glorious mysteries: The Resurrection of our Lord, the Ascension, the Descent of the Holy Spirit, the Assumption of our Lady, body and soul, into heaven, the Crowning of Mary by the Blessed Trinity.

(Note: Present day Catholics would naturally be adding the Luminous Mysteries instituted by Pope John Paul II.)

One may also choose any of the following prayers: the Rosary of six or seven decades in honor of the years our Lady is believed to have spent on earth; the Little Crown of the Blessed Virgin in honor of her crown of twelve stars or privileges; the Little Office of our Lady so widely accepted and recited in the Church; the Little Psalter of the Blessed Virgin, composed in her honor by St. Bonaventure, which is so heart-warming, and so devotional that you cannot recite it without being moved by it; the fourteen Our Fathers and Hail Mary's in honor of her fourteen joys. There are various other prayers and hymns of the Church, such as, the hymns of the liturgical seasons, the Ave Maris Stella, the O Gloriosa Domina (O Glorious Lady) ; the Magnificat (the prayer of praise Mary enunciated when the angel told her of her role as mother of the Messiah) and other prayers which are found in all prayer-books.

Singing hymns to her or teaching others to sing them.

Genuflecting or bowing to her each morning while saying for example sixty or a hundred times, "Hail Mary, Virgin most faithful", so that through her intercession with God we may faithfully correspond with his graces throughout the day; and in the evening saying "Hail Mary, Mother of Mercy", asking her to obtain God's pardon for the sins we have committed during the day.

Taking charge of her confraternities, decorating her altars, crowning and adorning her statues.

Carrying her statues or having others carry them in procession, or keeping a small one on one's person as an effective protection against the evil one.

Having statues made of her, or her name engraved and placed on the walls of churches or houses and on the gates and entrances of towns, churches and houses.

Solemnly giving oneself to her by a special consecration.

117. The Holy Spirit has inspired saintly souls with other practices of true devotion to the Blessed Virgin, all of which are conducive to holiness… These devotions are a wonderful help for souls seeking holiness provided they are performed in a worthy manner, that is:
1. With the right intention of pleasing God alone, seeking union with Jesus, our last end, and giving edification to our neighbor.
2. With attention, avoiding willful distractions.
3. With devotion, avoiding haste and negligence.
4. With decorum and respectful bodily posture.

DR. RONDA'S CONTEMPORARY APPLICATIONS AND PERSONAL REFLECTIONS

One could say could say that St. Louis Marie de Montfort has haunted me all of my Catholic life! The reason is that even though I like almost everything he wrote and think it is true, I find his style of writing uncomfortable. But every place I have moved I have found myself in a group making the De Montfort Consecration with the many days of meditation taken from St. Louis Marie's writings. I always get many graces from making the consecration!

The most spectacular graces came to me from making the consecration with the statue of the Pilgrim Virgin of Our Lady of Fatima, brought to my home by women in my parish devoted to St. Louis Marie de Montfort. At this time I had many heavy family burdens and worries expressed by me through anger. For years after the consecration I was not only peaceful but full of contemplative graces as well.

Let me start with the great truth – that Mary, Mother of God, is essential to our faith, not some optional devotion suitable for the uneducated. An interesting confirmation of this point came from Carl Jung, the famous non-Catholic psychologist. Jung was thrilled when the dogma of the Assumption of Mary was declared by the Church in the 20th century. He thought that it signaled a better understanding of the role of the feminine in the whole universe.

For me, Mary symbolizes all the beautiful positive feminine traits I love such as compassion, helpfulness, sweetness, sensitivity, delicacy and long-suffering. These traits I always find in the famous paintings of Mary, from the Grunewald smiling Madonna to the exquisite pathos of the face of Our Lady of Guadalupe on the tilma of Juan Diego. On the other hand, Mother Mary also symbolizes the absence of such negative feminine traits as weakness, seductiveness, silliness and hysteria! When I am overcome by some of those negatives, just the sight of Mary's face is a help to me.

To my enormous surprise, sometimes people who know me now at 76 years old think that I have some of those positive feminine traits and even that I make them think of Mary!

St. Louis de Montfort

KATHLEEN'S CONTEMPORARY APPLICATIONS AND PERSONAL REFLECTIONS

I thank God every day for allowing me to be Roman Catholic. The Real Presence of Jesus in the Blessed Sacrament, devotion to Our Lady, and the ability to share in Divine Life and Love through the grace of the sacraments are the reasons I have chosen to remain Catholic after my conversion some 37 years ago.

Having read *True Devotion to Mary* and *The Secret of the Rosary* early in my faith life, I was convinced I would never have true devotion to Mary, and that I had never said a worthy Hail Mary. I continue to hope that, with God's grace and Our Lady's help, I will one day.

But in the meantime, I can't help but notice how Our Lady was the instrument of my conversion and, after bringing me to the Church, she gently but firmly helped me let go of her hand as she nudged me toward her Son. It was almost imperceptible as it was happening. I didn't believe in God for a time, was afraid of Him for another period, and Mary was the one to whom I ran in prayer. She continued to give me her love and remove my fear until, one day, I noticed I was talking to Jesus about everything, praying to Him regularly, and asking His help and His will. And I know that's what she wants. Her Son is God. She wants Him honored and loved and reverenced. She wants us to know His love for us and love Him in return. She wants us to make Him known.

I made an act of consecration to Our Lady as a member of St.

Maximilian Kolbe's Militia Immaculata. I pray the rosary daily. I still run to Mary when things are really difficult. But her "job" seems to be to make Jesus loved and I feel more and more that it's my job too. Of course, I will be better at helping others love Him when my love for Him is perfected. And the best way for that to happen is for me to imitate Our Lady as best I can. Most days, my best is not as good as I would wish. I know I am nothing like her. But I want to be.

It's remarkable to me that Jesus taught us by His words and also by His example. But He also gives us His Mother to be Our Mother. She is the example of God's grace at work in a soul. She is the example of truly putting the will of God above everything else in life. Her virtue, her beauty, her love of God, her humility, her obedience are there for us to imitate.

Wouldn't the world be amazing if every woman was like Mary? God help me to be truly devoted to Our Most Blessed Mother!

FOR PERSONAL REFLECTION AND GROUP SHARING

Write about or share orally about the history of your relationship to the Blessed Virgin.

Have you ever made the de Montfort consecration? If so, tell us about your experience. If not, google it and pray about giving it a try.

BLESSED JOHN HENRY NEWMAN (1801-1890)

John Henry Newman was originally a member of the Anglican Church, and became a priest in the Church of England. A leading member of the Oxford Movement, he wanted the Church of England to embrace the rites and faith of the Apostles. In writing tracts opposed to the Catholic Church, he actually discovered the truth contained there, and began to realize the Church of England was not for him. He became Roman Catholic in 1845, was ordained a priest in 1847, and was elevated to Cardinal by Pope Leo XIII in 1879.

Newman used his own spiritual journey and his great pastoral experience to express connection between a well-formed conscience and arrival at truth. He did not allow conscience to be an excuse for liberalism, or doing one's own will. Rather, he was convinced it would lead one to obedience to doctrine and to the sacraments.

Newman, probably the greatest Catholic writer of the 19th Century, set forth such works as *Apologia Pro Vita Sua*, *The Grammar of Assent*, *The Dream of Gerontius*, and *The Idea of The University*. He wrote the beautiful hymn, "Praise to the Holiest in the Height."

His famous poem, "Lead Kindly Light," follows below:

Lead, kindly Light, amid the encircling gloom, lead Thou me on!
The night is dark, and I am far from home; lead Thou me on!
Keep Thou my feet; I do not ask to see
The distant scene; one step enough for me.

I was not ever thus, nor prayed that Thou shouldst lead me on;
I loved to choose and see my path; but now lead Thou me on!
I loved the garish day, and, spite of fears,
Pride ruled my will. Remember not past years!

So long Thy power hath blest me, sure it still will lead me on.
O'er moor and fen, o'er crag and torrent, till the night is gone,
And with the morn those angel faces smile, which I
Have loved long since, and lost awhile!

Meantime, along the narrow rugged path, Thyself hast trod,
Lead, Savior, lead me home in childlike faith, home to my God.
To rest forever after earthly strife
In the calm light of everlasting life.

Blessed John Henry Newman

Excerpts from his sermon, "Mental Sufferings of Our Lord in His Passion[1]"

Every passage in the history of our Lord and Savior is of unfathomable depth, and affords inexhaustible matter of contemplation. All that concerns Him is infinite, and what we first discern is but the surface of that which begins and ends in eternity... (but we are obliged during Passion Week) to direct your thoughts to a subject, especially suitable now, and about which many of us perhaps think very little, the sufferings which our Lord endured in His innocent and sinless soul.

You know, my brethren, that our Lord and Savior, though He was God, was also perfect man; and hence He had not only a body, but a soul likewise, such as ours, though pure from all stain of evil... He took on Him a soul as the means of His union with a body; He took on Him in the first place the soul, then the body of man, both at once, but in this order, the soul and the body; He Himself created the soul which He took on Himself, while He took His body from the flesh of the Blessed Virgin, His Mother. Thus He became perfect man with body and soul; and as He took on Him a body of flesh and nerves, which admitted of wounds and death, and was capable of suffering, so did He take a soul, too, which was susceptible of

---

[1] Discourses addressed to Mixed Congregations by John Henry Newman (New Impression), Longmans, Green, and Co., 39 Paternoster Row, London, New York, Bombay. Alt. Citation: Newman, John Henry. (Rev. 2001, May) "Discourses addressed to Mixed Congregations ." *Newman Reader*. National Institute for Newman Studies. Retrieved from http://newmanreader.org/works/discourses/discourse16.html

that suffering, and moreover was susceptible of the pain and sorrow which are proper to a human soul; and, as His atoning passion was undergone in the body, so it was undergone in the soul also…

This it is very much to the purpose to insist upon; I say, it was not the body that suffered, but the soul in the body; it was the soul and not the body which was the seat of the suffering of the Eternal Word. Consider, then, there is no real pain, though there may be apparent suffering, when there is no kind of inward sensibility or spirit to be the seat of it. A tree, for instance, has life, organs, growth, and decay; it may be wounded and injured; it droops, and is killed; but it does not suffer, because it has no mind or sensible principle within it. But wherever this gift of an immaterial principle is found, there pain is possible, and greater pain according to the quality of the gift. Had we no spirit of any kind, we should feel as little as a tree feels; had we no soul, we should not feel pain more acutely than a brute feels it; but, being men, we feel pain in a way in which none but those who have souls can feel it…

Now apply this to the sufferings of our Lord—do you recollect their offering Him wine mingled with myrrh, when He was on the point of being crucified? He would not drink of it; why? because such a portion would have stupefied His mind, and He was bent on bearing the pain in all its bitterness. You see from this, my brethren, the character of His sufferings; He would have fain escaped them, had that been His Father's will; "If it be possible," He said, "let this chalice pass from Me;" but since it was not possible, He says calmly and decidedly to the Apostle, who would have rescued Him from suffering, "The chalice which My Father hath given Me, shall I not drink it?" If He was to suffer, He gave Himself to suffering; He did not come to suffer as little as He could; He did not turn away His face from the suffering; He confronted it, or, as I may say, He breasted it, that every particular portion of it might make its due impression on Him…our Lord felt pain of the body, with an advertence and a consciousness, and therefore with a keenness and intensity, and with a unity of perception, which none of us can possibly fathom or compass, because His soul was so absolutely in His power, so simply free from the influence of distractions, so fully directed upon the pain, so utterly surrendered, so simply subjected to the suffering. And thus He may truly be said to have suffered the whole of His passion in every moment of it.

…When we suffer, it is because outward agents and the uncontrollable emotions of our minds bring suffering upon us. We are brought under the discipline of pain involuntarily, we suffer from it more or less acutely according to accidental circumstances, we find our patience more or less tried by it according to our state of mind, and we do our best to provide alleviations or remedies of it. We cannot anticipate beforehand how much of it will come upon us, or how far we shall be able to sustain it; nor can we say afterwards why we have felt just what we have felt, or why we did not bear the suffering better…

He took a body in order that He might suffer; He became man, that He might suffer as man; and when His hour was come, that hour of Satan and of darkness, the hour when sin was to pour its full malignity upon Him, it followed that He offered Himself wholly, a holocaust, a whole burnt-offering—as the whole of His body, stretched out upon the Cross, so the whole of His soul, His whole advertence, His whole consciousness, a mind awake, a sense acute, a living cooperation, a present, absolute intention, not a virtual permission, not a heartless submission, this did He present to His tormentors. His passion was an action; He lived most energetically, while He lay languishing, fainting, and dying. Nor did He die, except by an act of the will; for He bowed His head, in command as well as in resignation, and said, "Father, into Thy hands I commend My Spirit;" He gave the word, He surrendered His soul, He did not lose it...

And now, my brethren, what was it He had to bear...He had, my dear brethren, to bear the weight of sin; He had to bear your sins; He had to bear the sins of the whole world. Sin is an easy thing to us; we think little of it; we do not understand how the Creator can think much of it; we cannot bring our imagination to believe that it deserves retribution, and, when even in this world punishments follow upon it, we explain them away or turn our minds from them. But consider what sin is in itself; it is rebellion against God...Sin is the mortal enemy of the All-holy, so that He and it cannot be together... Sin could not touch His Divine Majesty; but it could assail Him in that way in which He allowed Himself to be assailed, that is, through the medium of His humanity. And...in the death of God incarnate, you are but taught, my brethren, what sin is in itself, and what it was which then was falling, in its hour and in its strength, upon His human nature...

There, then, in that most awful hour, knelt the Savior of the world, putting off the defenses of His divinity, dismissing His reluctant Angels, who in myriads were ready at His call, and opening His arms, baring His breast, sinless as He was, to the assault of His foe… Are these the hands of the Immaculate Lamb of God, once innocent, but now red with ten thousand barbarous deeds of blood? are these His lips, not uttering prayer, and praise, and holy blessings, but as if defiled with oaths, and blasphemies, and doctrines of devils? or His eyes, profaned as they are by all the evil visions and idolatrous fascinations for which men have abandoned their adorable Creator? And His ears, they ring with sounds of revelry and of strife; and His heart is frozen with avarice, and cruelty, and unbelief; and His very memory is laden with every sin which has been committed since the fall, in all regions of the earth…Of the living and of the dead and of the as yet unborn, of the lost and of the saved, of Thy people and of strangers, of sinners and of saints, all sins are there…they are all before Him now; they are upon Him and in Him. They are with Him instead of that ineffable peace which has inhabited His soul since the moment of His conception. They are upon Him, they are all but His own; He cries to His Father as if He were the criminal, not the victim; His agony takes the form of guilt and compunction. He is doing penance, He is making confession, He is exercising contrition, with a reality and a virtue infinitely greater than that of all saints and penitents together; for He is the One Victim for us all, the sole Satisfaction, the real Penitent, all but the real sinner…

And then, when the appointed moment arrived, and He gave

the word, as His passion had begun with His soul, with the soul did it end. He did not die of bodily exhaustion, or of bodily pain; at His will His tormented Heart broke, and He commended His Spirit to the Father.

Excerpts from *The Heart of Newman*[2]

The saint differs from an ordinary religious man, I say, in this – that he set before him as the one object of life, to please and obey God; that he ever aims to submit his will to God's will; that he earnestly follows after holiness; and that he is habitually striving to have a closer resemblance to Christ in all things. He exercises himself, not only in social duties, but in Christian graces; he is not only kind, but meek; not only generous, but humble; not only persevering, but patient; not only upright, but forgiving; not only bountiful, but self-denying; not only contented, but meditative and devotional. An ordinary man thinks it is enough to do as he is done by; he will think it fair to resent insults, to repay injuries, to show a becoming pride, to insist on his rights, to be jealous of his honor, when in the wrong to refuse to confess it, to seek to be rich, to desire to be well with the world, to fear what his neighbors will say. He seldom thinks of the Day of Judgment, seldom thinks of sins past, says few prayers, cares little for the Church, has no zeal for God's truth, spends his

---

2 Erich Przywara, S.J., *The Heart of Newman* (London: Burns and Oats Limited, 1963). Archaic language changed to more contemporary language by the editors.

money on himself. Such is an ordinary Christian, and such is not one of God's elect. For the latter is more than just, temperate, and kind; he has a devoted love of God, high faith, holy hope, overflowing charity, a noble self-command, a strict conscientiousness, humility never absent, gentleness in speech, simplicity, modesty and unaffectedness, an unconsciousness of what his endowments are, and what they make him in God's sight. This is what Christianity has done in the world; such is the result of Christian teaching; vis., to elicit, foster, mature the seeds of heaven which lie hid in the earth, to multiply (if it may be said) images of Christ. (pg. 326-327).

God beholds you individually, whoever you are. He "calls you by your name." He sees you, and understands you, as He made you. He knows what is in you, all your own peculiar feelings and thoughts, your dispositions and likings, your strength and your weakness. He views you in your day of rejoicing and your day of sorrow. He sympathizes in your hopes and your temptations. He interests Himself in all your anxieties and remembrances, all the risings and fallings of your spirit. He has numbered the very hairs of your head and the cubits of your stature. He compasses you round and bears you in His arms; He takes you up and sets you down. He notes your very countenance, whether smiling or in tears, whether healthful or sickly. He looks tenderly upon your hands and your feet; He hears your voice, the beating of your heart, and your very breathing. You do not love yourself more than He loves you. You cannot shrink from pain more than He dislikes your bearing it; and if He puts it on you, it is as you will put it on yourself, if you are wise, for a greater good afterwards (pg. 168-169).

God has created me to do Him some definite service; He has committed some work to me which He has not committed to another. I have my mission – I never may know it in this life, but I shall be told it in the next…I have a part in a great work; I am a link in a chain, a bond of connection between persons. He has not created me for naught. I shall do good, I shall do His work; I shall be an angel of peace, a preacher of truth in my own place, while not intending it, if I do but keep His commandments and serve Him in my calling.

Therefore, I will trust Him. Whatever, wherever I am, I can never be thrown away. If I am in sickness, my sickness may serve Him; in perplexity, my perplexity may serve Him; if I am in sorrow, my sorrow may serve Him. My sickness, or perplexity, or sorrow may be necessary causes of some great end, which is quite beyond us. He does nothing in vain; He may prolong my life, He may shorten it; He knows what He is about. He may take away my friends, He may throw me among strangers, He may make me feel desolate, make my spirits sink, hide the future from me – still He knows what He is about. (pg. 204).

Christ finds us in the double tabernacle, of a house of flesh and a house of brethren, and he sanctifies them both, not pulls them down. Our first life is in ourselves; our second in our friends. They whom God forces to part with their near of kin, for His sake, find brethren in the spirit at their side. They who remain solitary, for His sake, have children in the spirit raised up to them. How should we thank God for this great benefit! Now especially, when we are soon to retire, more or less, into ourselves, and to refrain from our ordinary intercourse with one another, let us acknowledge the blessing, whether of the holy marriage bond, or of family affection, or of the love of friends, which he so bounteously bestows. He gives, He takes away; blessed be His Name. But He takes away to give again, and He withdraws one blessing, to restore fourfold. Abraham offered his only son, and received him back again at the Angel's voice. Isaac "took Rebekah, and she became his wife, and he loved her; and Isaac was comforted after his mother's death." Jacob lost Joseph, and found him governor of Egypt. Job lost all his children, yet his end was more blessed than his beginning. We, too, through God's mercy, whether we be young or old, whether we have many friends or few, if we be Christ's, shall all along our pilgrimage find those in whom we may live, who will love us and whom we may love, who will aide us and help us forward, and comfort us, and close our eyes. For His love is a secret gift, which, unseen by the world, binds together those in whom it lives, and makes them live and sympathize with one another (pg. 228).

Stay with me, and then I shall begin to shine as You shine; so to shine as to be a light to others. The light, O Jesus, will be all from You. None of it shall be mine. No merit to me. It will be You who shines through me upon others. O let me praise You, in the way which You love best, by shining on all those around me. Give light to them as well as to me; light them with me, through me. Teach me to show forth Your praise, Your truth, Your will. Make me preach You without preaching – not by words, but by my example and by the catching force, the sympathetic influence, of what I do – by my visible resemblance to Your saints, and the evident fullness of the love which my heart bears to You. (pg. 257).

O my Lord and Savior, in Your arms I am safe; keep me and I have nothing to fear; give me up and I have nothing to hope for. I know not what may come upon me before I die. I know nothing about the future, but I rely upon You. I pray You to give me what is good for me; I pray You to take from me whatever may imperil my salvation; I pray You not to make me rich, I pray You not to make me very poor; but I leave it all to You, because You know and I do not. If You bring pain or sorrow on me, give me grace to bear it well – keep me from fretfulness and selfishness. If You give me health and strength and success in this world, keep me ever on my guard lest these great gifts carry me away from You.

O You who died on the cross for me, even for me, sinner as I am, give me to know You, to believe in You, to love You, to serve You; ever to aim at setting forth Your glory; to live to and for You; to set a good example to all around me; give me to die just at that time and in that way which is most for Your glory and best for my salvation. (pg. 215-216).

DR. RONDA'S CONTEMPORARY APPLICATIONS AND PERSONAL REFLECTIONS

The writings of John Henry Cardinal Newman were part of my conversion fifty-five years ago. Even though this famous 19th century Catholic convert had a history and a mind very unlike my own, the universal truth in his writings was compelling to me. After long years of Catholic spiritual practices, it still amazes me how insightful Blessed John Henry Newman is in the way that he sees right into our minds as to the often-unconscious objections we have to important truths of the faith.

The hymn "Lead Kindly Light" always tugs at my heart in its admonition to see only one step ahead. I tend to obsess about the future. A mentor of mine used to say about this hymn that, in contemporary language, one could say that the light of Christ is not a floodlight giving us a vision for a wide area of our lives, but a small circle coming from a flashlight to give us direction for only one step ahead.

I find the graphic description Newman gives of the mental sufferings of Jesus in the passion so poignant for a specific personal reason. Psychologists distinguish between sanguine and melancholic types. The sanguines tend to be optimists, always thinking that things will get better. Melancholics are pessimists and generally think the worst will befall them. What I have noticed is that sanguines only feel sad or depressed if something terrible is happening. But melancholics, like myself, find life itself pretty sad and depressing. Realizing, from Newman's sermon, what Jesus underwent in His mental sufferings is comforting. Pondering the sins of all times and the consequences of them is not a sign of being morbid. Rather, it can be a participation in the sufferings of Christ, not only in the agony in the garden, but in all of His time on earth.

It isn't that we are to only suffer on this earth and never have joy, but our joy is in what we experience of the good, as a foretaste of heaven. Our joy should never simply be a nonchalance about the sin and victimization that is part of life until our heavenly reward.

KATHLEEN'S CONTEMPORARY APPLICATIONS AND PERSONAL REFLECTIONS

I was introduced to the writings of John Henry Cardinal Newman by one of my first, and most beloved, spiritual directors. His gift of *The Heart of Newman* is still one of my favorite and most treasured books. I feel a kind of kinship with Newman, since we both came to the Catholic Church after being raised in the Anglican – or in my case, Episcopalian – faith.

Shortly after my conversion, the writings of Newman made the truths of the faith clear to me in such a simple, common sense way. His own journey through doubt to faith makes his writing all the more convincing, because he knows how to present the truth in a way that speaks to our own doubts and questions. It always impresses me that, in addressing the errors and apostasy of his own time, he gives a brilliant defense of the faith for those who would minimize it today. We are in such need of his reminders to keep the focus on God, not to allow science and politics to distort faith and morals. Newman's explanation of doctrine and holiness is an invaluable resource for my work in teaching the faith. He just makes sense.

Each of these excerpts from *The Heart of Newman* made me

weep the first time I read it. Each one explains some aspect of Catholic spiritual life in a beautiful, encouraging, and completely logical way.

Whenever I find myself questioning what is happening in my life, it is good for me to read, "God has created me to do Him some definite service..." It is a beautiful reminder that everything happens for a reason. The longer I live, the more often I am reminded that this is true. It is such a blessing to be given the grace to see that some incident worked out for my good. It makes it easier to accept the next situation.

If I am troubled, or fearful, or despondent, praying, "O my Lord and Saviour in Thy arms I am safe..." brings me consolation and encouragement. And even when I pray it just because I haven't done so in a while, it always makes me weep. It is the most precious reminder that "it is better to take refuge in the Lord" (Ps 118:8).

Somehow, *The Heart of Newman* is my heart too. I wonder what it is about these two Englishmen, Blessed John Henry Newman, and St. Thomas More, that reaches right inside and touches me at the depths of my soul? My two favorites were the most difficult reflections to write.

FOR PERSONAL REFLECTION AND GROUP SHARING

1. Before reading Newman, had you often meditated on the mental sufferings of Jesus in His Passion? Select specific passages you found inspiring.

   Do the excerpts from *The Heart of Newman* touch your heart? Which one in particular? What does his writing on being a saint say to you?

SAINT THÉRÈSE OF LISIEUX (1873 – 1897)
DOCTOR OF THE CHURCH

Saint Thérèse, born Marie-Françoise-Thérèse Martin, was a French Carmelite nun. She is also known as "The Little Flower of Jesus"…

She felt an early call to religious life, and overcoming various obstacles, in 1888 at the early age of 15, became a nun and joined two of her older sisters in the cloistered Carmelite community of Lisieux, France. After nine years as a Carmelite religious, she died of tuberculosis at the age of 24. The impact of *The Story of a Soul*, a collection of her autobiographical manuscripts, printed and distributed a year after her death to an initially very limited audience, was great, and she rapidly became one of the most popular saints of the twentieth century. She was beatified in 1923, and canonized in 1925. Thérèse was declared co-patron of the missions with Francis Xavier in 1927, and named co-patron of France with Joan of Arc in 1944. On 19 October 1997 Pope John Paul II declared her the thirty-third Doctor of the Church, the youngest person, and only the third woman, to be so honored. Devotion to Thérèse has developed around the world.

The depth of her spirituality, of which she said, "my way is all confidence and love," has inspired many believers. In the face of her littleness and nothingness, she trusted in God. She wanted to go to heaven by an entirely new little way. "I wanted to find an elevator that would raise me to Jesus." The elevator, she wrote, would be the arms of Jesus lifting her in all her littleness.

The Basilica of Lisiuex is the second largest place of pilgrimage in France after Lourdes. *(Bio from Wikipedia.)*

Quotes from *Story of a Soul*

St. Thérèse's First Communion

8th May 1884

Source: Story of a Soul [St. Thérèse's autobiography], (Rockford, Illinois: TAN Books and Publishers, Inc.)

At last the most wonderful day of my life arrived, and I can remember every tiny detail of those heavenly hours: my joyous waking up at dawn, the tender, reverent kisses of the mistresses and older girls, the room where we dressed—filled with the white "snowflakes" in which one after another we were clothed—and above all, our entry into chapel and the singing of the morning hymn: "O Altar of God, Where the angels are hovering." I would not tell you everything, even if I could, for there are certain things which lose their fragrance in the open air, certain thoughts so intimate that they cannot be translated into earthly language without losing at once their deep and heavenly meaning. How lovely it was, that first kiss of Jesus in my heart—it was truly a kiss of love. I knew that I was loved and said, "I love You, and I give myself to You forever." Jesus asked for nothing, He claimed no sacrifice. Long before that, He and little Thérèse had seen and understood one another well, but on that day it was more than a meeting -- it was a complete fusion. We were no longer two, for Thérèse had disappeared like a drop of water lost in the mighty ocean. Jesus alone remained—the Master and the King. Had she not asked Him to take away her liberty, the liberty she feared? She felt so weak and frail that she wanted to unite herself forever to His divine strength. And her joy became so vast, so deep, that now it overflowed. Soon she was weeping, to the astonishment of her companions, who said to one another later on: "Why did she cry? Was there something on her conscience? Perhaps it was because her mother was not there, or the Carmelite sister she loves so much." It was beyond them that all the joy of Heaven had entered one small, exiled heart, and that it was too frail and weak to bear it without tears. As if the absence of my mother could make me unhappy on the day of my First Communion! As all heaven entered my soul when I received Jesus, my mother came to me as well. Nor could I cry because you were not there, we were closer than ever before. It was joy alone, deep ineffable joy that filled my heart.

That afternoon I was chosen to read the "Act of Consecration to Our Lady." I suppose they chose me because I had lost my earthly mother so young. Anyway, I put my whole heart into it and begged Our Lady to guard me always. I felt sure she was looking at me with that lovely smile which had cured me and delivered me, and I knew all I owed her; for it was she herself, that morning of the 8th of May, who placed Jesus in my soul, "the flower of the field and the lily of the valley."

When evening came that lovely day, Father led his little queen by the hand to Carmel, and there I saw you made the bride of Christ. I saw your veil, all white like mine, and your crown of roses. There was no bitterness in all my joy, for I hoped to join you and wait for Heaven at your side.

I was very moved by the family feast prepared at Les Buissonets and delighted with the little watch which Father gave me. Yet my happiness was very tranquil, with an inward peace no earthly thing could touch. Night came at last to end my lovely evening, for darkness falls even on the brightest day. Only the first day of communion in eternity will never end.

When I looked upon the mystical body of the Church, I recognized myself in none of the members which St. Paul described... Love appeared to me to be the hinge for my vocation. I knew that the Church had a heart and that such a heart appeared to be aflame with love. I knew that one love drove the members of the Church to action, that if this love were extinguished, the apostles would have proclaimed the Gospel no longer,...I saw and realized that love sets off the bounds of all vocations, that love is everything, and this same love embraces every time and every place. In one word that love is everlasting. Then, nearly ecstatic with the supreme joy in my soul, I proclaimed: O Jesus, my love, at last I have found my calling: my call is love. Certainly I have found my proper place in the Church, and you gave me that very place, my God. In the heart of the Church, my mother, I will be love...

What a comfort it is this way of love! You may stumble on it, you may fail to correspond with grace given, but always love knows how to make the best of everything; whatever offends our Lord is burnt up in its fire, and nothing is left but a humble, absorbing peace deep down in the heart."

Our Lord's love makes itself seen quite as much in the simplest of souls as in the most highly gifted, as long as there is no resistance offered to his grace.

The science of loving, yes, that's the only kind of science I want I'd barter away everything I possess to win it.

When I act as charity bids, I have this feeling that it is Jesus who is acting in me; the closer my union with him, the greater my love for all the sisters without distinction.

Above all it's the gospels that occupy my mind when I'm at prayer. "I'm always finding fresh lights there.

TRIAL OF FAITH: "I get tired of the darkness all around me."

The darkness itself seems to borrow, from the sinners who live in it, the gift of speech. I hear its mocking accents: 'It's all a dream, this talk of a heavenly country of a God who made it all, who is to be your possession in eternity!" "All right, go on longing for death! But death will make nonsense of your hopes; it will only mean a night darker than ever, the night of mere non-existence!"

Without love, deeds, even the most brilliant, count as nothing.

On the day of my conversion charity entered into my heart and with it a yearning to forget self always; thenceforward I was happy.

When charity is deeply rooted in the soul it shows itself exteriorly: there is so gracious a way of refusing what we cannot give, that the refusal pleases as much as the gift.

From letters and counsels:

Time is but a shadow, a dream; already God sees us in glory and takes joy in our eternal beatitude. How this thought helps my soul! I understand then why He lets us suffer...

VIII Letter to Her Sister Celine

How I thirst for Heaven—that blessed habitation where our love for Jesus will have no limit! But to get there we must suffer... we must weep... Well, I wish to suffer all that shall please my beloved, I wish to let Him do just as He wills with His "little ball."

In Heaven the good God will do all I wish, because I have never done my own will upon earth.

Even now I know it: yes, all my hopes will be fulfilled... yes... the Lord will work wonders for me which will surpass infinitely my immeasurable desires.

DR. RONDA'S CONTEMPORARY APPLICATIONS AND PERSONAL REFLECTIONS

I chose St. Thérèse of Lisieux as my confirmation saint, not because I identified with her, but for the exact opposite reason—no one could have been more different. I was brought up as an atheist, she in a family of Catholic saints. I love dramatic apostolates, she popularized the little way of tiny deeds of love. I was an intellectual Catholic. Though bright and deeply wise, she moved from intuitions of the heart. I write in an analytic style, she writes in a personal manner.

I chose her to help form me as a confirmed Catholic because I wanted to be all that she was, and she has helped me throughout the decades of my Catholic life to the maximum. At key terrible moments in my life, she has suddenly given me a sign of hope. Twenty years ago, I learned from the California police that my son's body had been found, proof of his tragic suicide. My brother-in-law, who had never heard of little Thérèse, smelled roses where there were none and couldn't have been blooming in February in that locale.

Most of all I love the famous photos of her. You might look for them on the web because there are more than you might think.

KATHLEEN'S CONTEMPORARY APPLICATIONS AND PERSONAL REFLECTIONS

Perhaps nowhere is the example of true love of God seen so perfectly and so simply as in the life of St. Thérèse of Lisieux. Perhaps there is no other subject or saint where I can so truly say, "it's that simple." St. Thérèse might be the easiest of saints to teach. Anyone can grasp her notion to be little and to love God above all else. Each time we find struggle in the pursuit of holiness we need only remind ourselves to keep on for the love of God.

The first time I read *The Story of a Soul* I found St. Thérèse to be a spoiled brat. She had to have everything her way. She pushed and pushed until she got her way to enter the convent early. I saw no humility in her (a funny thing coming from a person with no humility!) It took me a long time to see her true holiness. One of the greatest lines I've ever read is her encouragement that if we pick up a pin for the love of God it will bear much fruit. Now when I struggle for self-mastery I remind myself to keep my opinions to myself "for love of You, Jesus." I remind myself not to snap at someone, "for love of You, Jesus." I resist the urge to defend myself, "for love of You, Jesus." I continue to fast on difficult days, "for love of you, Jesus." I try to take 100% responsibility for every relationship in my life and never blame someone else for my behavior, "for love of You, Jesus."

Mind you, I have not "arrived." I struggle almost every moment of every day. I slip into unloving words and actions far more often than I overcome those temptations. But, the few times in a day I might remember to discipline myself I do so, "for love of You, Jesus."

One of the best lessons in loving others is one I learned from St. Thérèse. Her admonition to pray for someone we dislike and, thereby, learn to love them, is a wise and simple means to obtain a change of heart – not in others, but in ourselves. We pray for others, and God changes our hearts. The example she gave of praying for the nun who disliked her and the aim to become her "best friend" was such a great story to exemplify God's grace at work in us, changing our hearts to be more loving. St. Thomas More says it is a great waste of time to dislike someone for this short time on earth when we either will love each other heartily in heaven, or have pity for ones who will not share eternity with God.

Our success in the spiritual life lies in our attitude and perspective. Just a tiny change in outlook can allow God's grace to work wonders in our hearts. If our focus is on His great love for us, then we can be humble enough to accept what comes into our lives knowing it was sent or allowed by His love for us. If we desire to give Him glory, then we can develop a desire to become what He wants us to be, and to allow Him to work in us until we are that person. We will love others because He does. We rely totally on God and His grace, realizing that apart from Him we can do nothing, become nothing, acquire nothing. We will not seek riches or fame or material possessions because God's glory will be of paramount importance. Instead of becoming puffed up, we will seek to become little, as little children trusting in God to provide what we need, to lead us in right paths, to pick us up when we fall, to feed us when we are hungry (physically and spiritually), to achieve in us any measure of good.

Mother Teresa of Calcutta said we cannot do great things for God. We can only do little things with great love. St. Thérèse of Lisieux shows us how to do that. Her "little way" shows us how to be little, and how to do little things with great love. Her love for God is so great that it wasn't enough for her to work for His glory in this life only. She vowed to spend her heaven doing good on earth – all for the glory of God. She wanted to win souls for God while she lived on earth, and to continue to do so when she attained heaven.

It is likely because of her littleness and simplicity that so many souls on earth love her and can relate to her. She shows us that we don't have to be great in order to love God and give Him glory in the everyday-ness of our lives. She shows us how to become as little children in the eyes and heart of the Father Who loves us. In doing so, He allows us to achieve real greatness – eternity with God in heaven.

FOR PERSONAL REFLECTION AND GROUP SHARING

What lines from the writings of St. Thérèse meant the most to you?

Try living the little way of love for a few days and make note of incidents, prayers, and insights you have.

CONCLUSION

We hope that following our program *Spirituality for All Times* has been inspiring.

In our introduction we suggested you consider yourselves to be "Called by Name" to a holiness that takes a form befitting the way God has created you with your own specific talents, such as "I am loving service," or "I am a father to my family and to all I encounter." Describe your spiritual "name" now as you understand it after reading this book:

Spirituality for All Times

You might want to copy lines you always want to remember from these readings in the spiritual classics. We suggest that you write them here, free hand, and then type them in a nice format and print them out. In this way, you will have these beautiful sayings handy when you go for a time of quiet prayer each day or, paste them on the door of your fridge!

Conclusion

You may also want to compose a short, easy to remember, prayer to offer to God each day:

www.ingramcontent.com/pod-product-compliance
Lightning Source LLC
Chambersburg PA
CBHW031313160426
43196CB00007B/511